THE LIFE AND TIMES
OF SIR ARCHIE

A MODERN PORTRAIT OF SIR ARCHIE

From a painting by Martin Stainforth, based on Alvan Fisher's portrait from life and on various contemporary descriptions. It is now in the possession of the University of North Carolina.

THE
Life and Times
OF
Sir Archie

❦

THE STORY OF
AMERICA'S GREATEST THOROUGHBRED,
1805-1833

by
Elizabeth Amis Cameron Blanchard
AND
Manly Wade Wellman

Chapel Hill
THE UNIVERSITY OF NORTH CAROLINA PRESS

Copyright, 1958, by
Benjamin P. De Loache, Trustee for the Estate of
Elizabeth Amis Cameron Blanchard

*For the great love
of a great horse*

🟦 FOREWORD 🟦

MRS. Elizabeth Amis Cameron Blanchard was born in California, educated in Europe, and lived in New York; but traditions from the Southern side of her family were vivid with her, and these included tales of a celebrated Thoroughbred stallion, supreme as a race horse and unrivalled as a sire, which had belonged to her North Carolina ancestors. Nearly thirty years ago, visiting the South in search of family records, she found herself particularly drawn to the dramatic story of Sir Archie, pride of her forbears the Amises, and began collecting all available information about him.

For years she travelled, studied, questioned. In America and England she haunted libraries, visited old homes, consulted manuscripts, newspapers, and turf records. She was pursuing with great vigor her organization of material at the time of her death in 1956.

Her notes toward a biography of Sir Archie are included in ten great typescript volumes, totalling some three thousand pages, besides a mass of original source material in the form of photostats, copies of rare documents, clippings from ancient papers and maga-

Foreword

zines, records of interviews and other matters that, like the treasure of Ali Baba, is better estimated by volume than by counting. Much of it is a rich reminder of what the classic racing world of America was like more than a century ago, and much more leads to other sources, authoritative and fascinating, that are all but forgotten except by sportsmen-scholars.

Mrs. Blanchard's study went far beyond her first project of establishing her family's ownership of Sir Archie and the facts of his career on the Amis family estate in Northampton County, North Carolina. It extended to a consideration of the development and flowering of American Thoroughbred racing and breeding. She sought for everything, and what she found she kept. The task of organizing a single-volume story of Sir Archie and the world he lived in and sometimes electrified has sometimes been embarrassed by the plethora of rich material.

Early in the pursuit of her project, Mrs. Blanchard realized that she might go far toward supplying a certain lack in the recorded consideration of American life and manners. The ways of antebellum Southerners have been much explored in recent years, by historians and novelists. Agriculture, slavery, politics, education, social customs, and finally military affairs most deservedly have inspired whole libraries of books. But an activity which fascinated Southerners of high and low estate, and which had its devotees only less preoccupied in the North, was the racing of horses. Upon his world of racing, Sir Archie made an impact as tremendous, certainly, as any impact made by other famous Americans on their worlds.

Here, then, is my own effort to finish what Mrs. Blanchard began. One may doubt if it goes near to realizing her dream, but dreams seldom come to a proper realization.

MANLY WADE WELLMAN
Chapel Hill, North Carolina

❦ ACKNOWLEDGMENTS ❦

    To thank, intelligently and properly, every person who has assisted in the gathering of material for a biography of Sir Archie is utterly impossible. They have been so many, and their contributions so various. To the names listed below, enough could be added, perhaps, to make a book by itself.

    Mrs. Blanchard, in her years of pilgrimage after material, was greatly aided by two turf historians who, like herself, have died. They are John Lewis Hervey of Chicago and Fairfax Harrison of Belvoir, Faquier County, Virginia. Her papers are full of grateful acknowledgment of the help of these experts. It is appropriate, in this connection, to acknowledge the good offices of A. Pendleton Whitehead, executor of Mrs. Blanchard's estate, and Benjamin De Loache, trustee for her literary material.

    The Jockey Club of New York City generously permitted quotation from Mr. Hervey's two-volume work *Racing in America, 1665-1865*.

    To this project, as to those of countless other students and writers of history, priceless help was rendered by the directors and staffs of

Acknowledgments

the Louis Round Wilson Library of the University of North Carolina, Chapel Hill, North Carolina; the Library of Congress, Washington, D.C.; the Municipal Library of New York City; and the Duke University Library, Durham, North Carolina.

Mr. Alexander Mackay-Smith of White Post, Virginia, expert on the turf past and present, read the working draft of the manuscript, gave authoritative advice, and contributed an appendix on the sons and daughters of Sir Archie. Robert W. Linker of Chapel Hill, North Carolina, volunteered to provide the index which appears at the end of the work.

A thousand various aids, when and where they were needed, were provided by the following:

W. Lunsford Long of Warrenton, North Carolina; Willie Jones Long of Longview, Northampton County, North Carolina; Henry W. Lewis of Chapel Hill, North Carolina; Mrs. Louis A. Froelich of Jackson, North Carolina; Hugh T. Lefler of Chapel Hill, North Carolina; Mr. and Mrs. John G. Burgwyn of Northampton County, North Carolina; George F. Scheer of Chapel Hill, North Carolina; and Mrs. James Boyd of Southern Pines, North Carolina.

Others who helped know that the help was welcome and appreciated; and all of them have the generosity to forgive the omission of their names here for lack of space.

M. W. W.

CONTENTS

Foreword		vii
Acknowledgments		ix
1.	Sir Archie's Ancestors	3
2.	Sir Archie Struggles in His Youth	18
3.	Sir Archie Outshines the Racers	34
4.	Sir Archie Outshines the Sires	51
5.	Sir Archie Reigns at Mowfield	69
6.	Sir Archie Glories in His Children	91
7.	Sir Archie Gets into Politics	110
8.	Sir Archie is Assailed by Scandal	141

Contents

9. Sir Archie Fulfills His Destiny ... 160

10. Sir Archie Lives in His Descendants ... 180

Appendices

    A. The Spelling of "Sir Archie" and "Mowfield" ... 187

    B. The Ancestry of Sir Archie ... 189

    C. The Birthplace and the Grave ... 191

    D. The Racing Record of Sir Archie's Sons and Daughters by Alexander-Mackay Smith ... 194

Notes ... 209

Bibliography ... 219

Index ... 223

ILLUSTRATIONS

A Modern Portrait of Sir Archie	*frontispiece*
	facing page
Mowfield Plantation	26
Trifle, the Brilliant Daughter	44
The Horse of Horses	66
Sir Archie in Business	67
Great among the Great Sons	82
Diomed, the Sire of Sir Archie	82
Sir Charles	83
One of the Consorts	83
Boston, the Grandson	106
Mansion of a Turfman	146
The Co-Breeders: Tayloe and Randolph	147
Some of the Amis Family	162
William Ransom Johnson	163
Allan Jones Davie	163
Robert Potter	163
John Randolph of Roanoke	163
Lexington, the Incomparable	182

The endpaper of the book pictures the Eclipse-Henry race. This is a contemporary sporting print showing the finish of the three brilliant heats of the greatest intersectional race in American sports history.

THE LIFE AND TIMES
OF SIR ARCHIE

And never today a champion
That on the turf wins fame,
But back in his breeding somewhere
You'll find Sir Archie's name.

     JOHN LEWIS HERVEY
      The Ballad of Sir Archie

I

SIR ARCHIE'S
Ancestors

THEY appeared as early, perhaps, as the recognizable ancestors of any of the mammals living today—almost at once in the Eocene epoch after the unexplained vanishment from earth of the dinosaurs. Among the towering screw-pines and tree-ferns, through the lush undergrowth of western North America scurried the little four-toed Eohippus, no larger than a big cat, yet foretelling by head and teeth and somewhat by body lines the horse he would become. In the branches above him, possibly, played the lemur-like forerunners of the monkeys that would in turn develop into men.

Forty million years ago the Eohippus throve, and in fullness of time developed into a larger animal, with fewer toes, cleaner limbs, a more graceful neck. Immemorial epochs succeeded each other. Changes, wondrous and sometimes destructive, wrought upon ancient strains of animals. The emerging horse, with single hoofs, round barrel, and fine swift legs, died out in America; but wandering herds had trotted across the land bridge to Europe in the early Pleistocene. At that time certain four-handed, hairy tree dwellers with inquiring minds pioneered on the ground, learned to eat flesh, and to use sticks and stones as the simplest of tools and weapons, looking, without knowing that they looked, toward a future as human beings.

The ground-walking children of the Tree People became cave dwellers and hunters. To them, in their food-stalking centuries, the horse—something like a zebra in shape and size, and possibly in pattern of hide—was a toothsome prey, and they outwitted his speed and furtive vigilance. They killed him and roasted his flesh on their fires. When men learned to scratch and paint pictures on cavern walls, horses appeared among the animals they represented.

The horses grew larger, swifter, and the men grew wiser, more complex of enterprise. Stone weapons were replaced by copper, then by bronze. Primitive settlements grew into cities and nations. Humanity learned to build houses, plant crops, weave cloth. The cow, the dog, were tamed. Horse speed and horse intelligence, once a frustration to meat-hunters, impressed developing man as something worth alliance with himself. The horse was taught to draw crude carts, to carry burdens and riders.

Mounted, the descendant of tree dwellers achieved journeys, migrations, great roaming adventures in trade or exploration or conquest. As barbarism refined into civilization in Asia Minor, along the Nile, and across India, the horse's hoof planted its round mark alongside man's footprint at history's threshold.

Assyrian and Babylonian warrior-kings galloped their horses over rival nations. Egypt's Pharaohs drove with regal dignity their own gold-mounted chariots. The Persians, mastering the world in turn, taught their sons that the three chief lessons in life were to ride, to shoot, and to speak the truth. In Greece grew the tale that the sea-god Poseidon had created and conferred the horse on mankind, and poets symbolized their soaring genius with white-pinioned, sky-aspiring Pegasus. Alexander, pointing his conquering phalanxes with cavalry, named a new city for Bucephalus, the horse he had loved in boyhood. Britain fell to Caesar's invasion, and in Bucking-

His Ancestors

hamshire the legions paused to gaze with wonder upon the broad hillside where turf had been stripped from the chalk to make the symbol of the White Horse, four hundred feet long.

New invasions overthrew old invaders. Mounted barbarian hordes crumpled Rome's defenses. The ages darkened, then lightened appreciably with the coming of chivalry, a word and an ideal founded upon horsemanship.

Mailed knights wanted and needed the proper horses to carry their weight of fighting equipment into worshipful battle. Horse breeding had begun before the invention of practical writing, and by medieval times it was something of a science. Nobles and gentry strove to produce a combination of size, swift vigor, and valor. There were polite tiltings with lances and the romantic adventures that *Don Quixote* would satirize but not wholly disparage. There were wars, too. Charles Martel's cavalry drove back the Moslems at Tours. William the Conqueror's mounted Normans beat stubborn Saxon infantry at Hastings. Christendom crusaded to win the Holy Sepulchre in Palestine and brought back, along with Arabic numerals, new scientific knowledge, several doleful diseases, and the Barbary, Arabian, and Turkish stallions to improve their own stock.

Beyond what had seemed nowhere's western rim was discovered the New World, husky with rumors of fortune and adventure. Into the Aztec Empire's unimagined wonder rode Cortez with his handful, and Montezuma's hosts, who might have braved the guns and the steel swords, broke before the sixteen chargers of the Conquistador cavalry. Into the land that would be the United States escaped Spanish horses to breed, on plains where once little Eohippus had flourished, the tough western broncho.

"A duller task could scarcely be undertaken," acridly declares the sportsman-encyclopedist A. E. T. Watson, "than that of endeavouring to trace the history of horse-racing from material furnished by the vague and contradictory accounts of the earliest writers on the subject. It may safely be assumed that racing dates from the period when two energetic men found themselves side by side on high-couraged horses."

Such impromptu competitions surely began before the dawn of written history, and the Greeks included horse races in the twenty-third Olympiad. Romans preferred chariot racing. In the Eastern Empire, guilds of charioteers rose to such power as influenced the crowning of rulers. From the Middle Ages onward, the best running horses were bred in England.

Richard Coeur de Lion's reign saw the laying out of courses. Richard's Plantagenet successors imported stallions from southern Europe and the East. As knighthood's flower faded, race horses became more popular than the great war horses. At Chester, in 1524, a regular race track was established with, as victor's prize, a flower-wreathed wooden bell.

James I shone as a royal breeder and racer of swift horses. His court at Newmarket became a center of racing events, and the track he established exists today. Nor did the vaunted best of foreign mounts excel the English. "When the best Barbaries that ever were in their prime," wrote Gervase Markham, not too quaintly vague in syntax to be authoritative, "I saw them overrunne by a black hobbye at Salisbury; yet that hobbye was overrunne by a horse called Valentine, neither in hunting or running, was ever equalled, yet was a plain bred English horse both by syre and dam."

Charles I held race meetings at Hyde Park. Cromwell forbade horse racing, but admired fine stallions and mares as breeding stock for cavalry mounts. Charles II entered, under his own royal name, horses at various courses, and Gervase Markham's early judgment of English racers as superior to Orientals was borne out by other observers. Indeed, Eastern horses seemed overspecialized—Arabians for speed, Barbs for strength and action, Turks for height and for length of stride. Breeding for combination of these traits proved practical, and several fine stallions won fame as sires. By the early

His Ancestors

part of the eighteenth century, three noble importations became cornerstones of the English racing breed.

First to arrive in England was a magnificent cavalry charger, ridden by Captain Byerly in King William's Irish wars, which between campaigns sired fine runners upon Irish mares. Captain Byerly brought him to England, where his sons and daughters became famous. He was called the Byerly Turk.

In 1703 a Yorkshire merchant named Darley imported from Aleppo another magnificent stallion who became known as the Darley Arabian. Some of his racing sons became progenitors only less celebrated than the Darley Arabian. Among these was Flying Childers, who outran a series of rivals and then sired winners like Blaze, Snip, Spanking Roger, and Roundhead.

Third of the triumvirate, and greatest as progenitor and as romantic legend, was the Godolphin Arabian. A tale followed him to England to the effect that he had been stolen abroad. As he began to win fame for the brilliance of his get, this report was forgotten in the rash of melodramatic folklore that broke out around him. He was said to have been a present from the Bey of Tunis to Louis XV of France, from whom, said some, he was stolen to be a woodcutter's drudge. At last, purchased by Lord Godolphin, the stallion reputedly crowned his career of toil and travel with a successful duel for love; he rivalled Hobgoblin, Godolphin's prize stallion at Gogmagog Hall, for the favors of the beautiful mare Roxana, vanquished Hobgoblin in a kicking, biting struggle, and claimed Roxana as prize of battle.

The facts were less dramatic. Hobgoblin had disdained Roxana, who was then offered to the Godolphin Arabian. The resultant foal was Lath, thought by some the finest racer since Flying Childers. Other champions by the Godolphin Arabian were Blank, Dismal, Cripple, Dormouse, Janus, Matchless, Regulus, Babraham, and Dimple. The Godolphin Arabian blood dominated succeeding generations of race horses.

Sir Archie

Of these three matchless sires, the Byerly Turk, the Darley Arabian, and the Godolphin Arabian, came descendants that became in turn important sires and founders of mighty lines.

King Herod, foaled in 1758, had as sire Tartar, great-grandson of the Byerly Turk, and as dam Cypron, granddaughter of the Darley Arabian. He won ten races out of fourteen, gruelling four-mile heats. To triumph over a field at that distance, the winner must excel in three heats out of five; it might mean twenty galloping miles in a single day. Nearly five hundred of King Herod's sons and daughters were racers, notably Florizel, Woodpecker, and Highflyer.

Matchem was the grandson of the Godolphin Arabian, and Matchem's dam was of the Byerly Turk line. Of his get, 174 won a total of $670,870 in prizes, not counting gold and silver cups and plates, and at stud he showed a net profit of $75,480. Some authorities call him history's most profitable horse.

Eclipse, foaled in 1764 on a day when the sun darkened, was sired by the Darley Arabian's great-grandson Markse upon Spiletta, granddaughter of the Godolphin Arabian. He won nineteen races, eleven of them for King's Plates. Never beaten, never even badly pushed, he retired for lack of competition and got 340 winning sons and daughters, including three Derby winners.

The first Derby of all, at Epsom in 1780, was won by Diomed, son of Florizel by a mare descended from both the Darley Arabian and the Godolphin Arabian. Six other races Diomed won that same year, conquering the best Thoroughbreds of the day.

Thoroughbreds had arrived before the term that was needed to define them as horses created for racing by complex heredity.

Lord Bristol wrote in 1713 to his son concerning "thoro-bred English horses," apparently referring to training rather than blood. A similar use of the word seems indicated in an advertisement in the *Racing Calendar* of Cheney for 1738; and Samuel Johnson's intriguing dictionary of 1755 flatly defines Thoroughbred: "Completely educated; completely taught."

His Ancestors

Something of another definition was hinted in America when, in 1778, a four-year-old colt was advertised for sale as "full-blooded and thoroughbred." Again this may be a distinction between the terms, or it may be redundant emphasis of the colt's pedigree. In any case, word and meaning were established shortly thereafter, to refer to pedigreed turf horses exclusively, in England and in America.

The first horses imported to England's American colonies had been eaten during Jamestown's melancholy Starving Time in 1609. Seventeen more arrived two years later to begin the establishment of a native breed. It was 1629 before horses and mares were shipped to Massachusetts. Earlier, however, Dutch stock had come to New Amsterdam and French animals to Canada. Interbreeding of these various strains produced by mid-century something of a representative American type.

Saddle stock of the colonies tended to be small but active, perhaps something like the later cow ponies of the West. Races were run, inevitably, by such steeds under vigorous pioneer horsemen. The early tracks where they existed at all, were impromptu and forbiddingly rough, and prizes varied from hogsheads of tobacco to the horses of the losers. Most courses were simple stretches of road or trail a quarter of a mile in extent, sometimes the main street of a village. Quarter racing, highly popular in the English colonies, developed famous little sprinters.

Richard Nicolls, who accepted Peter Stuyvesant's surrender of New Amsterdam and became New York's first English governor, made turf history by laying out, at the Hempstead Plains on Long Island, the first colonial race course of any adequacy. It was a two-mile oval, and Governor Nicolls offered, in 1666, the first of his series of silver cups as prize of the first American race meeting organized and conducted with formality. Appropriately, Nicolls named the course Newmarket after that historic race ground at the court of James I and announced that he offered prizes "not so much for the divertisement of youth as for encouraging the bettering of the breed of horses, which through great neglect has been impaired." One trophy, a simple but tastefully wrought porringer, exists today. Around its circumference is inscribed: "1668. wunn. att. hansted. planes. march 25." The name of the winner and the names of others who won races there have not survived in the records.

That 1668 porringer must have been the last prize offered by Governor Nicolls, for he returned to England later the same year and was killed in naval battle against the Dutch in 1672. But others gave trophies in his place, and the American Newmarket races continued throughout the Colonial period.

In 1689 William Penn imported to Philadelphia a stallion named Tamerlane and two mares for the breeding of racing animals. No pedigree of Penn's importations survives, and the first known stallion with any claim to Thoroughbred ancestry to reach North America was Bulle Rock, or Bully-Rock, brought to Virginia about 1730.

In Virginia, more than in the Northern colonies, a cavalier gaiety had made racing popular almost from the first appearance of horses on Tidewater soil. Some jealously distinguished the sport; Colonial officials made a law that restricted racing to the gentry. On September 10, 1674, a York County tailor named James Bullocke, who did not qualify as a gentleman, was fined a hundred pounds of tobacco for matching his mare in a race.

That sort of law did not long endure. Tailors, laborers, and others won the right to race and had the best of example. A notable figure in the early history of the Virginia turf was the energetic and versatile clergyman, the Reverend Dr. James Blair, who strove with equal fervor for the founding of William and Mary College, the moving of the Colonial capital from Jamestown to Williamsburg, and the establishment of the Williamsburg Jockey Club. On at least one occasion he served as an official at a race which needed his reverend testimony in court to establish the winner. Later in the seventeenth

His Ancestors

century, at about the time the Puritan communities of New England passed laws against horse racing, Williamsburg became the acknowledged center of the sport in Virginia, and Virginia was the chief of the colonies in the practice and development of racing.

In 1736 the Virginia *Gazette* began publication at Williamsburg and told much about the races and the horses that ran them. In January of 1739, a three-day meet was announced for Gloucester County, with a purse of thirty pistoles for the winner on the first day; a saddle, bridle, and housing for prize on the second day; and a saddle, bridle, and whip for prize on the third. Another account, in the *Gazette* for December 14 of the same year, describes a similar race, with a saddle as first prize, a bridle for place, and a whip for show.

Bulle Rock had been imported to Virginia some years earlier and, though his name appears in no official British stud book, he was announced as a son of the Darley Arabian, foaled in 1709, with a good racing record in England. He came into possession of Samuel Gist, a Hanover County merchant and, though no son or daughter of his achieved any fame, his blood descended in pedigrees for more than forty years. In 1733, Alexander Clarke imported a Godolphin Arabian mare into Virginia.

Other fine importations followed. Monkey, registered in the *General Stud Book* of England, came to Nathaniel Harrison's plantation in Prince George County in 1737 and later went to North Carolina. Before his death in 1754, he had sired full three hundred sons and daughters, many of them respected as racers and progenitors. Traveller, brought as a two-year-old to Virginia by Joseph Morton in 1749, raced for three years and then was placed at stud, bringing to America the blood of the Byerly Turk.

The colonies had become civilized, populous, and rich. Racing achieved an importance, especially in the South, hard to understand and evaluate today.

For almost everybody in Virginia, the Carolinas, and Georgia went racing. There was no other spectator sport of any consequence. From quarter races at frontier posts, between valiant scrubby little beasts, to elaborate and mannered meets at established courses on the seaboard, all classes and professions gathered. The Reverend Dr. Blair was but one of many clergymen who loved to watch the horses run. Governors, military officers, wealthy planters, tradesmen, and servants risked the much or little they had in ready cash on the outcome of notable races, at four miles, two miles, a quarter mile. George Washington, in 1761, was steward for the races at Alexandria. John Randolph of Roanoke competed as a jockey in his boyhood, as later would Stonewall Jackson.

Between 1760 and 1770, 115 Thoroughbred horses and mares were imported to the colonies, and racing came to something of a height in Maryland, midpoint between Northern and Southern turf stalwarts. Annapolis, then Baltimore, became a focus of rivalry and interest. In 1770 the growing dispute with the mother country brought about the non-importation movement, and the stream of English Thoroughbreds ceased, but native stock flourished and competed nobly for glory and prizes.

Then the War of Independence began, and the racing gentry became cavalrymen, and the blooded horses were spoil of battle. The British, holding New York against surrounding Continentals, organized race meetings on Long Island. The Americans, too, sometimes raced between battles, chiefly in western Maryland and along the boundary between Virginia and North Carolina. Destruction along Virginia's seaboard was great, and the British, sailing away at last, took with them many captured horses. Some of the best had been saved, however, and sent by their owners to points less likely to be raided. When peace and independence were assured to the new country, the courses echoed again to hurrying hoofs.

While the scarred Virginia Tidewater struggled to regain its fortunes, the southern part of the new state, with that area of North

His Ancestors

Carolina just below, moved into prominence as a breeding and racing region.

The North Carolina counties of Halifax, Warren, and Northampton had suffered comparatively little from the war; when Cornwallis' army retreated through the region on its way to Yorktown and disaster, it was too depressed and too hurried to sweep up all the Thoroughbreds. Great turfmen rose with the end of the conflict. Colonel Jephta Atherton, Willie and Allen Jones, General Stephen Carney, and Marmaduke Johnson bred and trained fine colts and fillies to vie with each other and with the best blood of more remote districts.

Four-mile heats became popular, as in England, and demanded strong, swift, and resolute racers. Such competition produced animals larger and longer-winded than the explosive quarter horses, and bottom and smooth action were ideals both in the breeding and the training.

Shrewd strategy, often verging upon the deceitful, sometimes obtained, as at a quarter race arranged in the 1780's by Jephta Atherton and Allen Jones.

Colonel Atherton had brought to North Carolina a swift Virginia sprinter named Mud Colt, which he offered to match, with £165 up, against any horse Jones could produce, not over fourteen hands high, to carry 130 pounds. The side bet was a tidy £500 in English money—none of your depreciated Continental paper—and the match was set at Tucker's Paths, a haphazard quarter-mile straightaway course.

Atherton appeared with Mud Colt, and Jones brought a fine horse of his own with racing tackle and jockey in a light cart drawn by a small, rough-coated beast of no immediately apparent distinction.

The bets were placed, and the numerous spectators made their own considerable wagers. Judges measured Mud Colt, then Jones' entry. This latter horse was pronounced full three-quarters of an inch above the fourteen hands specified as maximum. Jones beckoned his groom.

"Pare away his hoofs to bring him to the proper height," ordered Jones, and the groom did so, with file and knife. Again the horse was measured but proved still to be a trifle above the fourteen hands.

A second time the groom whittled at the hoofs. Colonel Atherton, observing the poor creature's toes to bleed, sent a messenger to advise certain of his friends to bet largely and confidently. Jones looked, as though on inspiration, at the shaggy horse that had drawn the cart.

"Is he not a horse of tolerable speed?" Jones was heard to ask.

"He is surely a better chance than a horse with no feet," replied the groom, dolefully sententious above the bleeding hoofs.

Gruffly Jones ordered that the animal be led from between the shafts and saddled. This impromptu entry proved to be well below fourteen hands. Gleefully, Colonel Atherton's friends staked their every shilling on Mud Colt.

The two horses were placed at the mark and the signal given. Instantly, Jones' cart horse shot ahead, kept and widened his lead, and won the race by full twenty-seven feet. As bets were paid, the truth came out. That unprepossessing winner, which bore the significantly appropriate name of Trick'em, had been brought, ignominiously uncurried and harnessed, for the very purpose of deluding Atherton and his backers.

Meanwhile, in Virginia, the center of racing shifted from Tidewater tracks like those at Williamsburg to Richmond, Petersburg, and the Southside. Petersburg had managed to hold meetings during the Revolutionary War, and by 1785 the community was so race-crazy that sober town officials passed an ordinance forbidding it on Sundays. On the south side of the Appomattox River, before the end of the eighteenth century, a splendid mile course was laid out in the form of an oval, and, like that other track on Long Island, was called Newmarket. Sand and loam made the track firm

His Ancestors

and fast. The stand was spacious, and dinners and drinks were served on race days. Quickly the Newmarket course became first for popularity in all the South.

North Carolina Thoroughbreds came there, contending on equal terms with the best in Virginia. The great Carolinian turfmen, Johnson, Carney, the Joneses, and Atherton, were seconded by newer vigorous venturers, the Longs, the Bynums, and William Amis. But a formidable Virginia partnership for breeding and training was that of Colonel John Tayloe III and Colonel John Hoomes.

Tayloe's home was Mount Airy, a magnificent country estate on the northern bank of the Rappahannock. The Tayloe stud and stable had come through the war not too greatly impaired. Hoomes, the other partner, was master of the Bowling Green in Caroline County and an earnest contender for supremacy on the American turf. He imported from England a number of leading stallions. Of these the greatest was Diomed, winner of that first Derby at Epsom.

Diomed, a splendid chestnut sixteen hands high, showed no white except a spot on the heel of his right rear foot. He had been foaled in 1777, and, like his grandsire Herod and his sire Florizel, challenged the racing world. After a brilliant beginning as a three-year-old, however, he seemed to lose races, perhaps because of poor conditioning, and in 1785 was placed at stud. However, he did not prosper as a sire in his native England; one expert sternly called him "a *tried* and *proved* bad foal-getter." In the spring of 1798, agents of Colonel Hoomes bought Diomed for the modest sum of £50 sterling and shipped him to Virginia. At the ripe age of twenty-one, Diomed began his first season at the Bowling Green.

Hoomes was enthusiastic about his stallion. "I wish you could see Diomed," he wrote to Tayloe. "I think him the finest horse I ever saw: fully as handsome as Cormorant if not more so, and a great deal larger. He is near sixteen hands and much admired by everyone who has seen him."

15

Sir Archie

But Hoomes sold Diomed a year later, as he had sold other of his imports. Thomas Goode and Miles Selden paid for him with £1,000 Virginia money, approximately $1,500.

However much Diomed had failed in his prime at home, in his ripe years he was an immediate and astounding success in Virginia. By 1803 his first American-born sons and daughters, Madeira, Peace Maker, Diomeda, Lavinia, and others, had defeated fine competition on a number of courses. His get were large and fine animals, promising from colthood.

Hoomes's friend and partner Colonel Tayloe had also made purchases of English Thoroughbreds at about the time Hoomes bought Diomed. In August of 1799, the *Tyne* arrived at a Virginia port with six British horses for Tayloe. Among them was a two-year-old filly named Castianira, dark brown, rangy, and crop-eared after a fad of mutilation that happily did not long endure. Her sire was famous Rockingham, of the King Herod line, and her dam was Tabitha, descended from Highflyer, King Herod's great son.

Tayloe was happy about her purchase, as Hoomes had rejoiced in Diomed. His English agent, James Weatherby, had written of Castianira: "She is a fine looking filly, with good action," but had added with something of pessimism: "...rather high upon the leg, and, when in training, I should be afraid will be light and leggy." She had cost one hundred guineas.

In 1800 Castianira raced and beat a horse hopefully named Celerity, but thereafter she failed on the track. The following year, at the age of four, she was put to breeding, and in 1802 produced a black filly by Mufti, a stallion belonging to Tayloe. In 1803 Tayloe turned her over to the elegant Captain Archie Randolph of Ben Lomond, in Cumberland County below the Appomattox, to breed on shares; and in the spring of 1804, Castianira was led to Selden's estate, Tree Hill, where Diomed, at twenty-seven years of age, was making his seventh American season at stud.

His Ancestors

Poor Castianira, a failure at racing, had become blind. She arrived at Tree Hill under the care of Thomas Larkin, an English groom who had made the trip on the *Tyne* in 1799 and had entered the service of Tayloe as a trainer. A Negro servant, Nat, also came from Ben Lomond with Castianira. Larkin and Nat were present when Castianira was offered to Diomed, and so was young J. M. Selden, son of the proprietor of Tree Hill. These witnesses had occasion to remember the day after a quarter of a century had passed.

Back to Ben Lomond, Castianira made her dark journey. Eleven months followed, and another spring was upon Virginia when Castianira's time came.

Surely the great horse-gods and horse-spirits of antiquity took note of the spring day in 1805 when a bay colt was born of Castianira—totter-legged and fuzzy-tailed, with, as with Diomed, only one small patch of white on the heel of his right hind foot. But his awkwardness did not hide from expert eyes the promise of a mighty future.

❦ II ❦

SIR ARCHIE
Struggles in His Youth

THE age and the land in which blind Castianira's little colt steadied his long shaky legs and lifted his baby head viewed with tremendous preoccupation the breeding and training of horses.

It is difficult to appreciate that preoccupation today. Horses were of a vital necessity to the America of the early nineteenth century and particularly to the agrarian South. Before the coming of the railroads, they were the only means of transportation other than sailing vessels and pole-driven flatboats on navigable waters. Ridden or driven, horses carried lawyers to court, doctors to the sick, students to college, statesmen to the capitol. Great wagons, drawn by fours and sixes of powerful draft animals, bore away the crops of tobacco and cotton and grain, fetched back furniture, food, clothes, tools, and books. Coaches trundled between towns, great journeys and small. Horses dragged ploughs on the farms and plantations, powered the machinery of sugar mills, tobacco presses, cotton gins. The mails rode horseback. So did ministers on wide circuits, and fond lovers seeking the doors of their ladies, and outlaws galloping from holdup to holdup. The towns, villages, and lonely

Sir Archie Struggles in His Youth

homesteads would have perished in isolation without horses. The economy of the nation necessarily used the harness and the saddle.

Along with this great fabric of necessity existed and grew a fabric of luxury, beauty, and excitement carried by the Thoroughbreds.

In that world of plantations, forests, and farms, the post-Revolutionary South had almost no cities or towns worth the name. Southerners, whether great barons of cotton and tobacco or individualistic yeomen, grew and made what they could of needed possessions and had other things brought them. They left home, by choice, for only three reasons—worship, the law, and racing.

Churches, courthouses, and race tracks often were located at strategic points in the little communities, near whatever crossroad huddles did duty for towns. Not infrequently did all three of these centers of interesting activity occur close together and, for the most part, saw the same people in attendance. Blood horses were tied to the hitching rails in front of the meeting houses; attorneys argued eloquently to juries, and at the end of court week went to wager on races. People took their personal interests strongly to heart. Great revival meetings saw hosts swept into loud and spectacular confession of sin and promise of living the godly life. Criminal and civil trials were deemed fascinating events, with a whole countryside crowded into the courtroom or bunched at the doors and windows to hear the thunderings of mighty giants of the law. And the race tracks exerted a universal fascination even greater than that of Colonial days.

For, outside the few cities, there was no other organized public spectacle. Races, in default of theaters and team games, were the one recreation of country dwellers. Crowds swarmed to the courses. Great Americans, from presidents down, gave prayerful attention to the breeding and training of racing champions. The names of the swiftest horses were spoken like the names of national heroes, which indeed such horses became. The most splendid and potent stallions sired whole dynasties of sons and daughters for a glory to the civilization of the thirteen original states, to help that civilization extend itself westward into the wild new lands lately wrung from Indians by buckskin pioneers.

Some of the blood of the noblest horses mingled with that of plainer mares to produce the crossbred hunters and fine saddle stock—cocktails, these animals were sometimes nicknamed—that made glad the hearts of all men. This mixed descent would produce, at last, the final great pageant of Confederate chargers during the Civil War, with names to thrill a nation and a century. Such war horses would include Bedford Forrest's fierce King Philip, who fought blue enemies with his hoofs; Jeb Stuart's Virginia, who led the swift raids around and around George B. McClellan's unwieldy invading army; giant Butler, on whose back giant Wade Hampton rode with drawn saber to the forefront of hand-to-hand battle; and gray Traveller, who with Robert E. Lee in the saddle remains a symbol of high military genius and great military tragedy.

In his office at Mount Airy Plantation, Colonel John Tayloe III opened his carefully kept stud book to the page of Castianira's record and penned a notation:

"1805 May 1st. By a bay coat named Robert Burns 150."

The date was not that of the foaling, but the official birthday specified by turf custom of the time for all foals of that season. The figure 150 meant the estimated value of Castianira's colt. The name suggested a love of certain lyric poems. It was not the name under which that bay colt would thunder to destined glory.

Before he was many weeks old, little Robert Burns travelled forty miles with his mother to Tree Hill where he had been conceived; for Castianira returned, probably in June of 1805, to be mated again with kingly old Diomed. For the colt that meant days of roaming the tree-bordered paddocks at the Selden estate, growing stronger and steadier daily, and a return to Ben Lomond, the

He Struggles in His Youth

miles easier now, for further growth as the summer moved toward fall.

The clumsiness of the baby legs was refined, and muscles clothed their long bones. The furry tippet of a mane, the ludicrous little tussock of a tail, grew into graceful and glossy hair. Thomas Larkin, the trainer who had come from England with Castianira, studied the growing colt with careful eyes, looking for the faults that refused to appear.

Captain Archibald Cary Randolph seems also to have given Robert Burns some attention. The captain was of the romantic strain of John Rolfe and Pocahontas and was a cousin at several removes of John Randolph of Roanoke. To judge from a surviving silhouette likeness, he was gracefully and even delicately handsome. He was unlucky as well.

There hung over Archie Randolph the muttered story, told half with a leer and half with a shudder, of the weird family scandal. In 1792, at a house party at the home of Randolph Harrison, Archie's lovely cousin Nancy had borne a child, said to be fathered by another cousin, Richard; the baby disappeared, and Nancy and Richard were tried for its murder, with Archie as a witness. Once he had courted Nancy; most horribly cured of all affection for her, he had married Lucy Burwell, daughter of sturdy Colonel Nathaniel Burwell up in the Blue Ridge country. Captain Archie Randolph was thirty-six years old in 1805 and in financial difficulty at Ben Lomond. In July of that year one of the Randolph children died, probably at about the time Castianira, having conceived again by Diomed, was led home with Robert Burns beside her.

They had not long to remain at Ben Lomond. Captain Randolph was obliged to sell his estate that summer and to move with his family to Carter Hall in Frederick County, the home of his father-in-law Nathaniel Burwell.

Here was a substantial though not distinguished dwelling house with impressive stables. Burwell had imported English stallions, notably Young Trumpator and Rustic, to improve his stock, and he trained several home-bred colts and fillies for racing. Other Burwell activities included an iron works, a vineyard, a tanyard, and a distillery.

Castianira seems not to have come at once to Carter Hall. Little Robert Burns, however, arrived at the Burwell home, and family tradition says that he was specially privileged by being allowed to play on the great front lawn of Carter Hall. Captain Randolph was less happy and carefree. Another of his children died that September, and business reverses dogged him, along with the sadness.

He continued his efforts at horse breeding. In 1806 Castianira produced a bay filly, full sister to Robert Burns, and her name was Miss Monroe. That year Randolph sent Castianira to the Bowling Green to mate with Hoomes's imported stallion Buzzard.

Hoomes had died in 1805, the year that Robert Burns was foaled. A creepy legend grew up around the tragedy; now and again through the years, Hoomes had sworn to the thunder of invisible hoofs on the private track outside his dining room window, and each time, as that ghostly clatter died away, some member of the Hoomes family died with it. One day at the table, he started from his chair, gazing intently toward the track. He had heard galloping, and he had seen nothing.

"Another death!" he cried, and within twenty-four hours he made good the prediction by his own decease. He was fifty years old.

Within his last few months of life, Hoomes had imported Buzzard, another of the fine sires that replenished and ennobled the Thoroughbred stock in Virginia, and by Buzzard, Castianira produced Hephestion in 1807.

Robert Burns was a two-year-old by then. At such an age, horses emerge from final coltish awkwardness into youthful strength and assurance, and Larkin began the preliminaries of training for Robert Burns's debut on the turf. Such a program meant careful

He Struggles in His Youth

diet and exercise, gentling, and assurance while the youngster grew accustomed to the saddle girth, the bit and the strap, and the guidance of reins by his trainer walking beside him. Meanwhile, Captain Randolph continued in bad fortune and felt forced to sell more of his possessions. Among these was his share of the promising colt.

He found an eager purchaser in Ralph Wormeley IV of Rosegill, son and grandson of Virginia turfmen.

Wormeley assumed Randolph's share of Robert Burns and wanted to enter him in races for the following year; but Archie Randolph had too many worries, and too few resources, to continue the supervision of any training regime at Carter Hall. On May 15, 1807, he wrote to Tayloe:

"I have sent *our fine colt* for you to take and do with as you please. I am not able to do him that justice such a horse is entitled to. He is thought to be the best colt that is anywhere. Larken says the finest two year old he ever saw. Mr. Wormeley will inform you what are his engagements; any part of which you may take. I have named him *Robert Burns* under which name he is entered."

Mount Airy was a magnificent new home for the colt. Tayloe's mansion was of massive stone with walls three feet thick. Closed galleries, also of stone, connected the spacious wings. A terraced slope behind gave a view of the Rappahannock River. There were splendid stables filled with Tayloe's mighty Thoroughbreds; for Tayloe, though of late he had relaxed his turf activities, was considered the foremost of successful breeders and backers of race stock.

Tayloe had been educated in England and knew books as well as he knew horses. In 1807 he was thirty-six years old, a man of massive good looks and great presence. From the age of twenty he had raced, and by 1806, when his interest lagged, his record of fifteen years of campaigning showed that his entries had won 113 races out of 141 starts. When Robert Burns arrived from Carter

Sir Archie

Hall, Tayloe opened his stud book and added to the entry concerning Castianira's colt that the name was changed to Sir Archie in honor of the former master of Ben Lomond.

Scant respect, beyond the affectionate rechristening, did Sir Archie gain at Mount Airy. Something about him did not please the otherwise horse-wise Tayloe, nor could the golden opinions of Captain Randolph and shrewd old Thomas Larkin persuade Tayloe that Sir Archie would uphold the great record of Tayloe racers. It is possible that Tayloe did not want to own a horse in partnership with Wormeley, who might stand stubbornly by his own notions of how Sir Archie could be trained and ridden. Too, there was a certain mare named Young Selima, bred in Tayloe's stables, by his prize stallion Yorick out of Black Selima. Tayloe had sold Young Selima to Wormeley, and he wished he had her back again. Now an opportunity had risen.

The two bargained one bright June day, and then Tayloe opened the stud book again to a page that bore the heading: "Sir Archie, formerly Robert Burns." Under this he wrote:

"My half of this colt I have given to Mr. R. Wormeley for the sorel mare Selima. June 17, 1807. (N. B. I gave $400 to boot.)"

Generous, indeed, those terms; more generous than Tayloe guessed, perhaps more generous than Wormeley guessed too. Selima's later career, if any, does not survive in turf records. Sir Archie went with Wormeley to Rosegill, his fourth home in something like twenty-six months of life.

With Sir Archie, and perhaps other horses once belonging to Randolph, went Thomas Larkin to train Wormeley's racers. At beautiful Rosegill on the Rappahannock, once called a glory of Tidewater Virginia, Sir Archie continued to make ready for his debut in the lively world of racing.

Other descendants of Diomed ruled that world. In 1804 Ball's Florizel, whom Diomed got upon a mare by Thomas Goode's imported Shark, had begun a career of brilliant victory. In two

He Struggles in His Youth

years he had beaten the darlings of all the principal stables—Tayloe's Top Gallant, Selden's Lavinia, Wade Mosby's Amanda, Hoomes's Peace Maker, and the great Northern horse First Consul. Retired to stud in 1806, Florizel at once fathered colts that bore the aspect of future winners. Potomac, a Diomed colt foaled in 1803, had endured disparagement because of a rumor, sworn as fact by serious Thomas Haskins of Prince Edward County, that his dam Fairy was not Thoroughbred. But in 1806 Potomac, after losing his maiden race to Stump-the-Dealer, won two others. In 1807 he was five times winner over fine contenders like Stump-the-Dealer, Rattray, Sir Peter, and Doctor. A sixth race of that fall, at Belfield, found no rival turfman with the confidence to enter a horse against Potomac, who plodded around the course in solitary grandeur to take the prize money. Greater things still were expected of him for the coming spring and fall.

Racers of other strains offered competition to the Diomeds, notably Postboy and Oscar, sons of imported Gabriel, and Floretta and Maid of the Oaks, daughters of imported Spread-Eagle.

Diomed was thirty years old in the spring of 1807 when he accomplished his final season at stud. Fruit of that season included Haynie's Maria, a mare destined for greatness both as racer and progenitrix. On April 15 of 1808 Diomed died, while nobody looked for sure victory from any but his sons and daughters and, possibly, from their descent. Thomas Goode, Diomed's last owner, buried him with affectionate and completely appropriate ceremony in a plot looking down upon the Appomattox.

The autumn sweepstakes at Fairfield Course on the edge of Richmond had attracted some promising colts. Wormeley entered Sir Archie. The field would include three more sons of Diomed—Virginius, Wrangler, and St. Tammany. Young William R. Johnson of Warrenton in North Carolina had entered True Blue, son of imported True Blue. There were also Palafox by imported Jonah and another colt named Moloch.

Sir Archie

Thomas Larkin's preparation for a race extended over an eight-week period, to build from a comparative briskness of activity to strenuous full-time conditioning. He liked his horse to be in good flesh at the beginning. For eight days he gave such a candidate a four-mile walk night and morning, under horse clothes and a blanket. Feeding and watering were rigidly supervised. Twice a day there were oats, chopped corn, and hard-twisted bundles of corn blades. Water, also twice a day, was limited to no more or less than forty swallows at a time. The horse underwent thorough rubbings with wisps of straw for the body and woolen cloths for the legs and washings with water and Castille soap.

The second eight days saw the regime stepped up with morning gallops of two miles. These conditioning workouts prepared the entry for longer and harder trials, with a rider not exceeding the weight to be carried in the coming race; sweats were followed by washing, cooling out, and rubbing until the horse's coat shone; there were regular and hearty feedings of selected grain and forage, with a muzzle to be worn at night to discourage nibbling at the straw on the floor of the stall.

While Sir Archie's training continued thus under Thomas Larkin, Ralph Wormeley found that racing, his family's deepest joy for three generations, had palled on him. On August 19 he published an announcement in the Fredericksburg *Virginia Herald*:

"Being determined to quit the turf, I offer for sale the following horses which may be purchased with or without their engagements, very low for cash, or on good terms and twelve months' credit.... The horses are in good condition and now training at Prospect Hill where they may be seen and their prices known by application to Mr. Thomas Larkin or the subscriber...."

He named four horses for sale, including Sir Archie, and his advertisement concluded: "Sir Archie is engaged in the great sweepstakes at Fairfield next October."

No purchaser came forward for Sir Archie, though many felt he

MOWFIELD PLANTATION

From a water color by Edward Hopper, presenting a good impression of what the Amis family mansion was like in its great days. The house still stands in fair condition but is empty.

He Struggles in His Youth

would make a splendid showing. Miles Selden, who owned Wrangler, was particularly respectful. On August 23 he wrote to his friend Tayloe in terms that may have impelled that astute horseman to regret a certain swapping of the previous summer:

"... [The Fairfield race] will be a grand stake, and who will win it is uncertain. The contest will be between Sir Archie, St. Tammany, Mr. Wilkin's colt, and Wrangler. Larkin and Wormeley have high expectations of Sir Archie, and I dread him more than any other colt; although I think Wrangler will beat any colt in America. Sir Archie will make a fine stallion after he has done running."

The young pretender to racing greatness was, by all accounts, a joy to look upon now that he had gained his full size and power.

He was sixteen hands and a fraction of an inch high—just under five feet five inches at the withers. He appeared vigorous, clean-limbed, and swift. His proportions were considered ideal in a race horse. Of special and significant strength were his shoulders, high at the withers and sloping toward the short, well-knit back and the lower-set hips behind. His thighs and forearms showed long, smooth musculature. Grace and pride were in the rise of his neck. His eye was brilliant, and in profile his head showed a concave nose, the mark of Arabian blood.

Wormeley, while waiting for a purchaser for Sir Archie, felt ambitious enough on his account to enter him in the Washington Sweepstakes, two-mile heats, to be run before the Fairfield meeting at Richmond. After those races, and the chances of victory in both were good, Sir Archie might look to his fourth year and the height of vigorous maturity, with perhaps something like the successes enjoyed by Ball's Florizel and Potomac.

But, while Wormeley and Larkin meditated thus, bad luck turned in at the stables and hitched to the rail. Sir Archie contracted a case of distemper.

This disease, which bears the impolite nickname of bastard strangles, is apt to assail young horses. It is induced by a special equine streptococcus which is picked up in food or water. In Sir Archie's day, ignorant of how germs infect an organism, it was compared by turfmen and veterinarians to human measles, a troublesome affliction apt to attack almost every horse in his youth, with immunity thereafter. Some efforts had been made to inoculate against it, using the pus of afflicted animals, but no great approval of such treatment was voiced in 1808.

As suffered by Sir Archie, it was a melancholy disease, beginning with coughing, a soreness of the throat, and a high fever that took away the strength and the appetite. This was followed by swelling of the glands beneath the jaw and behind and under the ears. Abscesses formed under the skin. The feet became unsteady, the knees trembled, the head drooped, and the nose ran, dolefully and profusely. Wretched Sir Archie stood trembling and burning, while his flanks heaved and his head drooped almost to the floor.

There was no curing of this disease save by allowing it to run its course. For two weeks or more, the poor ailing beast was tended skilfully and delicately. Treatment included poultices for the swellings to induce them to ripen and break. Sir Archie was confined to his stall in as cool an atmosphere as was possible in the Virginia summer. His grooms mixed warm bran mashes and coaxed him to eat and drink.

Fortunately, there were no complications of influenza or pneumonia. Larkin and his helpers, anxiously nursing Sir Archie, did not expect him to die, but his training stopped, of course, as soon as the first fever slowed and staggered him. The wretched colt was forced to mope indoors, feet weakly spraddled, fine head hanging to his very straw litter, until such time as the abscesses broke and discharged their unlovely burden of pus. Then, and not until then, did the fever abate, did he eat properly and begin to gain back his health.

Apparently Sir Archie endured his siege of distemper with a patience and stamina that were personal traits to be noted as life-long

He Struggles in His Youth

in his character. Healed at last, he returned to light exercise, then to galloping, but it was too late for him to regain the form and speed that had delighted Wormeley and Larkin and correspondingly had daunted Selden.

Forfeits had been posted for Sir Archie's running in the races at Washington and Richmond. Lest that money be lost, Wormeley bade Larkin do what he could to get the colt into shape. There was some last-minute training at speed over the two-mile distance Sir Archie must run, with medicines and mixtures of egg whites and wine in his food. The day of the Washington race arrived, and Sir Archie was as ready as he could be made.

It was, of course, a noisily brilliant occasion. President Thomas Jefferson, who once had owned a colt that beat George Washington's prized Magnolio, may have forgotten the cares of office for a brief hour in watching the horses run that day. Much more certainly, Senator John Randolph of Roanoke was there, for he bred and trained his own horses, had in his boyhood ridden races, and was as enthusiastic about Thoroughbreds as he was about states' rights.

If such distinguished spectators were present, they could not have admired Sir Archie to any great degree. The poor convalescent did his best, and that was nowhere good enough. Bright Phoebus, a Northern colt by imported Messenger, won the race decisively, his only distinguished performance to survive in fame, while Sir Archie finished nowhere.

Tingling from this defeat, Sir Archie was led back to Prospect Hill for further training and improved somewhat before he went to Richmond for the Fairfield Sweepstakes. But the day of that contest found him still poor in flesh and far below his best potential form.

The Fairfield track was on the northeastern edge of Richmond. It was unevenly kept and was considered slow running at best, but its convenience to the town made it popular. From the grandstand spectators had a splendid view of the city. On race days, wrote one who loved to go there, "... grave judges adjourned their courts, presidents of banks deserted their seats, and distinguished lawyers dropped their briefs to dispense, respectively, the light of their learned and financial phizzes on the occasion of some great contest of frantic interest to tiers of counties on either side of the upper or lower James." The day of the Fairfield Sweepstakes for 1808, says another reminiscence, was fine. Probably it was bright, mild Southern autumn weather.

Throngs of spectators had come, in carriages or on horseback, to range themselves in close order along the edge of the track. At the word of the judges, the horses were brought to the starting post.

They were seven, ridden by Negro jockeys. Sir Archie found himself ranged with his brothers Wrangler and Virginius, the North Carolina colts True Blue and Palafox, Moloch, and one other whose name does not survive in the account. No general favorite was recognized, though Selden's friends gave Wrangler some advantage. An onlooker recognized "diversity of opinion everywhere," and undoubtedly handfuls of gold and silver, sheafs of bank notes, were wagered throughout the crowd.

A drum tap, and they were away for the first heat.

Palafox, not widely fancied, instantly extended himself to go to the front. He took the lead around the first turn, kept ahead of the others on the back stretch, and at the second turn seemed to be winning. But Wrangler, plucky son of Diomed, found within himself resources and will to achieve a final spurt. He caught up in the homestretch, shot ahead within a few yards of the winning post, and was declared winner over Palafox by a scant but glorious eighteen inches.

Selden and his friends were jubilant. The backers of Palafox did not despair. A thirty-minute space for breathing and rubbing down, and again the seven colts mustered for the second heat.

As before, Palafox proved himself a quick starter and gained the foremost position, with True Blue and Moloch fighting to overtake

He Struggles in His Youth

and pass him. Wrangler ran confidently behind. The spectators could see that he was being held for another homestretch effort.

They came to the second turn. There, one segment of the track provided better footing than the rest. Wrangler's jockey rode wide to take advantage of this, but Wrangler blundered into Virginius. He lost his balance and went down in a heavy floundering fall.

On past the squirming body of Wrangler shot the others, Virginius, unshaken by his collision with Wrangler, regained his stride, made a spirited effort, and passed Moloch to contend with True Blue and Palafox. These three came down the homestretch close together, fighting almost to the last yard for victory. True Blue won.

When the third heat was called, the owner of Palafox, observing that his colt was exhausted by his pacemaking for most of two heats, withdrew him. Wrangler, evidently incapacitated by his fall, did not come to the post. Moloch and the unnamed colt, neither of whom had come close to making a figure in the first two heats, likewise were withdrawn.

But Sir Archie responded. With four of the seven entries scratched, he contended only with True Blue, hard pushed to win that second heat, and Virginius. If Sir Archie could win the third heat, the race might be decided by a fourth, and in his favor. Convinced that Sir Archie still had a chance, Wormeley and Larkin sent him to the post, hoping to see him win reputation and money.

New wagers were placed upon Virginius. He had shown in the second heat, and that after dangerous jostling which might have thrown a lesser horse clear out of competition. The three came to the starting post. Once again the signal, and away they sped.

At once it became a fierce contest between True Blue and Virginius—"a most beautiful heat," one spectator would remember for nearly a quarter of a century. Gallantly and brilliantly, the two colts fought for the lead all the way around the course. Again at the very last, victory-savoring True Blue made good his flying place in front, but up behind him and the hotly rivalling Virginius came Sir Archie, badly out of condition and making none of the appearance of the horse he could be. He had only heart on which to run, and on that he ran. When True Blue shot home the winner, with Virginius a close second, Sir Archie managed to make a good third in the heat.

The blue October sky rang and trembled with cheers for the victor. True Blue was properly paraded and honored, and those who had fancied Wrangler or Virginius paid their bets. Attention fixed itself, naturally, on True Blue—but not all attention.

True Blue's owner was there, as striking a figure as one might look for, even among Southern plantation aristocrats of the early nineteenth century.

At twenty-six, William Ransom Johnson was a man of graceful figure and bold handsomeness. His hair, prematurely white, flowed like a great snowy mane. He had level dark eyes, a proudly curved nose, a strong, well-cut chin. His dress was unostentatious but rich. His manners were impeccable. His critical knowledge of horseflesh was unsurpassed.

He had been born in Warrenton, North Carolina, in the heart of the rising center of Thoroughbred racing, but he owned Virginia plantations and was as well known in Virginia as in his own state. The year before he had been elected to the North Carolina legislature, though politics were, with him, of an importance secondary to horse breeding and training. His father, Marmaduke Johnson, had tried to implant other interests in him, but from boyhood William Johnson had proved himself a genius of the turf. True Blue was his sixty-first winner among entries in sixty-three races during the past two years. William Johnson was accustomed to winning.

Perhaps that habit of victory enabled him to expect it and to receive it with cool blood and clear eyes, so that he could watch other horses than his own. He could recognize, as did others of less gift, that considerable good luck had attended True Blue's triumphant performance. During the three heats at Fairfield he had been watching another man's horse—unhappy Sir Archie, who had made no figure in the first two heats, whose brave effort had brought him free of ignominy in the third.

It was said of Johnson that he had only to look at a horse to see how well he could run. If so, it must have filled his pockets with the money of turfmen less sharp-sighted. Now at the Fairfield track, Johnson felt that he saw how well Sir Archie would run, on another and healthier day than this.

Dodging the duties of a winning colt's owner, he sought out Ralph Wormeley and came to the point at once.

It was plain to Johnson how Sir Archie might perform when he was right; aye, and he had not been right today. Distemper, was it not, and the poor colt scarce cured? And had not Mr. Wormeley advertised, back in August, that he wanted to sell certain horses, including this one? What, then, would Wormeley consider a fair price for Sir Archie?

There was not much haggling. William Johnson paid $1,500 on the spot for the losing colt, led him aside, and surveyed him expertly.

At once he perceived that Sir Archie was in poor flesh and still short of complete recovery from his bout of distemper but in no way permanently damaged. What he needed just now was a season of coddling and conditioning.

Back to Warrenton rode Colonel William Johnson. Along with victorious True Blue, the groom led Sir Archie.

III

SIR ARCHIE
Outshines the Racers

THE new home to which William Johnson conducted Sir Archie was a paradise for horses and those who loved and understood them.

The misfortunes of war had been only the start of the downfall of Virginia Tidewater turfmen. Tobacco, which had made their Colonial forebears great and wealthy, had taken its payment from their soil. Starved acres sprawled where rich and royal crops had been grown and reaped, and planters went shabby and debt-ridden or moved away inland and southward to fatter holdings. The beautiful Roanoke River country now dared to challenge the rest of America for racing supremacy.

Warren County lies in the northeastern part of North Carolina, just below the Virginia state line. In 1808 beautiful little Warrenton, the county seat, included but a few houses along its quiet, tree-shaded streets, but among these were beautiful residences inhabited by men and women of notable character and charm. Small fields and great stretched in all directions around the town, making their owners wealthy with mighty yields of tobacco, cotton, and grain.

Sir Archie Outshines the Racers

The climate and the atmopshere of Warrenton were considered healthful, and many invalids and convalescents came there to rest and grow strong. A chief boast was the Warrenton Academy for boys, which bore the reputation of a splendid school and was attended by sons of many distinguished Virginians and North Carolinians.

Colonel William Johnson's plantation lay just below the south edge of Warrenton with the Halifax Stage Road running between his home and the town. The lady of his magnificent house was Mary Johnson, daughter of Dr. George Evans of Oakland on the Appomattox in Chesterfield County, Virginia. The hospitality she dispensed was called remarkable, even in a land and time that held hospitality to be a sacred duty and supreme pleasure.

This was the heart of the Roanoke region, and its horses became increasingly important on the track as the first decade of the century progressed. The climate may have been a factor. The grazing was good, and the flat, firm ground was excellent for race courses. But most important of all were the method and temperament of the men who lived there.

Marmaduke Johnson, father of William Johnson, was the pioneer of the turf in his home district. Tradition says that he began his career as a horseman in a somewhat offhand manner. One morning, as he came out to mount his fine horse, sired by Janus' prolific son Meade's Celer, he paused to admire the graceful lines of the animal. He asked the Negro groom who held the bridle if the horse could run. That he could, replied the groom; it was mighty hard for the boys to catch him in the pasture.

Pondering this information, Johnson rode into Warrenton and dismounted at a tavern, where his friend Kemp Plummer sat at backgammon. What, inquired Johnson, did Plummer think of organizing a race.

"What will you start?" asked Plummer.

Johnson indicated his mount. "My nag against the best riding horse in town."

"Done, sir," was Plummer's eager reply. "Your nag against my Bessy."

"It's a bet," agreed Johnson, "and I'll have a quarter-of-a-mile race track made on my land."

He did so at once. A smooth, straight quarter-mile stretch was soon finished, while the town's best saddler achieved a masterpiece for Johnson's horse to wear in the contest. The people of the town and the surrounding country turned out on race day to watch and wager, and Johnson's Celer horse badly trounced Plummer's Bessy. In time, the track was extended into a three-quarter-mile curve. Other and larger tracks were laid out later to make Warrenton a center of racing.

Before the match staged by Johnson and Plummer, North Carolina's horses had been running against each other more or less haphazardly. Stores at country crossroads, taverns on the edge of hamlets, did duty as highly irregular jockey clubs, and ill-trained mounts with reckless riders sometimes drove to fatal accidents as they won or lost. Marmaduke Johnson wanted something better than that. He recognized the fading of the Virginia Tidewater from the turf, and the rise of the Roanoke region above Warren County. He saw a chance to prepare and compete, and he began to build up his stable.

One of his earliest important purchases was a fine racing filly, daughter of Medley, who won for him and later became a successful matron. Her sons and daughters, by the end of the eighteenth century, began to reap glory on Virginia tracks.

Johnson's North Carolina neighbors and friends felt stirred to emulation. They, too, spent money and made careful plans for turf successes. A masterfully individual set of men, these new assailants of racing citadels.

In most cases they were new in the land they cultivated and

He Outshines the Racers

dominated. Many of them were Virginians by birth or immediate descent, and among them were a number of veterans of the Revolutionary War. Others prized commissions in the state militia and were addressed as Colonel, Major, or Captain. Successful, proud, confident, they numbered their acres by thousands, their slaves by scores. Most of them could display legs bowed by long years astride good horses. Formal education was apt to be limited, but they had polite upbringing and were capable of speaking well. They danced as skilfully as they rode and held their liquor as gentlemen of their sort were obliged by custom to hold it. They were splendid shots, whether in pursuit of deer and partridge or in settling some difference of opinion with hair-trigger pistols at twenty paces.

Their pleasures were vigorous and competitive. They wagered on everything, and heavily. A main of fighting cocks, a game of cards, a local election, a horse race—such was occasion for backing one's considered judgment with all the money in one's pocket, and perhaps with one's horse, plantation, or most valuable slave as well. The classic story of a wager in that community concerned Nathaniel Macon, Warren County's most distinguished son and long North Carolina's outstanding political leader.

Coming home to North Carolina from Revolutionary War battlefields, tall young Nat Macon was staggeringly smitten with the beauty of Miss Hannah Plummer, for whose attention a whole platoon of admirers contended. Assiduously Macon paid court to her until he had disposed of all rivals save one. Miss Hannah smiled upon both Macon and this survivor of the competition, ravishingly and with a maddening impartiality, until the evening when both swains came to call.

The three of them sat in the parlor, and the two young gentlemen found themselves able to speak, in each other's presence, with the utmost frank admiration of Miss Hannah. Each said unequivocally that he wished to offer marriage. Macon unsmilingly proposed that he and his rival play a hand of cards then and there; the winner to go unopposed in his future wooing, the loser to depart from the Plummer home and importune the lady no more.

It says volumes for the regional acceptance of gambling that neither did Miss Hannah consider herself insulted, nor did the other suitor seem amazed by this grotesque challenge. Cards were brought, and the two dealt and played. Within moments, Macon lost.

He then crowned his fantastic gamble with what may well be the most sensational instance in all North Carolina history of welshing on a bet. He rose from the card table, quivering in every fiber of his six-foot frame.

"Hannah," he mumbled brokenly, "I have lost you fairly, but love is greater than fortune—I still love you as much as ever!"

Beautiful with instant tears, the winsome prize of the game flung herself into the arms of its loser. He who had thought himself the winner took his hat, went out of the door, and strode away, forgotten by Macon and his sweetheart, and almost forgotten by later generations who told the tale.

The North Carolinians who wanted to become great in the world of swift horses had an early fortunate advantage in various stallions and mares of blood that had been sent down from Virginia to save them from the hands of thieving Tories. The get of these sires and dams came into the possession of Marmaduke Johnson, his friends, and opponents, and numerous other fine animals were purchased elsewhere in the colonies or imported outright.

Governor James Turner of Warren County owned the imported stallions True Blue, Magic, Jonah, and Bryan O'Lynn. In neighboring Halifax County, bluff General Stephen W. Carney became proprietor of imported Phoenix and Citizen and two excellent British brood mares, Honeysuckle and Allegranto. Willie Jones of the Grove in Halifax, patriot leader during the Revolution and later so earnest for states' rights that he avoided shaking hands with President George Washington, owned Whirlagig and by him bred a whole squadron of racers. Willie Jones's brother Allen of Mount

He Outshines the Racers

Gallant gained fame with imported Partner. Other Halifaxians who helped make this a leading Thoroughbred region were John Hamilton, John Dawson, and John Drew. In Northampton County, Jephta Atherton and his sons Jesse and Wade presented more competition, and William Amis, who had come out of the Revolution with the basis of a fortune by sales of military supplies, also turned to horse breeding.

But young William Johnson, improving on his father's start, was master of all these.

At about the time he brought Sir Archie home to Warren County, William Johnson's numerous sensational victories on Virginia's most fashionable courses had won him the nickname of the Napoleon of the Turf. Admiring ladies liked better to call him the Irish Beauty. From somewhere had come a colonelcy to tack itself in front of his name. At twenty-seven, he was considered the prince of all those who judged, trained, and raced horses. The best of aspiring horsemen begged him to supervise the training of their own colts, and a man whose hopeful entry was raced under the Johnson colors—blue cap and blue jacket—considered himself specially and fortunately singled out. Johnson's decisions on pedigree, conformation, soundness, and racing class went undisputed throughout the whole South.

Despite the advantage of living within a few minutes' ride of that fine Warrenton Academy, Johnson's education, like that of many of his contemporaries, was haphazard. He parrotted the boast of Andrew Jackson that he had never read a book through and liked also to say that nothing was better for the inside of a man than the outside of a horse. Though he was active in politics throughout the whole of his long life, he seems to have said and written very little except for business and racing reasons. Yet he was neither unintelligent nor uncouth. At a time when North Carolinians did not greatly shine in the eyes of Virginia aristocrats, Johnson was welcome in the homes of the best Tidewater barons, including those where horses were not the chief topic of conversation. His manner of speech, said

Sir Archie

a contemporary, was of "oracular sententiousness." He stood as a model of grace and dignity from his youth upwards.

Before coming with Johnson to the Warren County plantation, Sir Archie had lived on a variety of estates under several masters, but a constant factor in his daily life from foalhood had been the friendly care of his trainer, Thomas Larkin. Now Sir Archie passed into the hands of another trainer, and that, perhaps, the greatest trainer of the time in all America.

Like Larkin, Arthur Taylor had come from England. As a boy he had been a jockey, and a good one. But he had brains, too, where horses were concerned, enough to gain him quick promotion from riding winners to training them. He was twenty years old in 1808, a small young man, lean and hard and springy as a hickory stave, with bowed legs and a habit of carrying his head to one side. Along with his reputation for brilliance as a trainer, he cherished a name for honesty in all dealings. William Johnson habitually addressed him as Governor. When Johnson won the title of the Napoleon of the Turf, Taylor came to be called Talleyrand. Quite probably, a reckonable measure of Johnson's supremacy on track after track was due to Taylor's fine and faithful trainership.

Into the skillful care of Taylor, Sir Archie was delivered to undergo, first of all, a pleasant regime of feeding and light exercise to restore his health. When he started to put on weight and his hide became loose and glossy once more, his new schooling began.

Sir Archie's performances on Johnson's private track promptly convinced both owner and trainer that he was a natural four-miler of fine promise. Toward that popular and gruelling distance he was educated.

Races of four-mile heats had been popular in England for a century, and, early in the 1800's, they represented the cream and the jam of racing on both sides of the Atlantic, though the popularity of the swift-sprinting descendants of the great imported Janus still

He Outshines the Racers

held attention to quarter-racing. Thrilling to watch, four-mile contests were also exhausting to perform.

"The heroic distance," such a race was called, and a horse must be excellent of his kind to run it with any success. Four-mile heats could mean a lot of running in a single day. Even in a match of two, the best two heats out of three, twelve miles of superb performance often were required. With a field of several hard-running entries, as many as five heats might be run before the victor was named—twenty miles at a killing pace with but thirty-minute rest periods between heats.

That required the utmost in speed and bottom, along with the most rigidly achieved condition. Ball's Florizel, a son of Diomed out of a Shark mare, had outclassed all competition in 1805 because, it was insisted, he had achieved a raking stride of twenty-eight feet. Nor was such racing for young colts, still short of their utmost in powerful mature performance. Too quick an introduction to the heroic distance might mean an early breakdown of a swift and spirited animal; turf history was full of examples. Four-year-olds usually were introduced to four-mile heats after a third year that showed ability at the shorter distances, with a winter to give solider bottom, sharper reactions, and shrewder judgment to complement the riding of a good jockey. Some of the best horses thus intelligently prepared continued to excel on the four-mile track for years, scoring victories in their veteran years.

Arthur Taylor himself must often have ridden Sir Archie on exercise gallops during that mild North Carolina winter and the early spring of 1809; at other times he closely supervised Sir Archie's improving performances with the capable Negro exercise boys who were another example of Johnson's fine critical selection. No doubt, agreed Taylor and Johnson, that here was a four-miler for the ages, better than anything either of them had offered in competition before; better, particularly, than True Blue, who had been preternaturally lucky to win the Fairfield Sweepstakes the previous fall.

Sir Archie

When the spring meets began, Sir Archie was taken to Richmond to run in the Annual Post Stakes on the Fairfield track where he had known undeserved humiliation.

The field assembled for the event was headed by Miles Selden's Wrangler. This horse, too, had been less than lucky at Fairfield last spring, and during the winter he had developed, like Sir Archie, into a four-miler of promise. The day before the Post Stakes, Wrangler had fairly flown to glorious victory over all rivals for the Jockey Club Purse, but those who saw and respected the confidence of Colonel Johnson were immediately ready to back Sir Archie against the field.

Those bets on Sir Archie paid off. He won splendidly, and Colonel Selden and others of the Wrangler faction must have goggled rather foolishly. Was this the same horse which, six months earlier, had done so little worth a turfman's serious notice at either Washington or Richmond? Damned odd, gentlemen. Anyhow, Wrangler had run under some disadvantage; he had been somewhat tired from the previous day's race for the Jockey Club Purse. Another day, perhaps.

The two Diomeds were matched for the following week, at Newmarket Course northwest of Petersburg, for another Jockey Club prize.

Newmarket was becoming more popular than any of the courses around Richmond. For one thing, the track was smoother, firmer and faster than Fairfield. For another, accommodations for spectators were better. Banks Moody, the proprietor, had advertised Newmarket's attractions the year before:

"The subscriber who keeps the New Market Course has proved from long experience that to serve the public attentively and moderately are the most certain means of being remunerated for his labor, that he is therefore determined that every exertion shall be made on his part to promote the convenience and add to the amusements of those who may visit the races. An elegant stand 100 feet in length is already built on the field in which sumptuous dinners will be served up each day of the races. The advantages of being protected from inclement weather or the hot sun, feasting on the fat of our land and quaffing the choicest liquors all in full view of the contending coursers must greatly add to the gratification of the gentlemen...."

Hedgelike stretches of trees and shrubs enclosed the back stretch and the two turns of the oval track, with a fence along the front. Careful draining kept the course firm even in bad weather, and the space enclosed by the oval was sown that spring to wheat.

When Sir Archie and Wrangler came to the post with the other entries, a large crowd was present as usual, distinguished by high society and high officialdom. Probably William Haxall, auctioneer and horse-breeder, sat his saddle and trumpeted his predictions. Dash, the dog that always haunted the judges' stand, must also have been a spectator, and the stand was crowded by those who loved good food, good drink, and good racing.

Wrangler vindicated the claims of Selden that day by taking the first heat decisively, ahead of Sir Archie and the other entries. The second heat saw Sir Archie fighting Wrangler every step of the way and coming up along the home stretch to what looked like a tie. The judges pondered and argued long before they awarded that second heat to Wrangler.

Colonel Selden himself may have appeared surprised at hearing his horse declared the victor. Johnson, unconvinced, sought Seldon and challenged to a match between Wrangler and Sir Archie on the spot—a single heat of four miles for a substantial side bet.

Selden declined. He still dreaded Sir Archie.

Back to Warren County, Johnson took his new favorite for a summer's further conditioning and training. Sir Archie continued to improve. The victory at Fairfield and the harrying of Wrangler at Newmarket had been but a hint of what he might become. Confidently Johnson entered him for the autumn in yet another race at Fairfield, the fall Jockey Club Purse, four-mile heats.

Sir Archie

Again Wrangler would be his swift opponent. Another would be Rattray, also a darling of the Selden stables, beaten in 1807 by Potomac but greatly improved since then and a dangerous contender. There were also Minerva, by Diomed out of a Highflier mare, and Tom Tough, an entry from the brilliant Hoomes stable at Bowling Green who was all that his name implied.

Of the string of horses Johnson mustered for his autumn campaign, Sir Archie plainly was considered the star; and Sir Archie's foremost rival still would be Wrangler, the high hope of Selden.

The two Diomeds, Sir Archie and Wrangler, as intelligent Thoroughbreds, must have been horsily aware of each other as opponents. They had raced three times, each time to the utmost of their powers. At their first meeting, Sir Archie, still groggy from his ordeal of distemper and only partially trained, had seen Wrangler's heels in the first heat and had passed him in the second only because Wrangler had stumbled clear out of the running. Their next trial against each other, at the Fairfield Course for the Post Stakes in the spring of 1809, had been a clear win for Sir Archie, but Wrangler's backers had complained that their horse had been weary from a hard race the day before. The Newmarket contest had seen Wrangler win only by a vexed decision. Clear-cut settlement of the gallant rivalry was still to be achieved.

However, early fall again brought the spectre of bad luck to threaten Sir Archie. Only a few days before Johnson's horses were to take the road for Richmond, Sir Archie went out for a conditioning canter, and the exercise boy found it difficult to control him. Startled or irritated, Sir Archie ran away with his rider, and, when pulled up at last, proved to be limping.

Unlike Wormeley a year before, Johnson did not consider sending his horse to run if it meant defeat. Johnson departed with the rest of his string. Sir Archie stayed behind in the stables with instructions to his handlers that, should he show an unexpected good recovery, he should be brought on.

TRIFLE, THE BRILLIANT DAUGHTER

From another of Edwin Troye's splendid portraits, reproduced through courtesy of the National Museum of Racing, Inc., at Saratoga Springs, New York. Small, delicately made, but of gigantic speed and stamina, Trifle was worthy of her sire Sir Archie as a race winner and later proved herself as a dam of outstanding turf champions.

He Outshines the Racers

Within short days he recovered from his lameness with a heartening completeness, and a groom followed Johnson's main party with Sir Archie on a halter. They arrived at Richmond before race time.

Johnson examined his pet contender. Several days of enforced idleness had put some flesh on Sir Archie's flanks, and Johnson would have preferred him much trimmer for so important a trial. But, when the field assembled for the Jockey Club Purse, Sir Archie joined Wrangler, Rattray, Tom Tough, and Minerva at the starting post.

Sapient observers in the stand and along the track told each other that Johnson's entry, so high in flesh, could never survive a series of fast four-mile heats, but betting on him for the first heat was immediate and lively.

The signal was given, and away went the five horses.

Favored Wrangler, swift as lightning, jumped into the lead. Sir Archie was close behind him. The others strove but fell back with each stride. Plainly the heat would be decided between the two splendid four-year-old Diomeds that represented Johnson and Selden. Wrangler seemed to know it, and he ran, undoubtedly, the best race he had ever run in his fine career.

Around they went, and around, Wrangler still fighting gamely to stay in front. At midpoint of the four miles, watches showed that Wrangler had run those two miles in three minutes and forty-six seconds, the fastest time for that distance ever recorded on the Fairfield Course. Brave fellow! But—

Scarcely had the watches snapped shut before Sir Archie slid past the striving Wrangler.

Now the watchers from stand and trackside could see that Sir Archie had run second so far only because he had been saving himself. Still under a pull by his jockey, he drew away from Wrangler by a neck, a length, two lengths. For half a mile more, Wrangler did his frantic best to recapture that lost lead, but he could not even hold his own. Back he was forced to drop, and back. At the end of two and a half miles, Wrangler gave up the effort to win. As for Rattray, Tom Tough, and Minerva, they loped far behind, hopelessly outclassed and distanced.

From then to the winner's post, it was a question only as to whether Wrangler or any other horse could save his distance and escape disqualification. That did not happen, even when Sir Archie reduced his own magnificent speed and finally, as his jockey pulled him up, actually walked home a winner.

No question was entertained further as to whether Sir Archie could survive a succession of exhausting heats. He had distanced and disqualified his opponents without any seemingly great effort. The race was won, the purse awarded, and the bets paid on that decisive single heat.

So much for poor outrun Wrangler, and so much for Colonel Miles Selden who had hoped for miracles from him. Colonel Johnson made his habitual bows to the applause for a magnificently chosen and trained winner and took Sir Archie twenty miles southward to the Newmarket Course, where Wrangler had been victor in the spring.

Wrangler did not compete a week later when another field of hopefuls assembled to run four-mile heats for the Newmarket Jockey Club Purse. Sir Archie came to the post with all a conqueror's confidence. What happened was, to those who had followed the racers down from Richmond, almost boringly repetitious. Sir Archie quickly and decisively ran away from his competition, distanced everything, and again won his race in a single heat.

Yet another brilliant event was coming, the Belfield meet in Greensville County, just above the North Carolina border as Johnson and Sir Archie headed home, but Johnson did not offer to start his brilliant protege there. A crack field had been assembled, and the favorite was Blank, the talented charge of General Stephen Carney.

Blank was the son of imported Centinel, a sturdy and consistently

He Outshines the Racers

victorious horse in England. Earlier in 1809 Blank had won brilliantly. He crowned his autumn campaign at Belfield by beating a field of seven, which included two sons of Diomed—Gallatin and Dinwiddie—and Rainbow, son of Tickle Toby.

William Johnson may have been present at Belfield to watch Blank's feat, or he may have heard of it in Warren County. In any case, he instantly challenged Carney's horse in Sir Archie's name.

Two weeks after Blank's day of glory at Belfield, he and Sir Archie were brought to Scotland Neck in Halifax County, there to run four-mile heats against each other. No other horse seemed so gifted, even in the optimistically distorted regard of his owner, as to be entered with these two paladins of the year.

Johnson appeared confident again, indeed more confident than ever. Already he had written to a friend: "I would match Sir Archie against any horse for $5,000 or $10,000, four mile heats, being satisfied that he is the best horse I have ever seen." Nobody was inclined to dissent from that judgment, save possibly General Carney.

A banner crowd of Virginia and Carolina enthusiasts lined the sides of the course at Scotland Neck. The two horses came to the post. At the signal, they were off.

They started almost exactly together. To some watchers, they appeared to run cautiously, even deliberately, but that may have been because at first their strides were so well matched. For the first two miles they raced thus evenly with Sir Archie a few feet in the lead. Then Blank exerted himself, seeking to draw ahead.

Sir Archie's pace quickened on the instant. He kept in front, not widening the gap, but running faster and yet faster as Blank attempted a spurt. Indeed, it seemed that Sir Archie had tremendous reserves of strength and speed on which he drew only a little at a time, just enough to stay that short distance ahead. In they came, Sir Archie winning the heat by something more than a length, and the judges compared their watches.

Seven minutes and fifty-two seconds—that made it the fastest four

Sir Archie

miles ever run by any horse south of the James River, and the last two miles, with Blank making his greatest effort, had been accomplished by Sir Archie in three minutes and forty-six seconds. Do the sum in your head, gentlemen; the first two miles must have taken full four minutes and six seconds. Slow, when it was Sir Archie running. Manifestly he had held himself back to let Blank make what contest he could.

Cheers and applause. Bets were paid, new bets offered and taken. Then the second heat was called.

Again a start almost together, again Sir Archie forging ever so slightly to the front, again Blank doing his best to overtake Sir Archie, and again Blank failing utterly to do so. Sir Archie won the second heat in the same manner he had won the first, not a great distance ahead and quite clearly not extended to anything like his utmost. The time was eight minutes flat. Sir Archie had but accommodated himself to the supreme effort of his opponent.

In the thick of the tempest of excited adulation, Johnson must have pondered that this was something of a climax to his swift, brave horse's running career.

Sir Archie's life, up to the point of that victory at Scotland Neck, had been brief, suspenseful, troubled, and dramatic, and now it was crowned with the highest and most richly deserved success. Underappreciated in his colthood, passed from hand to careless hand by turfmen whose usual good judgment about horses had seemed to falter where he was concerned, Sir Archie from the first had contained within his splendid bay body every single quality that became a prince of race horses. Even so, he had come to his first colt races virtually as a convalescent from a serious and wasting disease. Against crack opponents he had been able to show only one quality of a champion, that of tameless courage. His mighty heart had been strained by the ordeal, but it had not been broken.

Then, after so unhappy a beginning, he had come by a gratifying reversal of fortune into the keeping of William Johnson and Arthur

He Outshines the Racers

Taylor, greatest trainers of their age, and they had guided him into a new career of unsurpassed brilliance.

On the record, Sir Archie had lost three races and won four. Like most oversimplifications, that did not begin to tell the true story of his performance. At his best, Sir Archie had shown himself to be so much better than anything else on four legs that the competition was no competition at all. There was simply no gainsaying him. He had run and won without extending himself, and even so had set a four-mile record that was not to be beaten in all the horsey South. As to what horse was second best, that was of small importance now.

For there was no second place. Sir Archie had distanced his best and sternest opponents. He had virtually driven them from the turf, and he might look in vain hereafter for any further challenge. Owners of race horses were not so foolhardy as to send their favorites to certain failure against Sir Archie.

That side bet Johnson had offered to post—$5,000 or $10,000, whichever sum any adversary might care to risk—went uncovered. Sir Archie was finished with racing, as utterly as though he had broken all four of those bewilderingly swift legs of his, but Colonel Selden once had foretold for Sir Archie a great future as a stallion, the sire of champions.

Up to that time, imported stallions had chiefly impressed the leading breeders. General William R. Davie had seen the race with Blank at Scotland Neck, and he knew all about those other races that Sir Archie had won at Richmond and Petersburg.

General Davie was fifty-four years old that autumn. Born in England, he had come with his parents to South Carolina at the age of eight and had been a student of law when the war with England broke out. Spending his last shilling to recruit and equip a mounted company, he had swiftly become a hard-riding, hard-fighting raider chief of a class with Marion and Sumter, finished the war a hero, and settled in Halifax County to become a wealthy planter. He was a general of the North Carolina state militia; he had been importantly active in the founding of the University of North Carolina; and he had served as governor of the state and as a special envoy of the United States to France. He was energetic and knowledgeable about horses, too. At Scotland Neck he was an impressive figure, recognized by all turf lovers, and he knew what he wanted when he saw it.

He offered Johnson $5,000 in cash for Sir Archie. The sum seemed impressive to all who heard of it.

Johnson knew that Sir Archie could race no more for him, and at the time he had no ambition to maintain a stallion. He accepted Davie's offer. One last hope remained. Perhaps, when other turfmen were told that Sir Archie no longer belonged to Johnson, some audacious seeker of racing glories might defy him.

With Sir Archie he gave General Davie a letter containing an earnest paragraph:

"I have only to say, that in my opinion Sir Archie is the best horse I ever saw, and I well know that I never had anything to do with any that was at all his equal and this I will back, for if any horse in the world will run against him at any halfway ground, four mile heats, according to the rules of racing, you may consider me five thousand dollars with you on him. He was in good condition this fall and he's not run with any horse that could put him at half speed towards the end of the race...."

After such an endorsement from such an imperial expert, Sir Archie's descendants would have to run fast and far to be worthy of their sire. For a sire was what Sir Archie would be. He accompanied Davie to another home plantation, called New Hope, and traded one great career for another.

IV

SIR ARCHIE
Outshines the Sires

GENERAL DAVIE'S purchase of Sir Archie in 1809 was one of the general's last important business transactions in North Carolina. He was in the process of quitting the state which had seen his many successes in varied fields and which looked upon him as a living tradition of heroism.

His decision to leave North Carolina saddened his friends, but he was stubborn about it. New Hope, his Halifax home, had come to him in 1783, part of the marriage portion of his bride, Sarah Jones. For twenty years William and Sarah Davie had been the pattern of a happily married couple, gracious, attractive of person, parents of six children. But Sarah Jones had died, and New Hope was filled with the gray shadows of mournful memories. General Davie did not wish to live there a widower.

Lately he had tasted the strange flavor of defeat in a Congressional election. Somewhat against his will, he had been coaxed into opposing his old neighbor, Willis Alston. The campaign had been marked with lively bad feeling between the rival factions, and when Alston had won, Davie felt shamed and rejected. He turned his gaze

Sir Archie

back to South Carolina, where he had spent his boyhood and where he now owned a vast plantation on the Catawba River.

When Sir Archie came to New Hope, therefore, General Davie had no notion of remaining there with him. Davie's oldest son, Allan Jones Davie, was twenty-four years of age, eager to succeed in life for himself, and had begun to gain reputation as an accomplished horseman. The general made Allan a present of New Hope and of Sir Archie as well, then he quitted Halifax County and North Carolina.

In January, Allan Jones Davie published an elaborate announcement in the Petersburg *Intelligencer*, with the dateline Halifax, January 1st, 1810:

"The celebrated racer Sir Archie, a fine bay, five ft. 4 inches high, gotten by old Diomed, out of Castianira who was imported by Mr. John Tayloe of Mount Airy, Virginia, and sent over to him as the best blood stock in England, she was got by Rockingham out of a Trentham, &c. Will stand at Newhope, two miles out of the town of Halifax, N. C., the ensuing season, which will commence the 15th day of February, and end on the 1st day of August, to cover mares at Forty Dollars the season, which may be discharged with the payment of Ten Pounds, Virginia currency, by the first day of January 1811.

"Good and extensive pasturage and servants' board gratis, and the mares if ordered will be fed with corn at a low rate, and every possible attention paid to them, but I will not be accountable for accidents of any description.

"As a *racer* or *blood horse*, Sir Archie is inferior to no horse ever bred or trained in this or any other country. At New Market and elsewhere, he has beaten the following famous horses: Wrangler, Tom Tough, Pallafox, Minerva, Rattray, Gatiun, &c., also General Carney's celebrated racer, Blank by Citizen [sic], never beaten before or since...."

These were boldly spoken claims, even though true ones. Sir

He Outshines the Sires

Archie, standing at so high a fee before being proven as a sire, represented a challenge to the notion, ingrained throughout the wealthy horse-breeding plantation society, that only imported sires were worth patronizing. Ten pounds in Virginia currency, or $40, was not much less of a fee than had been commanded by the best stallions from England—Diomed had last stood in 1807, at $50 the season or $100 to insure a living foal, and other homebred stallions, even great turf champions like Potomac, commanded fees of $25 or so. Sometimes the pedigrees of these American sires were attacked, spitefully and fantastically.

To back up his advertised opinion of Sir Archie's qualities, Allan Davie quoted from William Johnson's letter the offer to bet $5,000 on Sir Archie against any entry in the world, four-mile heats. And hopefully he concluded the notice:

... "Mares now in foal should be sent before the time of foaling to avoid travelling the colts too young. One dollar will be expected by the groom for each mare."

In February, Sir Archie began his career as a sire. He was a healthy and vigorous young stallion, not yet five years of age, and to him this new life must have been a horse's dream of paradise.

No more, for him, the grind of training and conditioning for those bitterly taxing four-mile heats, no skimping of hay lest it affect his wind. He had a comfortable, pleasant stall for meditative lounging and a fenced paddock, carpeted with the most succulent grass and clover, in which he could lope, trot, or walk at his own pleasure to stretch his muscles. His tub was filled with water, his rack and manger with food, for a stallion should be in good flesh. White men and black tended him with the utmost of flattering respect, and to him, all through the spring and into the summer, day after bright day, were brought the most fashionably bred mares.

Nor need he exert himself unduly and frustratingly, even in the wooing of his mates. Thoroughbred mares often are coy with the lovers to which they are hopefully offered. New Hope stables, therefore, provided teasers—less renowned and less purely descended stallions, whose thankless employment it was to carry on the preliminary courtship of each mare as she was presented.

Prancing, whinnying, pleading, caressing, the teaser seductively importuned the mare. For a short time or a long one, he pursued and blandished her. Finally, when the lady's blood flowed swift and hot, when she, too, frisked and whinnied and betrayed a melting mood of surrender—then a strong-handed groom unsympathetically twitched the poor teaser's halter rope and hustled him away, out of sight and reach. The door of Sir Archie's stall opened, and he appeared, majestic and triumphant, to accept as his effortless due the now eager mare.

Such a drama was played, sometimes several times in a single day with a succession of consorts, and certain mares, stubbornly slow to conceive, returned again and again to Sir Archie. Lodging was provided for them, and some produced offspring of other stallions before being presented to Sir Archie.

Colonel William R. Johnson paid his forty dollars and sent over from Warrenton Sir Archie's own sister—Miss Monroe, daughter of Diomed and Castianira—to mate with the horse which Johnson thought the finest he had ever seen, in hopes that this inbreeding would produce a colt of the same great talents. William Edward Broadnax, the great turfman of Brunswick County, Virginia, sent his cherished matron Meretrix, the daughter of the celebrated Magog. From the plantation of Colonel James Moore of Orange County, North Carolina, came Bay Doe, daughter of Little Driver, a mare as pretty as her name and as fleet. Harold Jones, of the Halifax County family that had risen above the banality of its surname to high distinction and great wealth, brought over Annoplede to tempt Sir Archie. Two mares by Sir Archie's sire Diomed appeared—Miss Selden, bred by Colonel Miles Selden who once had predicted for Sir Archie an illustrious career as a stallion, and an unnamed mare owned by Thomas Friend Wilson. Allan Davie himself bred Sir

He Outshines the Sires

Archie to a daughter of Gamenut, and there were Thoroughbred daughters of Wild Medley and Grey Medley.

All of this new employment was highly pleasurable to Sir Archie and reckonably profitable to Allan Jones Davie. William Johnson, observing, may have felt that for once he had done himself less than financial justice in selling his great winner of races. Sir Archie, under Allan Davie's management, seemed dramatically and instantly successful.

But in other matters, the son of General William Davie was proving less fortunate.

Allan Davie is remembered in surviving accounts as a man of charm, presence, and plausibility, with considerably better education and higher intellectuality than many of his contemporaries of the era's Southern horsey set. He had attended the State University his father had done much to establish, though he did not take his degree, and had been a founder of the Dialectic Society there. His various essays on the breeding and training of race horses are evidence of a witty and articulate style as well as original critical opinion on matters of the turf. But he was given to bitter dislikes and enmities. These he prosecuted with spite and sometimes with baseless slander, to his own discredit and damage. He liked to play cards, too, and his judgment of the infallibility of certain hands was far inferior to his judgment of the excellence of certain horses.

Almost as soon as General Davie had made permanent his move to South Carolina, the general's son found himself in want of money. His gambling losses were considerable and his management of New Hope Plantation less than efficient. Probably his need of ready cash forced him to listen when William Johnson offered to lease Sir Archie for the season of 1811.

That spring, therefore, Sir Archie again spent at the Johnson plantation outside Warrenton, while the mares bred to him in 1810 produced his first sons and daughters. From the very hours of their foaling, these had the aspect of potential winners. Johnson was especially happy in the bay colt born to Miss Monroe, naming him Spring Hill and destining him for future training. William Edward Broadnax, up in Virginia, was similarly pleased with the foal of Meretrix, which he christened Director and planned to develop into a race horse. Further, Broadnax offered to lease Sir Archie's services for the season of 1812, and, again, Davie felt obliged to accept.

Broadnax promptly advertised in the Petersburg *Intelligencer*, in January of 1812:

"The celebrated race horse Sir Archie, six years old last spring, a fine blood bay, upwards of 16 hands high, and in high condition, will stand at my stable, in Brunswick County, the ensuing season, (which will commence the 15th of February, and end the 15th of July)—and as times are difficult, and money scarce, he will be let to mares by the season, at the reduced price of Ten Pounds, payable the 25th of December next, or Twenty-five Dollars if paid within the season, or Fifty Dollars to insure a mare to be in foal, or the property of the mare is changed; with Half a Dollar in every instance to the groom...."

Little Director, approaching his first birthday and manifestly a colt of promise, must have helped to inspire the last paragraph of Broadnax's advertisement:

"...Notwithstanding Sir Archie's emperor blood, and all that might so justly be said of his unsignalled form, yet a personal view of him and his foals would be a far greater recommendation with gentlemen, real judges of a Race Horse. As to Sir Archie's performance on the turf, in his day, both in Virginia and North Carolina, with great ease, having run 2 miles in a 4 mile heat in 3 minutes and 46 seconds and finished the heat in 7 minutes and 52 seconds under a hard pull. He has since been purchased, for his superiority as a Stud Horse, at the price of Five Thousand Dollars!— and has covered two seasons since, and thereby proved himself to be as sure a foal getter as any horse in the world."

This optimistic assurance was dated January 25, just three weeks

He Outshines the Sires

before Sir Archie would begin his season for Broadnax in Brunswick County. While he still lingered at New Hope Plantation, however, he met and accepted a mare of less than Thoroughbred ancestry, in what would seem violation of Davie's contract with Broadnax for Sir Archie's exclusive services for the spring of 1812; and the produce would make turf history both brilliant and intriguing throughout many Southern states.

On a day before the middle of February, Davie rode to the town of Halifax and on the street heard altercation. His friend Jared Weaver sat a white-footed sorrel mare and harangued Peter Fagen, a free Negro known as Cabin Point, insisting on payment of a hoary debt of twenty-five dollars.

Davie reined up beside Weaver. Cabin Point was well known to Davie, as to all happy folk of the region, as by far the finest fiddler up and down the Roanoke River. Why, inquired Davie, did not Weaver let Cabin Point pay his obligation in fiddle music?

Weaver shook his head. As he saw it, there wasn't twenty-five dollars worth of melody in any fiddle, not even though scraped by Cabin Point.

Now Davie eyed Weaver's mare. She was about fourteen hands high. Her sire was Dongolah, son of fleet old Mark Anthony and property of Davie's grandfather and namesake, Colonel Allan Jones. Her dam was a work mare of no blood whatever, and Weaver valued her at about forty dollars in the then scarce silver coin of the republic. Impulsively generous, Davie offered to pay Cabin Point's debt by mating the half-bred sorrel mare to Sir Archie.

Weaver agreed at once, and that very day went with Davie to New Hope, where the match was made and consummated. Not long afterward, Sir Archie was led off to Broadnax's plantation in Virginia, where was assembled for him a harem of beautiful mares far more renowned for blood and turf performance than the obscure hack of Jared Weaver. One of the first presented to Sir Archie was Broadnax's own prized Bet Bounce. Marmaduke Johnson, father of

Sir Archie

Sir Archie's great sponsor, again sent from Warren County his gray mare by Medley, which that same spring had produced a lively little filly, fruit of her previous year's visit to Sir Archie. And there were numerous others as attractive and as vigorously noticed by the young stallion.

Another war with Great Britain came upon the country in 1812. The South was not invaded, but the scarcity of money earlier recognized by Broadnax became a sore one, particularly with turfmen. Down at Charleston, where thriving sea traffic was almost at a standstill, hard times beset the Washington Course and its race meetings, and Jockey Club purses there sagged in value from $1,000 to less than $300. In the spring of 1813, Sir Archie was back at New Hope once more to begin his third season at stud, and fees were fewer in the austere war times.

Meanwhile, seven colts of his first year's siring underwent preliminary training toward future races. Six of his second crop, yearlings in the spring of 1813, were destined for something of fame. And in 1813 was dropped a plain but sturdy and well-proportioned chestnut colt, result of the impromptu mating with Jared Weaver's crossbred saddle mare.

Because a quarter-strain of this youngster's blood was of workaday ignobility, Weaver gelded him. Three of Sir Archie's 1811 crop of sons, Allan, Blucher, and Brown Bob, had undergone similar surgery, and their masters would live to deplore such short-sightedness.

During the 1813 season, Sir Archie was patronized at New Hope by a number of notable Virginia turfmen who offered him their best Thoroughbred mares. Nathan and James J. Harrison—they were not close kin, but brotherly on the turf—sent daughters of imported Bedford and imported Sir Harry. Jonathan Forrest's mare by imported Alderman also appeared at New Hope, as did Thomas Norfleet's mare by imported Phoenix and Colonel Mark Alexander's mare by imported Buzzard.

He Outshines the Sires

The service of these and others put some money in Allan Davie's limp pockets, and the produce of the matings, attractively vigorous and handsome from foalhood, added to the growing luster of Sir Archie's reputation.

On November 14 of that year, up at Carter Hall where he had lived as a pensioner of his father-in-law, Captain Archie Randolph died. Few beyond his neighbors and family were aware of his death, but loudly rang the praise of his namesake at New Hope, and, by the following spring, reports flew concerning Sir Archie's first crop of sons and daughters and their chances of victory on the race track. Another busy season awaited their sire.

No less than seven of Sir Archie's get were now ready to try their fortunes in that last year of the war. These were Johnson's Spring Hill, Broadnax's Director, Harwood, Tecumseh, Castel, and the geldings Allan and Blucher. Another, brought along less slowly but expected to shine in future turf seasons was Brown Bob.

So well did Director's training performance please William Edward Broadnax that the horseman returned Director's dam, Meretrix, to New Hope for remating with Sir Archie. Two of Diomed's daughters, Dr. Cutler's Lady Rabbit and Henry Macklin's Sally Duffy, also made honeymoon trips from Virginia to New Hope. General William Wynn, appropriately nicknamed Racing Billy, sent two mares, one of them a daughter of imported Citizen. Other Virginia mares to join Sir Archie's seraglio included the daughters of such great imported sires as Sir Harry, Precipitate, Druid, and Dare Devil. Among Davie's North Carolina neighbors to pay their fees for Sir Archie's services were Major John R. Eaton, P. Hawkins, and the clear-thinking, dollar-wise planter William Amis of Northampton County. From South Carolina, still hard hit by the British blockade of Charleston, Colonel William Alston could afford to send up pretty sorrel Lottery, daughter of imported Bedford and descendant of the Darley Arabian, who had won twenty-one times out of twenty-two starts.

Sir Archie

By autumn, Sir Archie's first racing sons had attracted attention from war news by their successful debuts. Notable among them, understandably, was William Johnson's carefully schooled and conditioned Spring Hill, who won a $750 purse at Newmarket, scene of Sir Archie's valiant defeat and splendid victory. Allan, Blucher, Harwood, and Director also established themselves as winners. Poor Castel died that same fall before he ran his first race. Allan Davie's Tecumseh, after an early success, added to his owner's ill luck by breaking down.

Then came peace, the return of prosperity, and full attention to the importances of the turf. The spring of 1815 would be a lively one on Southern tracks, and the newcomers of Sir Archie's blood could expect stiff competition from a number of swift nags, notably Johnson's Sir Hal, Wynn's Merino Ewe, Abner Robinson's vaunted Optimus by Potomac, and Tuckahoe, a great son of Ball's Florizel, seven years old and by many reckoned unbeatable.

Edward Broadnax had sold Director to James J. Harrison, and was planning mightily for Director's younger full brother, Virginian. Harrison trained Director wisely and matched the fleet four-year-old against Abner Robinson's Optimus for two-mile heats at the Newmarket Course on April 27. Each would carry a hundred pounds, and the side bet was $5,000. Much was expected from this match which, forecast in a broadside dated March 8: "... will, in all probability, exhibit a contest more interesting to gentlemen of the turf, as well as others, so fond of this fashionable and pleasing amusement, than was ever expected at any race ground."

That broadside came close to the truth. Excitingly and decisively, Director beat Optimus. John Forrest then bought Director from Harrison to run in the autumn races, along with Sir Archie's daughter of the 1812 year, Betsey Mitchel.

Other Sir Archies of the 1812 crop were ready, brilliantly so, by autumn. Of these, most immediately notable was Lady Lightfoot, got by Sir Archie from John Tayloe's mare Black Maria by imported Shark.

Lady Lightfoot was a pretty brown filly, just under sixteen hands high, and Tayloe felt that she would be a credit to him. "Let her alone," he snubbed an overseer who complained of Lady Lightfoot's plunderings of a Mount Airy corn patch. "She is worth your whole field." In the summer of 1815, after preliminary training by reliable old Thomas Larkin, she dazzled all beholders by running a two-mile trial, under blankets and wearing exercise shoes, in three minutes and fifty seconds. Her companion on the gallop, Revenge by Ball's Florizel, came in lengths behind her.

"No better nag in the world," Colonel Tayloe praised her.

But even as he spoke, it was in his heart to quit his active role as a turfman. In October, when Lady Lightfoot made her debut, Tayloe announced himself ready to sell her at any fair price.

On October 14 Lady Lightfoot entered the Sweepstakes at Washington, where she distanced a field of four abashed competitors to take a $1,800 purse, and that with no evidence that she was running her best. Two days later, she was an entry for the Jockey Club Purse, $1,500 this time, three-mile heats over the same course. Dr. Brown's Stranger and Avery's Childers were among those brought to the post with her. As in the Sweepstakes, she won the first heat with careless ease.

Abner Robinson, still tingling from that spring defeat of his Optimus by Director, stood watching with the longest of faces. He had wagered against Lady Lightfoot to a far greater sum than he could afford to lose. Now he moved to redeem his poor judgment with remarkable presence of mind. While the competing horses breathed gratefully during the half-hour between heats, Robinson fairly scuttled to Tayloe's side. He bought Lady Lightfoot then and there for $1,500 and withdrew her from the next heat before she could beggar him by winning it. His sportsmanship, on this occasion, was considered to be far below his ingenuity. The Washington

Sir Archie

Jockey Club met after the race and voted a new rule prohibiting any future imitations of the Robinson bet-hedging method.

Racing Billy Wynn took charge of the further training of Lady Lightfoot for her new owner, and in November she ran away from yet another field of rivals at King George Court House, earning back $900 of her purchase price.

Considerably less fortunate that autumn was Director, who had been sold again, this time to Jona Forrest. William Johnson's dynamic Sir Hal beat Director at Newmarket. Later, at Warrenton, Sir Hal defeated Director's half-sister and stable mate, Betsey Mitchel. At the same Warrenton meet, Director faced another Johnson entry, Walk-in-the-Water by Bedford. Splendidly trained like all of Johnson's horses, and starkly brave to boot, Walk-in-the-Water nevertheless was pushed to his last fiber of endurance and beyond to beat Director in two bitterly contested heats. Staggering from the judge's stand after being declared the winner, valorous Walk-in-the-Water fell dead from his desperate exertions.

The autumn racing season for 1815 came to an end with Lady Lightfoot hailed as a daughter to make Sir Archie proud. She was seen as the chief rival of Johnson's Sir Hal and Wynn's fine fast mare, Merino Ewe, in the coming year's contests.

But early in 1816, Lady Lightfoot contracted her sire's old ailment, distemper, and suffered even more miserably than had he in 1808. She choked, staggered, and went through bouts of exhausting fever. The spring campaign opened without her.

Then a new hero of the Sir Archie blood came galloping into the picture. This was Timoleon, a colt of the 1813 crop out of a mare by imported Saltram. In color he was a light chestnut, with a white star on his forehead. He scaled an inch under sixteen hands at the withers. He looked long-barrelled, clean-cut, with powerful limbs.

James J. Harrison, who had first raced Director, trained Timoleon. Harrison brought his latest pet to Newmarket as an entry in a sweepstakes with one-mile heats. John Worsham, too, was there, with a son of Potomac from which he expected wonders. Harrison and Worsham appear to have argued, in friendly but emphatic fashion, the merits of their respective racers. Then they made a wager. At sunrise of the day of the sweepstakes, Timoleon and the Potomac colt were matched for a half-mile race for a side bet of $100. Timoleon easily outran his opponent and later that same day entered the sweepstakes with a field that included two other Sir Archies, Sambo and Fair Rosamond.

The first heat was well run by several, but Timoleon was so unbrotherly as to beat both Sambo and Fair Rosamond, finishing the mile in a minute and forty-seven seconds. This, said students of the racing calendars, was within four seconds of the legendary record set by Timoleon's ancestor, the English champion Flying Childers. The second heat was won by Timoleon more handily still, though his time was a single second slower. Racing Billy Wynn, delighted with the new colt's showing, bought him from Harrison for $2,500 and put him under intensive training for the autumn races.

Elsewhere in Virginia and in North and South Carolina, various other Sir Archies underwent similar schooling—Blank, Columbia, Lady Burton, Reaphook, Vanity, and, of the 1813 crop that had produced Timoleon, the mare Coquette and Johnson's highly rated filly Reality, the latter out of Marmaduke Johnson's Medley mare. At the same time, racing attention was drawn to a more doubtful stable, which housed the chestnut son of Sir Archie and Jared Weaver's little crossbred Dongolah saddle mare.

He had grown into a sizable and lively gelding, fifteen and a half hands high, with especially fine and graceful hoofs. A crossroads race of rustic nags—a "corn race," such an event was called in those days—had been planned, and one Henry Coates asked Weaver if he might train the chestnut. Weaver agreed. The gelding responded smartly to a brief twelve days of work, and when the corn race was run he badly skunked all his fellows on the makeshift track.

Still struggling in the coils of financial embarrassment, Allan

Sir Archie

Davie had leased Sir Archie again, this time to Edmund Irby of Nottaway County, Virginia. Irby, a gentleman planter and horseman whose manners were gracious even among his ante-bellum neighbors, was delighted with a colt got by Sir Archie from his favorite Dare Devil mare. News of what Sir Archie's sons and daughters were beginning to do against all comers helped the foremost breeders of the South to make up their minds.

William Johnson sent his mare, Miss Halifax by imported Phoenix, to the stallion at Irby's plantation. James Selden paid the stud fee for his Beauty, Sir Archie's half-sister by Diomed. Irby's neighbor and close friend, John Randolph of Roanoke, professed deep admiration for Sir Archie, whose services he bespoke for two priceless imported mares, Dutchess and Lady Bunbury. Phil Claibourne of Brunswick County returned his Druid mare Poll to Sir Archie, in hopes of another colt as good as her yearling Carolinian by the same sire.

While Sir Archie blithely consummated union with these and a pretty host of other mates, his sons and daughters of earlier years prospered in their preparations to better, if possible, his turf record. Autumn came, and race meetings were scheduled on a number of tracks.

Unhappy Lady Lightfoot had thrown off her siege of distemper, but the attendant fever had caused all her sleek brown hair to fall out. She looked unrecognizably ugly while it slowly grew back in. Johnson's master trainer, Arthur Taylor, watched her as she resumed exercise and soberly opined that she could not run. She remained languishingly convalescent, and was not started in the early fall.

But two other Sir Archie mares, Vanity and Reality, came upon the turf in October, upholding the colors of William Johnson. Vanity made her debut at a Washington race, four-mile heats. The field seemed dominated by Florizel's sprightly son Tuckahoe, seven years old in 1816 and called invincible by his owner, John Wickham of Richmond. Other entries were Columbia, Young Florizel, Stranger, and Oscar's son Northampton.

He Outshines the Sires

In the first heat, all of these proud horses had an excellent but disheartening view of Vanity's trim bay haunches, speeding far in advance of them. She won that heat with the same unhurrying grace displayed by Lady Lightfoot on the same track the previous autumn. Tuckahoe, the boast of his invincibility blown away by the wind of Vanity's passing, was ignominiously withdrawn from the second heat, which Vanity won almost in a walk.

At the Newmarket races that same season, Timoleon and Reality were both entered in the two-mile sweepstakes with three other colts. At the starting signal, Timoleon fairly soared to the front. His jockey found himself unable to control the straining, speeding horse, who outran Reality from the first stride. He won the heat, and Reality was only a poor second, more than sixty yards behind him.

That runaway performance had wearied Timoleon, and the half-hour rest did not wholly restore him. Reality, better ridden and fresher, fought him all the way in the second heat and managed to win, having sped two miles in three minutes and forty-seven seconds, a tie of Timoleon's fast time in the spring. In the third heat it was again a duel between the two Sir Archies, and Reality nosed ahead of Timoleon once more to win the race. The others had been so badly beaten as almost to escape notice.

The victory by Reality had been a fantastic bit of luck. Nobody who watched the race questioned Timoleon's superiority. At Belfield, not a single horse presumed to contest the $250 Proprietor's Purse with him, and he walked around the course alone to take the money. At Tarboro in North Carolina, Lady Lightfoot appeared at last to run against Timoleon for the $400 Jockey Club Purse. Still she was far from her best after that summer of illness, and Timoleon beat her decisively. At Warrenton, he beat Harwood, another of Sir Archie's get.

Wynn's happy enthusiasm for Timoleon must have been tremendous, but he had interests in other horses and other races, great and small. With John Amis, son of the master of Mowfield Plantation in Northampton County, North Carolina, Racing Billy partnered to enter a horse in a minor post stake at Scotland Neck. Time grew short before this event, and the two sportsmen found themselves with no reliable entry on hand.

Then one or the other of them remembered Jared Weaver's cocktail victor in that obscure corn race. They sought out Weaver at Halifax and bought his chestnut gelding for $500. He was entered at Scotland Neck under the name of Young Timoleon, and Amis and Wynn watched smugly as he outgalloped rivals of purer breeding but slower pace.

That victory was a sensation of sorts. Who was this Young Timoleon, anyway? The story of his haphazard origin was told by a score who remembered various versions of it. Wynn raced him successfully thereafter. John Amis' brother-in-law, Wade Bynum, later took over Young Timoleon and changed his name to Walk-in-the-Water, after William Johnson's brave horse that had killed himself to win from Director. The gelding won more races in Virginia, the Carolinas, and eventually in the new, horse-hungry western states. Colonel W. J. Hamlin bought Weaver's little sorrel mare, vowing to mate her again with Sir Archie.

Thus the eleventh autumn of Sir Archie's life found him a fascinating topic wherever turfmen gathered to talk about horses. His brief career as a race horse had ceased only for lack of opposition. William Johnson and others had called him the finest horse ever to set hoof on a track. Now, as a sire, he was proving greater still.

Director, son of Sir Archie's very first year at stud, had shone like the morning star even among his competent kinsmen. The second season had produced the great mares, Lady Lightfoot and Vanity. Then from the 1813 crop had come the peerless Timoleon, Reality, which had contrived once to beat him, and Walk-in-the-Water, whose quarter-strain of humble blood had not kept him

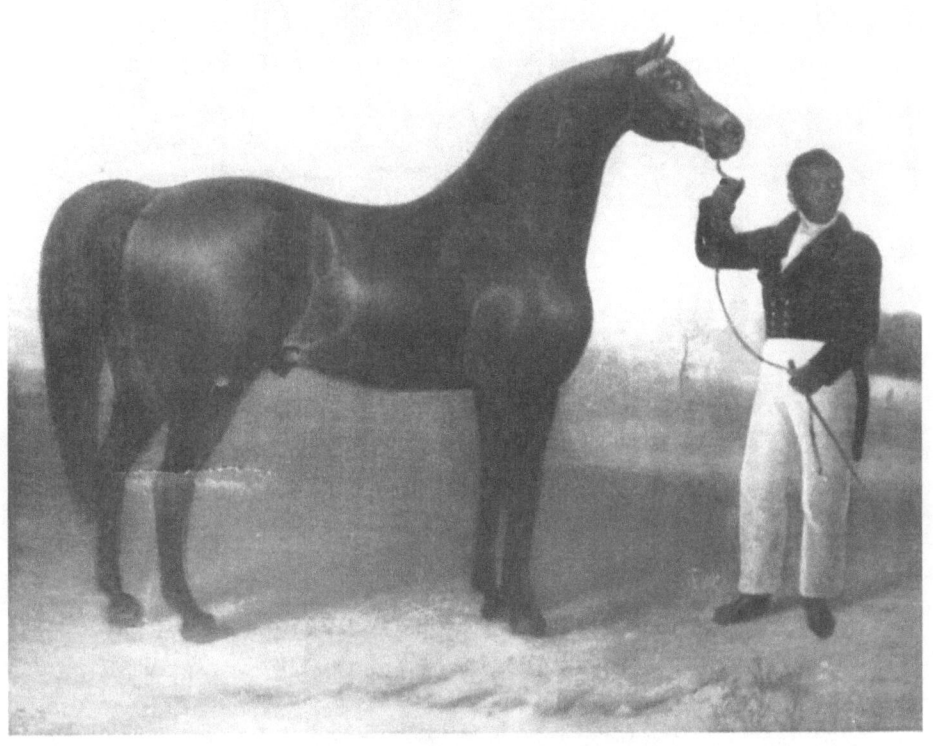

THE HORSE OF HORSES

From the only surviving portrait of Sir Archie from life, executed by Alvan Fisher at Mowfield, probably in 1823 or 1824. It was commissioned by Charles Henry Hall of New York and for decades was thought destroyed. At last it was found in the collection of George N. Ellis, Jr., of New York and Hot Springs, Virginia, who courteously allowed it to be copied for the present work. Though Fisher was no finished artist, he achieved a likeness that contemporaries thought striking. Uncle Hardy, the faithful groom, holds Sir Archie's halter.

SIR ARCHIE IN BUSINESS

This broadside advertising the services of the great stallion was circulated by William Amis early in 1817. The woodcut was said by many to be a true portrait of Sir Archie. Turf authorities have called this perhaps the most interesting of such broadsides ever to be printed.

He Outshines the Sires

from the winner's post in early modest rivalries, while now he headed for greater conquests.

These fine winners might be considered enough, and more than enough, to establish Sir Archie's reputation as a sire; but others were on the way, bidding fair to challenge the best of the older sons and daughters.

Outstanding among the Sir Archie colts of 1816 was a sturdy young chestnut on the farm of Peyton Maughn in Halifax County. In form he was very like his sire—high in the withers and strong in the well-sloped shoulders, well-proportioned throughout, clean and powerful before and behind. He was named Sir Charles. Of the previous year, those who promised most were Edmund Irby's Contention, Major Phil Claibourne's Carolinian, and William Edward Broadnax's Virginian.

These, and others who most probably would follow them, seemed certain to complete the rout of runners by all other sires earlier preferred to Sir Archie. The question that now seemed to rise was not whether a Sir Archie would dominate the race courses, but which of the Sir Archies would outclass his brothers and sisters to reign supreme. Who of all turfmen but must envy Allan Jones Davie the fortunate ownership of so instantly and sustainedly brilliant a progenitor of all these champions?

Yet, if his acquaintances wished they could change places with him, Davie must have been wishing that he could change places with one of them, any one of them who was able to meet his bills and pay his debts.

For six years Davie had lived beyond his means and had gambled beyond his purse. The New Hope Plantation, wedding gift of Sarah Jones to William R. Davie and paternal present of William R. Davie to his improvident son, must be sold. Allan Davie looked away to where he dared dream there were newer hopes still, the opportunity-rich lands of Tennessee. He would go there, and to make the move

Sir Archie Outshines the Sires

he must settle his obligations. That meant selling everything, including Sir Archie.

The great stallion's services were widely sought and richly purchased. No doubt but that he was profitable. But, after all, you had to trust gentlemen horse breeders. They sent you their mares to tend and mate, and they paid you some time around next Christmas. That was not much help for Allan Jones Davie, who needed money and lots of it, right now in 1816.

William Amis was one of Davie's many creditors. Sir Archie went to settle what Davie owed the master of Mowfield. Once again, Sir Archie changed homes. From New Hope in Halifax County he went to Mowfield in Northampton and into the Amis stables.

Davie bade his stallion farewell with sorrow and affection, and he said good-bye to Amis with something of chilly formality.

V

SIR ARCHIE
Reigns at Mowfield

IT WAS to the pleasant stables at Mowfield Plantation that Sir Archie came home at last.

In eleven years he had lived on eight estates, and on but one of these for much more than a single unbroken year. From Ben Lomond, where he had been foaled and where he had spent his first few months of existence in 1805, he had gone to Carter Hall. In May of 1807, Archie Randolph had sent him to John Tayloe at Mount Airy. After a stay of short weeks there, Sir Archie had been transferred to Ralph Wormeley's Brunswick County estate, had gone at the beginning of the next summer to Prospect Hill for training, and in the fall of 1808 had journeyed with William Johnson to Warren County, North Carolina. The following autumn, after campaigning on Virginia and North Carolina race courses, he had been sold to General Davie, who took him to New Hope Plantation in Halifax County.

The Davies had owned Sir Archie for seven years, but he had not spent all that time at New Hope. The season of 1811 had found him back at Johnson's plantation on lease. The following stud sea-

69

son he had spent with William Edward Broadnax in Brunswick County, Virginia. His next three years, again at New Hope, had been his longest residence at one place, and in 1816 Irby had leased him to stand in Nottaway County, Virginia.

At last, after so many changes of owner and residence, he had ceased his pilgrimages. More than 60 per cent of his life remained to Sir Archie, and he spent nearly all of it, quietly, happily, and usefully, at Mowfield.

The family history of his new owner was a fairly colorful example of how a Carolina planter of Jeffersonian times arrived at affluence and position. The Amises looked back to forbears among the gentry of Norfolk in England, where, in 1445, Thomas Amis had presented a chapel to the Church of St. Michael and All Angels at Barton Turf. The name was also spelled Amyas and Amias. The first of the family to come to America seems to have been another Thomas, who settled on Virginia's Eastern Shore before 1620. His descendants upheld, to their own damage, the violent uprising of disgruntled tobacco planters in 1682 short years after Bacon's Rebellion. As with that larger and fiercer flouting of Colonial laws, the tobacco troubles were put down only by Colonial militia and the execution of two ringleaders. The Thomas Amis of that period —Thomas was a Christian name in every generation of the house— was tried in court for his part in the disturbance, but escaped serious punishment.

John Amis, born in Middlesex County, Virginia, in 1724, was the first of the family to come to North Carolina. He settled in Northampton County about the middle of the eighteenth century and built, of locally molded bricks, a house which was given the uncomplimentary name of Mud Castle. At least one of his six children, William, was born to him at Mud Castle. John Amis died in 1764, leaving a will that disposed of fruitful lands, considerable money, and nine Negro slaves.

To young William had been left the Mud Castle estate, to be

his after the death of his mother, Mary Dillard Amis. William came to the threshold of manhood as the Revolutionary War started and, on May 6, 1776, he was appointed commissary to the Third Regiment of North Carolina Continental Troops, then being mustered in his part of the state. The post carried with it a lieutenancy.

A commissary combined the duties of quartermaster, purchasing agent, and ordnance officer. Press of private business caused Lieutenant William Amis to ask for leave of absence in December of 1776, and his older brother, Thomas, became commissary of the Third Regiment in his place, with rank of captain. Later on, William resumed commissary duty at the town of Halifax and sometimes served as confidential messenger to Governor Richard Caswell. He was trusted with the guarding and wise expenditure of considerable sums of public money, on one occasion as much as $30,000. Sometimes he met critical shortages from his own pockets, trusting the hard-pressed and dilatory Continental treasury to pay him. No record of his military services after 1779 has been found, but a family tradition says that, as a private contractor, he sold supplies to Washington's army at Yorktown and thereby laid the foundation of a fortune greater than that left by his father.

As an officer of the army that had won independence for the new nation, he received other rewards, including large tracts of land. Probably soon after the end of hostilities, he married his cousin, Susan Wilburne.

By that time he owned several plantations in the Gumberry District along the Roanoke in Northampton County. A ferry crossed the river to Halifax on the other shore. His neighbors considered that he had done very well indeed for himself. His education was limited, but he was a good man of business, perhaps apt to look closely at both sides of a dollar. While still young, legends grew up around him in the region. Some neighbors swore that in one of his fields he had discovered a big metal strong box which proved to be full of money—hidden there, elaborated the gossipers, by

Sir Archie

Cornwallis on his retreat through North Carolina. In politics he adhered to the development of Federalism. When the nineteenth century came to its third decade, and Northampton County grew strongly Democratic and Jeffersonian, William Amis and his son and grandsons were staunch Whigs.

The family name was pronounced with a long *A*. Some Northampton County neighbors did not sound the final *s*.

A son and daughter, John and Mary, were born to William and Susan Amis during the 1780's. For a time William Amis was active in politics, being elected in 1791 and again in 1792 and 1793, to serve during not particularly distinguished sessions of the General Assembly of North Carolina. He was also appointed overseer for the building of roads in Northampton County.

His plantation house at Mowfield, set nearly a mile north of the road that ran from Warrenton and Roanoke Rapids southeast to Jackson, the little county seat of Northampton, was of his own design. It was built of wood, painted white, and was massive but handsome, with a steeply pitched roof and a broad and lofty porch surmounted by a covered balcony. Huge hand-dressed timbers served as beams, joists, and rafters. Inside, a hall ran from front to back, with a winding staircase that mounted to rooms above. Ceilings of the rooms were lofty, and there were solid chimneys of brick and fireplaces large enough to roast whole hogs or sheep. The house stands today and reflects the definite and individual taste of its builder and master. Outside, gardens and hedges and tall trees graced the surrounding yards. Beyond these, level fields and meadows stretched for miles.

At left and to the rear of the house stood the stables and barns. Behind was laid out a quarter-mile race track.

For horses were among the enthusiasms of William Amis, else he would have been eccentric in his land and time. He owned, among other animals, a fine stallion and former racer named Chanticleer, dark brown with white-blazed face and two white hind feet. Chanticleer's reputation for speed was matched by one for bad temper—"a very vicious horse, and one of the most ungovernable kind," remembered one who knew him well. Among the mares at Mowfield were one by Planter, which had been mated with Sir Archie during his first season at New Hope, and a fine daughter of Bellair, which had gone to Sir Archie in 1814 and the following spring had produced a likely bay colt which William Amis named Sir Sampson.

The Amis children, John and Mary, had grown up to be handsome and personable. Wise enough to deplore his own lack of formal education, William Amis had hired private tutors for them and in 1802 had sent John to the University of North Carolina. John had studied there one year, and probably he saw much of Allan Jones Davie in the classroom and dormitory, but John was at home again in time to attend, in July of 1803, the marriage of his sister to Lemuel Long of Quankey Place. Mary's husband was the son of Colonel Nicholas Long who, as commissary-general for North Carolina during the Revolutionary War, must have been an old acquaintance of William Amis.

John Dillard Amis was married, not long after leaving the university, to Elizabeth Bynum, herself the daughter and granddaughter of turfmen. For his bride, John Amis built a home called the White House, on a plantation several miles south of Mowfield, and began to win fame for high and gay hospitality. He was almost as good a businessman as his father and, by all surviving accounts, of considerably more social habit.

He played cards, too, and that with sense. Indeed, neighbors whispered of a slight disagreement between William Amis and his son John concerning the purchase and ownership of Sir Archie. John, said some, thought that he had won the stallion during a brisk night of gambling with Allan Jones Davie. William was equally certain that Sir Archie was his, by bill of sale in settlement of a debt. If this difference of opinion did exist, John did not make a serious issue of it. Sir Archie lived at Mowfield, and William Amis, as his proprietor, set about gathering him a new harem for the spring of 1817.

Amis felt that the return of good times, with the fully established reputation of Sir Archie as a foal-getter, deserved an increase in stud fees. Accordingly he prepared for publication a handbill advertisement:

THE CELEBRATED HORSE

SIR ARCHIE

WILL STAND THE ENSUING SEASON

At my Stable in Northampton County, North Carolina, about three miles from the Court House, nine miles from the town of Halifax, and twenty-one miles from Belfield, Virginia.

He will Cover Mares at Fifty Dollars the Season, payable on the first of January next, or Forty-Five Dollars if paid within the Season. (with one dollar to the Groom in all cases.)

Such of Archie's Friends, that lives [sic] at a distance, will send their Notes with the Mares, payable on the first of January next— Also, feeding of the Mares to be paid when taken away.

The season will commence the first of February next, and terminate the Fifteenth of July—Extensive fields of Small Grain and Clover are sowed for the benefit of the Mares, (which may be left with the Horse) with the addition of grain feeding, at 25 cents per day.—Separate enclosures are provided for Mares with Colts.— No pain will be spared in taking the best possible care of Mares, &c., which may be left, but no responsibility for escapes or accidents.

SIR ARCHIE'S BLOOD, GREAT SIZE.... Performance on the Turf, and celebrity as a Foal getter, are sufficient recommendations.

WILLIAM AMIS.

He Reigns at Mowfield

This bill he decorated with a spirited woodcut of a ramping stallion, prancing with forefeet in the air to dwarf a rather harassed groom who clung to his halter. Whether meant as a true portrait of Sir Archie or not, it was widely recognized as such.

If Sir Archie had made a pleasant end of his travels, such was not the case with his fleetfooted sons and daughters. In mid-February, at about the time the sire began his advertised season at Mowfield, various outstanding horsemen of the upper South turned their eyes to South Carolina, where the first important races of the year would take place.

The historic South Carolina Jockey Club had known disbanded years during the Revolutionary War while Charleston was a battleground and members of the club rode furiously on other than racing matters with Marion, Sumter, Moultrie, and the first Wade Hampton. It had reorganized in 1792 and had built a splendid oval mile track some four miles northwest of the City Hall of Charleston, near the shore of the Ashley River. This course was named for William Washington, cousin of the president, hero of Cowpens, and a passionately active turfman.

The brief recession of racing during the War of 1812 had been forgotten with the advent of greater activity than ever and the return of large purses. Race Week in February once more was a gay, swift-galloping event to challenge the best and most popular meetings in Virginia and other states to the north. What might be lacking in the cosmopolitan variety of crowds at Washington or Richmond, Charleston made up in rich elegance and fantastically cordial manners. Race Week was the height of Charleston's social season, comparable to New Orleans' Mardi Gras.

The 1817 week would begin on Monday, February 24. Each day would see a thrilling contest, with heats of two, three, or four miles. The South Carolina Jockey Club had hung up three purses. There were also two splendid silver prizes and one stake race for colts. Above all material rewards of victory would be reputation, perhaps

75

Sir Archie

such as would dominate throughout the South or even the whole nation, for the rest of the year and beyond.

William Johnson did not make the trip to Charleston. His wise eyes had looked long and calculatingly toward residence in Virginia, where his chief campaigns had been waged and won. At about the time of Charleston Race Week in 1817 he completed a move from his boyhood home in Warren County to Oaklands in Chesterfield County on the Appomattox, formerly the property of his father-in-law. There he supervised final training regimes for Vanity and Reality, his chief hopes for the spring season. His friend Racing Billy Wynn marched southward with his consistently victorious Merino Ewe and his two equally prized Sir Archies, Timoleon and Lady Lightfoot. James Harrison, too, headed for Charleston, with Director.

Charleston awaited these Virginians in carnival mood. Courts were adjourned, schools let out, stores closed, for Race Week. Plantation grandees in London-tailored clothes, ladies in exquisite frocks and bonnets, came to the Washington Course in splendid carriages. Along with such equipages appeared liveried outriders. Countrymen gathered, in buckskin breeches and boots. Grave judges, high officials, clergymen, merchants, sat together in the stands. The holiday included Negro slaves, who, freed from their toil in field or kitchen or barn, perched in rows on the rails or climbed the roof of the grandstand. The only care was for horses entered in this event or that; the only time regarded was that which elapsed between explosive start and straining finish.

The elite of the South Carolina turf welcomed Wynn and Harrison, offering them hospitality and predicting defeat for the horses from up the road.

Most to be feared of all the Palmetto sportsmen was, perhaps, Colonel James B. Richardson of Sumter County. In 1811 he had dominated Race Week with the great four-miler Virginius, son of Diomed, and he proposed to do the same in 1817 with that champion's children. He had led to Charleston a splendid Virginius filly, Transport, and her two brothers, Lycurgus and Eclipse, as well as Lady Jane, a mare by Potomac.

Equally zealous and confident appeared Richard Singleton of the High Hills of Santee. He had brought Little Johnny, son of Potomac, who at two previous Race Weeks had taken the four-mile heats, and also a daughter of Sir Archie, Young Lottery, which he had purchased from his friend William Alston of Waccamaw. In Singleton's High Hills stables were two younger Sir Archies; Kosciusko had also belonged to Alston, and the filly Blank had been sold to Singleton by General John McPherson, president of the South Carolina Jockey Club. Both of these youngsters were destined for great things to come.

John Taylor of Columbia appeared with a colt, Playfair. Peter Brown entered his filly Maria, and a turfman named Green hoped to win with his colt Bedford. Thomas Watson had brought Sir Archie's five-year-old daughter, Black-Eyed Susan.

The taste of spring was in the air, and thousands of onlookers lined the rim of the Washington Course on Monday, February 24, when the drums beat for the Colt Stake, two-mile heats.

Five subscribers had posted $200 each to be forfeited in case entries did not appear, but three of the group shrugged and yielded when Wynn announced that Timoleon, still classed as a three-year-old and therefore eligible for colt races, would represent his stable. The only rival to field an entry was Colonel Singleton. Timoleon distanced this rival in the first heat and finished the two miles in three minutes and forty-nine seconds. Wynn picked up the stakes of $1,000.

Again the eager crowd gathered on Tuesday for the running of two-mile heats for the $400 silver cup offered by the proprietors of the course. Timoleon rested after his first day's victory, and Wynn started Lady Lightfoot. Singleton's Young Lottery lined up with her and so did Black-Eyed Susan, Lady Jane, and Roe's

Sir Archie

Orlando. Maria and Little Witch, earlier announced, were withdrawn before post time.

Richardson, tingling from the defeat of his Monday's entry, ordered a hard ride of Young Lottery, who outdid herself to snatch and keep a lead in the first heat. She came home a winner in three minutes and fifty-five seconds, just ahead of Lady Lightfoot, but in so doing taxed her strength too far. Lady Lightfoot, strong and fresh, outran her in the second heat to win. The third heat, too, went to Lady Lightfoot, with Black-Eyed Susan only a fair second and poor tired Young Lottery lagging back to third place.

For proud Colonel James Richardson, this new reversal must have required a brave effort to keep his face from woeful scowling, his excuses from irritated whining. Two of his colts thrashed in two days, each by a Sir Archie from up there in the Roanoke District. Colonel Richardson liked it not a whit. On Wednesday, February 26, the high point of Race Week was called, four-mile heats for the $1,000 Jockey Club Purse. Richardson entered his bravest and best, Virginius' bay daughter Transport.

Harrison brought forward Director, and Wynn entered Merino Ewe. Four more entries came to the post.

That Wednesday, Transport vindicated her owner's fondest hopes. She won the first four-mile heat in splendid order, while poor Director, somehow off form, was distanced. The second heat, too, was Transport's. Richardson beamed, as well he might. He enjoyed himself to the full that night at the traditional Jockey Club Dinner held on Wednesday of each Race Week in Charleston.

There was good food and plenty of wine throughout the evening, with toasts to those who had won already and to those who would win during the exciting days to come, and the singing, as custom demanded, of *The Highmettled Racer*, song of songs for the South Carolina Jockey Club. But this was a relaxation only temporary for those who attended, and, for those whose horses were entered for the following day's event, probably a relaxation only partial at best.

On Thursday, the Jockey Club offered another purse, $600, for the winner at three-mile heats. Richardson ordered Transport's brother Lycurgus to be saddled for the event. Lady Jane had been sold, after her defeat on Tuesday, to O. Ree, who optimistically sent her in. Black-Eyed Susan, too, would contend for the purse after a day's rest. Singleton brought Blank from the High Hills. Timoleon, already victor over one Richardson colt, was the fifth in that field of entries.

He was unquestionably first at the judge's stand in straight heats, another victory scored with the same apparently effortless address that had characterized Sir Archie at his best in 1809. Timoleon's total winnings for the week were $1,600, less the $200 posted for his appearance in the Monday Colt Stake, and Racing Billy Wynn gratefully sent him to rest in his stall. Lady Lightfoot would uphold the Wynn colors on Friday.

The race on that day was at two-mile heats for the Jockey Club's third purse, $500 this time. Richardson produced his last unused Virginius colt, Eclipse. Singleton called up Young Lottery, who, after all, had taken one thrilling heat from Lady Lightfoot on Tuesday. Green's Bedford and Taylor's Playfair were the other entries.

Four of those five contestants might as well have stayed idle at their mangers. Lady Lightfoot won in straight heats as overwhelmingly as had Timoleon in his banner performance of the day before. Cheers, shouts, the waving of tall hats and dainty handkerchiefs; then, as usual on Friday night of Race Week, the Jockey Club Ball.

This was recognized as the outstanding occasion of Charleston's fashionable season. It was graced with the presence of the reigning beauties from all the great plantations. The fashionable ball dresses of these princesses of the cotton and rice aristocracy were set off by the snug court breeches, long silk stockings, and buckled dancing pumps of their escorts. Club officials presided with overwhelming ceremony, and badge-decked managers bustled and gestured to marshal the grand marshals to organize the polkas and reels. There was a sumptuous supper, and even more sumptuous courtesy. Everybody went to bed late, and on Saturday rose to watch the final event of Race Week, the Silver Plate Handicap.

Desperately Richardson ordered the grooms to lead out Transport, his stable's choicest flower and three days earlier a glorious winner of the four-mile heats for the $1,000 purse. Singleton's entry was Little Johnny, hero of the 1815 and 1816 Race Weeks. Brown sent in Maria. Along with Lady Lightfoot, Wynn entered Merino Ewe.

This was a distinguished field, and betting must have been lively and widespread. The question seemed to be between the two fine bay fillies, Lady Lightfoot and Transport, in many ways similar.

Each was rising five years of age, each had been rigorously and knowledgeably trained, each had run to victory earlier in the week, each carried exactly ninety-nine pounds of diminutive jockey. Possibly a trifle more money favored Transport; after all, she had idled and rested since Tuesday, while Lady Lightfoot had won a swift-galloped race on the day before. And, too, this was South Carolina, home grounds for Richardson and Transport.

Transport, splendid daughter of a splendid sire, did her brave and magnificent best to win the silver plate that Saturday, but Lady Lightfoot was swifter than she and better ridden.

No whit of fatigue remained to hint of Lady Lightfoot's Friday winning of the third Jockey Club purse. Despite a gallant bid by Transport, Lady Lightfoot came in well ahead in the first heat, three miles in five minutes and fifty-four seconds. In the second heat, Transport strove again, extending but not threatening Lady Lightfoot, who won in a second less time than before. The others—Merino Ewe, Little Johnny, and Maria—never presented any great show of competition.

He Reigns at Mowfield

Race Week was over in Charleston, with Wynn the invader-hero of the meet. Out of six brilliant events, three had been won by his Lady Lightfoot, two by Timoleon, and the only other winner, Transport, had been humbled by Lady Lightfoot on the final day.

The performance of the beautiful filly against highly praised rivals was hailed as phenomenal. Back northward Wynn led his racers, with $2,100 in prize money and two glittering silver trophies, to plot new conquests on the courses of his native Virginia.

The news from Charleston hurried up behind him, may well have sped past him and through North Carolina and Virginia, to electrify all men of the turf, especially those with Thoroughbred mares. These fine four-footed ladies swiftly assembled at Mowfield, where not all of them were strangers to Sir Archie. John Goode's Robin Redbreast mare, which had produced two fine colts by Sir Archie, appeared in hopes of conceiving a third. Phil Claibourne sent back Poll, daughter of Druid, with, by her side, Sir Archie's little son Boxer of that same spring. William Amis' son-in-law Lemuel Long returned Bellona.

From South Carolina, Richard Singleton sent a trio of mares with cash to pay at once their stud fees and keep at Mowfield. He wanted Sir Archies of his own to run for him during other and happier Charleston Race Weeks.

The month of May saw men and horses gathering at Petersburg for the spring meet at the Newmarket Course. Timoleon and Lady Lightfoot were there, shining with their South Carolina victories. From Oaklands, William Johnson brought his two Sir Archie fillies, Vanity and Reality, to oppose these champions of their own kinship. No horse or mare by any other sire appears to have attracted serious attention or to have attracted much financial backing when the wagers were laid.

It was a bad May for the Napoleon of the Turf in his new home state of Virginia.

Reality had beaten Timoleon the previous fall, it was remem-

Sir Archie

bered. Widespread betting on the two was reported, with no odds offered by fanciers of either, when they were matched at Newmarket at the end of a dreary week of rain. The normally firm and swift track was slippery with mud, and for stretches the footing was hidden by brown puddles of standing water. All other contestants stood off, and the gray mare and the chestnut horse grimly splashed and floundered away. A tense throng watched Timoleon literally wade home in both heats. His time for each was in excess of eight minutes.

Vanity then challenged her full sister, Lady Lightfoot. The Jockey Club had offered a purse, but again no others were entered. Sir Archie's two daughters by Marmaduke Johnson's Medley mare went to the post for the first three-mile heat and were off.

Fiercely and stubbornly they fought for the lead on the muddy track. Lady Lightfoot managed to draw ahead, but her sister pressed her more closely than had any rival at Charleston. They finished the second mile with Vanity's nose close to Lady Lightfoot's streaming tail. Amid a storm of cheers, Vanity seemed to gain, by fractions of inches. Then—

Her hoof slipped into a hole on the rain-gouged track. Heavily she fell, somersaulted, and did not rise, while Lady Lightfoot forged on to win. William Johnson and others, hurrying to the fallen Vanity, found that she had broken her neck. It was the first race, and the last, in which she had been beaten.

That October, Wynn sold Lady Lightfoot to Dr. Gustavus Brown. At Washington she again beat her old rival Tuckahoe, who thereupon retired from the turf. At Shrewsbury, Virginia, she took the Jockey Club Purse. At Hagerstown, Maryland, after a crowd watched her trounce three other racers in straight four-mile heats, the toast at the Jockey Club dinner was "Sir Archie forever."

It was a fashionable toast echoed elsewhere. Timoleon helped his sire's reputation that same October by winning at Warrenton over Harwood and Optimus. At the Newmarket autumn meet, he found

GREAT AMONG THE GREAT SONS

Timoleon, by Sir Archie out of a Saltram mare, was foaled in 1813. He won thirteen out of fifteen races, and his two losses may be called bad luck. As a stallion he fathered many winners and, through his son Boston, continued what is probably the noblest sustained strain of the Sir Archie blood. This portrait is from an engraving included in the *American Turf Register and Sporting Magazine*.

DIOMED, THE SIRE OF SIR ARCHIE

From a spirited portrait by George Stubbs in the William Woodward Collection in the Baltimore Museum of Art. Painted in England while Diomed was still a formidable winner of races.

SIR CHARLES

From an engraving in the *American Turf Register and Sporting Magazine*. As race horse and as sire, Sir Charles was considered during his lifetime to be the best son of his father Sir Archie. Father and son died on the same day.

ONE OF THE CONSORTS

Transport, daughter of Virginius, and dam by Sir Archie of Sir William of Transport and Sir Archie Montorio, is here represented in her melancholy old age in a painting by Edwin Troye, now in the collection of Anna Wells Rutledge of Washington, D.C. Transport belonged to J. B. Richardson, of Sumter County, South Carolina. This appears to be the only traceable portrait of a consort of Sir Archie.

He Reigns at Mowfield

no horse to challenge him save Worsham's Florizel, which he disdainfully outran and distanced in one three-mile heat for the Proprietor's Purse of $300. He went on to Belfield, Halifax, and Scotland Neck vainly seeking competition. At each of those towns, with all other entries withdrawn to watch in sullen helplessness, Timoleon ambled around the course to make good his uncontested title to the purse. His autumn's winnings totaled $2,430, a small fortune as reckoned in those days. In a generous moment, Wynn sold him to William Johnson's brother Robert for $4,100, and ten days later sought vainly to buy him back for $5,000.

In Northampton County, John Amis of White House spent much of his time at Mowfield in interested study of Sir Archie and his get. The younger Amis aspired to breed and train race horses himself, and several times he sent colts to race under the management and colors of his friend William Johnson. It also occurred to John Amis that the American turf most embarrassingly needed something it did not have—an authoritative stud book, a record of the increasingly fine native horses and mares which enchanted throngs on tracks in the North and South.

Such a record had been published in England in 1808, Weatherby's *General Stud Book;* and as early as 1815, a Philadelphia bookseller by the name of Bioren had begun collecting pedigrees for a similar American work but had despaired of finishing when fire destroyed his shop with all his papers. John Amis never considered himself a writer, but he had education and enthusiasm. Might he not gather and publish invaluable pedigrees and listings for American racing and thereby win the gratitude of his whole world of the turf? He may have begun serious preliminary efforts toward assembling material in 1818, when the sons and daughters of Sir Archie seemed to have established their supremacy on race tracks everywhere.

Robert Johnson took Timoleon to Charleston in January of 1818 to be ready for the Race Week that would start that year on February 2. But distemper, the earlier plague of both Sir Archie and Lady Lightfoot, attacked Timoleon as he reached the stables at Washington Course. He lingered in his stall until Race Week started, while the spectators watched his sister Blank, so soundly beaten by him the year before, take two Jockey's Club purses on successive days.

On Thursday, February 5, Timoleon seemed to have made a plucky recovery, and Robert Johnson entered him for the $500 Proprietor's Purse, two-mile heats. Timoleon managed to win, and on Friday was entered for the Handicap Race, three-mile heats, with Transport his only rival.

Timoleon made a heartening try. For a mile and a quarter of the first heat he pressed Transport nobly, then began to choke and founder. Robert Johnson signalled the jockey to pull him up and take him off the track. Only slow travelling and anxious care brought poor Timoleon the long way home to Warren County.

Sympathy and praise came to him from the greatest turfmen. "I believe him superior to any horse that ever turned a gravel on any course in the United States," vowed Racing Billy Wynn, who had regretted selling him. Strong, too, was the endorsement of William Johnson, who had watched Timoleon beat Reality: "His performances, from one to four mile heats, have been such as would do credit to the best runner in either this country or Europe—and his style of going is the most superior action. His size and blood entitle him to first rank as a stallion...."

First rank Johnson assigned to Timoleon, but not the title of the best horse ever to run. That title Johnson still assigned to Sir Archie, though at times he wondered if Reality was not better.

Other breeders thought as did William Johnson and wanted to put their mares to Timoleon. Cautiously Robert Johnson allowed only one mating of his treasure that spring to a mare belonging to his father. He hoped to run Timoleon again that fall, but Timoleon was lamed in his summer training, and his retirement to stud was complete and permanent, first of Sir Archie's many sons and daughters to make him a grandsire.

Sir Archie himself was occupied with a multitude of mares in the season of 1818. As before, some of them were his old mates. John Goode's Robin Redbreast mare was back for the fourth time. Broadnax returned his Bet Bounce, whose daughter Coquette by Sir Archie had run well in 1817. Colonel Richard Singleton ordered Young Lottery, retired from the turf after her defeats by Lady Lightfoot, to be sent to Mowfield in hopes that she would produce offspring swifter than herself. And John Amis bred two mares to Sir Archie, intending to train and race the offspring.

The autumn saw Lady Lightfoot and Reality still winning with, as rivals, other Sir Archies, notably Rarity, Carolinian, and Contention. Nobody in the South seemed willing to send their horses against these paladins, and just then the South seemed the center and fountainhead of great racers—chiefly Sir Archie's get.

Of special significance were the triumphant performances at four-mile heats by the Sir Archies. Not only did they win over all contenders, but they won by setting new marks for speed. The old enthusiasm for the Janus blood, which surpassed chiefly at short distances, began to slack off as the Sir Archies grew mature and electrified race meeting after race meeting at the heroic distance.

In the North, anti-racing legislation from time to time had oppressed lovers of the sport. The great champion of the Northern turf had been First Consul, which in six years had won twenty-one out of twenty-five races and which in 1808 had been retired to stud, where he sired none to emulate him. A new Northern champion, American Eclipse, and a highly individual contender, Hermaphrodite, sometimes known as Swallow, dominated New York courses in the fall of 1818, when Lady Lightfoot, her reputation secure at shorter distances, was entered for four-mile heats at Marlborough, Maryland. Hermaphrodite came down to oppose her.

This horse, bred in New York by J. Lapham, was deformed sex-

Sir Archie

ually but had become a formidable winner. In October, Lady Lightfoot beat him at Marlborough in a close contest, two heats out of three. Shortly afterward, at Hagerstown, Hermaphrodite won in straight heats, by only a head in each, from Lady Lightfoot. Enthusiasm rose for a third match; but Hermaphrodite went lame shortly after the Hagerstown race and ran no more. After his retirement, the banner of the Northern turf was carried by American Eclipse.

Like the Sir Archies who looked to contend with him for national supremacy, American Eclipse was a grandson of Diomed. His Virginia-bred sire Duroc might have succeeded more brilliantly on the track had his hot temper and nervous jumpiness not given him a bad habit of bolting, which lost him races to horses probably his inferior in all but training and track wisdom. Sold north, he sired American Eclipse upon Miller's Damsel in 1814.

Fairly full records survive as to American Eclipse's rearing and training, and they tell much of how racing champions were made ready for their destinies.

He was the property of General Nathaniel Coles, and summers saw him running and grazing freely on the meadows of the Coles estate outside Queens City, Long Island. Winters found him snugly sheltered and fed royally on whole and ground oats and corn along with his hay. In the autumn of his second year he was carefully broken to the saddle, and at the age of three, in the spring of 1817, he was trained hard for nine weeks, then given another summer of free play and grazing outdoors, and another winter of high feeding. In May of 1818, after more training, he ran his first race at Newmarket in Virginia, easily beating Sir Archie's daughter Black-Eyed Susan for a purse of $300.

Then he was withdrawn from racing, for a final year of hard work to train and condition him to a razor edge. In 1819, while Sir Archie's increasing battalions of sons and daughters overwhelmed all opposition on the Southern tracks, American Eclipse piled up

He Reigns at Mowfield

easy victories at all distances in New York State. He was then owned by Cornelius Van Ranst, William Johnson's Northern opposite number as an emperor of the racing world.

But anti-racing legislation hampered American Eclipse's career. In 1820, when he was six years of age and without a serious rival in all his region, came the announcement that he had been retired to stud. This seemed a permanent change in his activities; during the season of 1821 he served eighty-seven mares at a fee of $12.50. Then the New York laws against racing were eased, and Van Ranst haled American Eclipse from his luxurious stables to train for the autumn season. At about this time he was called American Eclipse no more, but simply Eclipse, like the great horse of old England.

On Long Island, just west of Jamaica and eight miles from Brooklyn, a splendid new track had been finished, one mile and thirty feet in circumference. It was faced with well-packed, naked loam, and experts judged that horses ran a mile there from three to five seconds faster than on the turf of the ancient Hempstead oval. On October 15, 1821, the track was opened as the Union Course, with thousands present to watch and several to run.

Lady Lightfoot, nine years old, was present to race four-mile heats. The fall of 1820 and the spring of 1821 had witnessed her speeding to victory after victory in Virginia and Maryland and at Washington. With Timoleon retired, there seemed nothing left for her to conquer anywhere in the South. As she came to Long Island in search of new glories, she was a two to one favorite to take the $500 purse.

Against her were brought Schenck's Flag of Truce, Schomp's Heart of Oak, and Eclipse. He was seven that autumn, not immeasurably younger than Lady Lightfoot, and on the track again after a happy but understandably softening season with that harem of eighty-seven mares.

The first heat started with Lady Lightfoot promptly shooting into the lead, which she held while the contenders thundered thrice around the track. Then Eclipse put forth his great strength, not diminished after all, and sped to catch up. He fought his way past Lady Lightfoot and came in a winner by two lengths.

Flag of Truce and Heart of Oak, left pitifully far behind in that heat, were drawn in the second. Lady Lightfoot and Eclipse went to the post alone.

Again Lady Lightfoot sprang nimbly to the front, and for two miles she stayed there. In the third circuit of the course, Eclipse passed her as before, forged well ahead, and distanced her utterly.

Lady Lightfoot's backers paid their bets and took council.

Here was a new and untasty experience for them, after four years of watching the Sir Archies take first money everywhere and from everybody. Was it, perhaps, that Lady Lightfoot had outlived her swiftness? After all, this need not be a permanent championship for the North. Let poor nine-year-old Lady Lightfoot rest on her lavish laurels while Southerners found a younger and swifter successor to put this proud Eclipse in his place.

Sir Charles, foaled in 1816, was the son of Sir Archie and a Citizen mare belonging to William Johnson. Now he was the property of James Harrison. Since the autumn of 1819 he had raged through Virginia and the Carolinas like a devastating plague. Some enviously critical souls murmured that his blood was not Thoroughbred, but none could say that he had run behind anything for long. In May of 1821, for instance, he had seemed to be loitering as he led a field of frantic rivals at Newmarket, as once Sir Archie had loitered home in front of adversaries not worth his strife; but, ordered to extend himself, Sir Charles had in the last mile totally distanced all the others, and the Virginia experts pronounced him "able to run with any horse in the world." A leg injury midway of the 1822 spring season had marred what had promised to be another succession of victories, but in October, four times in as many weeks, Sir Charles won from the best in all the South. His only serious threateners had been other Sir Archies—Sir William, Van Tromp, Childers, and Muckle John.

All these successes impelled Harrison to issue a challenge to Van Ranst, who readily accepted on behalf of Eclipse. A match at four-mile heats would be run at the Union Course on November 20 for $10,000 a side. Each owner posted $5,000 as a forfeit in case his entry was withdrawn. A large and lively crowd gathered to watch, and money amounting to fortunes was offered and covered, backing this horse or that. The jockeys swung into their saddles—Sir Charles carried 120 pounds, Eclipse 126—and the rivals headed for the starting post.

Then Harrison hurried to the judges' stand. He said that Sir Charles had injured a tendon in exercise a few days earlier. Perhaps this was an aggravation of the laming accident of the previous year. Now, at the last moment, Harrison said he would pay the forfeit. However, he made haste to add, he would not allow the spectators to be disappointed utterly. He offered to bet $1,500 on Sir Charles against Eclipse for a single heat.

Van Ranst covered the money, as spiritedly prompt as any Virginian would have been in his place. Off darted the two horses at the signal, Eclipse capturing the lead. Sir Charles kept close behind, apparently holding himself ready for a spurt at the finish. Three times around, and then Sir Charles tried to put on all speed.

It was a tragically vain effort. His lame leg failed him, and he faltered as he ran, slowed down quickly, and limped to a halt. Eclipse, too, cut his pace and cantered in, an unthreatened winner of the heat and the wager.

Several grooms gathered around the pain-racked Sir Charles and helped him as he hobbled off the track. The loud applause for Eclipse savored of Northern sectionalism, and the men who had gathered from Virginia and the Carolinas glared and tightened their lips.

Their chief and spokesman was, of course, William Ransom

Johnson. White mane abristle with fierce determination, he sought out Van Ranst that evening with a new defiance.

Was Eclipse indeed the swiftest horse in all the North? Aye, that he was, came Van Ranst's reply; had Eclipse not just proved it, against the proudest boast of Virginia? Very well, rejoined Johnson, here was something for Eclipse and his friends to consider. He, Johnson, would bring a horse to beat Eclipse next spring, right here at Eclipse's own familiar Union Course—four-mile heats, best two out of three. The side bet? Johnson said that he spoke for a committee that would raise $20,000, and here ready in his hand was appearance money to the amount of $3,000 to post that moment as a forfeit with any acceptable stakeholder.

Van Ranst's friend and ally, John C. Stevens, instantly produced $3,000 from his own well-filled purse as forfeit on behalf of Eclipse. There followed conferences of backers and experts on both sides. May 27 of 1823 was set for the contest. Let the Southerners bring up their swiftest and best. The New Yorkers swore that Eclipse would run any rival into the ground.

Johnson said goodbye to the New Yorkers and reported back to his quickly-gathered associates from Virginia and the Carolinas.

They must find a pretender against Eclipse. And where else to look for such a pretender but among the descendants of Sir Archie?

VI

SIR ARCHIE
Glories in His Children

JOHN C. STEVENS of New York was thirty-seven years old at the time of William Johnson's challenge to Eclipse. The Stevens family was highly important in New York, socially, financially, and scientifically. John C. Stevens, Sr., brother-in-law of the statesman Robert Livingston, had perfected many aspects of steam engines and in 1804, three years before Robert Fulton's *Clermont*, he had sailed his own experimental steamboat on the Hudson with young John as engineer. He proved a better businessman than most inventors, and he and his sons became great in river and railway transportation.

Under John C. Stevens' dynamic urging a committee was organized among New York sportsmen, and the $20,000 side bet on Eclipse quickly subscribed. Stevens started the fund with a contribution of $6,000. Eclipse's owner, Van Ranst, made a substantial addition. So also did Stevens' kinsman John Livingston; William Niblo, the cafe owner; Stephen Price, manager of the Park Theatre; and Michael Burnham, publisher of the New York *Evening Post*. Twelve other New Yorkers made up the remainder of the sum.

Sir Archie

Back in Virginia, William Johnson completed the formation of his own syndicate. Among its members were John Randolph of Roanoke and the rising turfman Otway P. Hare. This group promptly amassed $20,000 to back its entry and put all matters of selection, training, and strategy into the highly capable hands of Johnson.

The Napoleon of the Turf had no intention of meeting a Waterloo at Union Course. He proposed to train no fewer than five horses and to wait until the very day of the race before announcing which of these he would start. From among the squadrons offered him, he chose three sons, one daughter, and one grandson of Sir Archie.

None of these were his own trainees, though in his Oaklands stables were several horses and mares of fine promise. Racing Billy Wynn's five-year-old John Richards and six-year-old Childers pleased him better. All the way from South Carolina he called Colonel J. R. Spann's four-year-old Betsey Richards, full sister of John Richards. Nearer at hand was Lemuel Long's Henry, not yet four years old. The grandson who made up the quintet of Sir Archies was Washington, son of Timoleon by that one mare sent by Marmaduke Johnson to Mowfield in 1818. Washington was highly rated by Robert Johnson, who may have helped to persuade his brother.

"I will run said colt against any colt or colts in a stake of $2,000 entrance," Robert had earlier defied the whole racing world on Washington's behalf; and Washington had upheld this good opinion by brilliant victory in 1822.

Of these candidates for the glamorous trial against Eclipse, six-year-old Childers and five-year-old Betsey Richards had repeatedly shown their prowess at four-mile heats. The younger horses had never raced at the heroic distance, but they had all looked splendid in training and in colt races at two and three miles, and all were in training for four-mile contests. William Johnson brought them together, drilled them in his characteristically severe training regime, and conferred soberly with Arthur Taylor and other experts.

Johnson favored Wynn's John Richards, despite the fact that both Sir Charles and Washington had beaten Racing Billy's horse a year earlier. John Amis, who had trained both John Richards and Lemuel Long's Henry, agreed with his friend Johnson. Amis had tried the two against each other on the Mowfield exercise track, and to his notion John Richards had shown better speed and form than Henry. To help himself arrive at a final decision, Johnson advised that all five of his selections vie with each other in earlier spring races in the South. Such contests would go far toward showing where lay clear superiority and would give Johnson a campaign-sharpened entry to boot.

To Charleston, therefore, journeyed Childers and Betsey Richards, both of which had won nobly against stiff competition at previous Race Weeks. They did not disappoint Johnson or their owners. Childers distanced his rivals in the first three-mile heat on Thursday, February 13. On St. Valentine's Day, Betsey Richards took straight two-mile heats from Sir Archie's daughter Princess and Richardson's Leonidas, a fast Virginius colt. The final day of Race Week saw both Childers and Betsey Richards entered for the climactic Handicap Purse, three-mile heats. Childers, carrying 112 pounds, beat the filly with 99 pounds up, while another son of Virginius, Corvisart, took an unsensational third place.

Then, early in May, these two victors and the three younger horses of Johnson's choice were in Virginia for further proof of their mettle. Most of the races in that state wound up as contests among the carefully selected five. At Nottaway, Childers narrowly won at two-mile heats from John Richards. On the Newmarket course, Henry brilliantly triumphed in his first four-mile heats, while the more seasoned Betsey Richards forced him to his utmost to win. Washington, on the same track, took the first two-mile heat against seven-year-old Sir William, another of Lemuel Long's Sir Archies, but was beaten in the second and third.

Sir Archie

From Petersburg, William Johnson and Arthur Taylor headed their troop northward. They made the journey by water to avoid a wearying overland march and possible strains or other mishaps. Down the James River from Richmond they voyaged, up the coast to Delaware Bay, and up the Delaware River past Philadelphia to the home of Johnson's friend Bela Badger, ninety miles from the Union Course on Long Island where Eclipse, unraced that spring, was already in training quarters. At Bela Badger's estate, final training began on May 15 with conditioning gallops on the adjacent Fairview Course.

Bad luck sat on the rail there at Fairview. John Richards, still Johnson's first choice for the race with Eclipse despite his defeat at two-mile heats by Childers, cut the frog of his foot on a rock while exercising and was retired to the stable. Washington, too, went suddenly off form and had to be dropped from the reckoning. About May 22 Johnson and Taylor appeared at the stables of the Union Course with Henry, Childers, and Betsey Richards.

New York City was a noisy jam of sports lovers. They had come from everywhere—the North and South and the West, jamming hotels, taverns, and boarding houses, while the homes of the hospitable were opened to guests from afar.

At that railroadless day, public transportation was by boat along rivers or by stage along slow, poor roads. Frequent transfers were necessary. Nobody liked such journeying, and probably a great proportion of the Southerners came to New York in their own carriages, whole families of the wealthy sportsmen. Others rode horses—some of these mounts were crossbred descendants of the finest Thoroughbreds in American history. A few may even have walked long distances. All in all, fully 20,000 spectators were reckoned to have come from the South. Their travel adventure had something of the aspect of a great migration.

The ordeal of such laborious and expensive journeying, through strange territory with pauses at roadside taverns or small-town hotels

He Glories in His Children

of dubious varying degrees of cleanliness and comfort, was a true proof of the people's great love of racing.

Once in New York, home-towners and visitors talked and talked about horses in general and the race in particular. Pocketfuls of gold, silver, and bank notes were wagered. It was the most important and most interesting occasion of all the country's turf history.

The meet began on Monday, May 26, when a Northern mare named Jane of the Green was victor. By comparison, this event attracted almost no notice. Everyone waited, with wire-taut impatience, for the following day's match between Eclipse and the Southern entry.

By sundown of the twenty-sixth, hosts of people had left New York to gather around the course outside Jamaica, camping like a great army on bivouac. By dawn of the twenty-seventh, the roads from New York were a great crowded mass of carriages, riders, and jostling pedestrians. Everyone, it seemed, was on his way to watch the race between the two best horses in America.

Well, not quite everyone; William Ransom Johnson would not be there.

The night of May 26 had been given over to celebration by sportsmen from near and far. At a Long Island hotel at a little distance from the Union Course, New Yorkers offered hospitality to the most distinguished Southern invaders. Johnson was an honored guest at a formidable feast of lobsters, and late that night he became seriously ill at his stomach. As the sun rose, bright and hot, on the twenty-seventh, he lay prostrate in his hotel room, with grave-faced doctors and busy nurses trying to ease the undignified agony of his indigestion. Outside rose the clamor of the gathering multitude. Johnson was totally unable to rise from his sick bed, much less command at the greatest turf battle of his career.

Fully 60,000 spectators, by far the largest gathering of humanity to have assembled at a sporting event in all the previous history of America, fought to enter the broad gates of the board fence that surrounded the track. Between that fence and the oval, all the way around, spectators were wedged like herrings in a barrel. Some climbed the fence itself to sit on its uncomfortable top and peer over the heads of the others. Inside the track, the acres of infield with their confining ring of poles were thronged with carriages and mounted watchers.

The grandstand overflowed with distinguished Americans from near and far. Young Josiah Quincy II, of the great New England family, had been given a ticket that allowed him to sit in the jockey box directly across from the judges' stand. Directly in front of him sat slender, excited John Randolph of Roanoke, and near Randolph was Arthur Taylor. Along the front of the stands Otway Hare walked his horse, pausing to discuss with Randolph points of Southern strategy that could not be settled by the absent William Johnson.

Diplomatically, the three judges had been chosen from the country between New York and Virginia. They were General Charles Ridgely of Baltimore, Captain Cox of Washington, and John Allen of Philadelphia. In the interest of exact timing of the heats, they were provided with imported chronometers that indicated split seconds, the first of such instruments ever to be used in America.

Time of coming to post was set for 1:00 P.M.

Hare and Randolph had seen to it that one of Johnson's demands was carried out. The Union Course measured thirty feet beyond an exact mile in circumference, and Johnson had insisted that the heats should be four miles exactly. The starting post stood midway of the quarter-mile forward stretch, and the finish line was now established well to the rear of that point, not far past the end of the track's second curve. As race time drew near and excitement rose in deafening yells, the Southerners announced Johnson's choice for the supreme effort of South against North.

It was Henry, attempting his second race at four-mile heats. He would be ridden by John Walden, a white jockey from Virginia, in the blue cap and jacket of the Johnson stables. Walden rode

He Glories in His Children

at 108 pounds, twelve more than would have been required for Henry on any course in the South; for the Union Course rules demanded that Henry, though his fourth birthday would not come until June, be officially reckoned a four-year-old as of May 1.

Eclipse, as an aged horse, must carry 126 pounds. He was used to that weight and had carried it to repeated victories. His backers had hoped that he would be ridden by Samuel Purdy, who often had guided Eclipse to triumph and who was considered the foremost jockey of the Northern states even at the ripe age of thirty-eight; but Purdy and Van Ranst were reported to have quarrelled, and Purdy was present only as a spectator, muffled in a loose coat. Therefore Eclipse would have Billy Crafts up, in the Van Ranst crimson. Crafts scaled at an even hundred pounds, which meant that an additional twenty-six pounds of dead weight must be added to Eclipse's burden.

Thousands of knowledgeable eyes strained to compare the rivals as they appeared.

The redoubtable Eclipse was of gleaming dark sorrel color, with a white star on his forehead and a white rear hind foot. By the official measuring standard of the Union Course he stood fifteen hands two inches at the withers. He looked massive for a Thoroughbred. At juncture of neck and jaw hung a puffy sag of flesh, evidence of his age. But his proportions were fine, and his points excellent. Turfmen admired his length of waist, the width and strength of his loins, his broad, massive chest and shoulders.

Henry was chestnut, and also showed white on his forehead and one hind foot, with mane and tail shades lighter in hue than his body. He was smaller than Eclipse—the standard showed that he lacked half an inch of fifteen hands. His build was compact, with a strong barrel and finely powerful forequarters and haunches. Eclipse's advantage of size and experience might be offset, hoped the Southerners, by Henry's unjaded youth, the wise and watchful training by

Johnson and Taylor, and the advantage of eighteen pounds in the weight he carried.

The toss of a coin gave Eclipse the choice of starting positions. His groom led him to the left, next to the poles at the inner edge of the track. Henry took his stand fully twenty-five feet away from his adversary. The waiting thousands ceased their hubbub to wait for the starting signal.

It came—the thump of a great drum. Instantly they were off.

Henry had the better of that start by the fraction of a second. Walden shot him ahead at the slightest of angles leftward to seize the lead as he moved clear of Eclipse, and at the beginning of the track's first turn Henry was in front. Smoothly, powerfully, Henry increased his advantage on the turn and came into the back stretch of the first mile a commanding three lengths ahead of Eclipse. Close, shrewd watchers saw that Walden rode Henry with a firm, wise hand on the reins, keeping a snug pull that controlled without hampering. Bravely Eclipse strove to come up from behind, but he could not close the interval. Thus the two pounded around the track for the first mile, then for the second and the third.

Inside the oval, near the last turn of the track, Cadwallader Rennselaer Colden of New York sat his horse among the carriages. He was forty-nine years old that spring, as knowledgeable about horses as most men present at the race and perhaps more articulate on the subject of racing than any. With him, also mounted, was John Buckley, a veteran jockey and trainer. They saw Crafts begin to strike Eclipse with his whip and dash in his spurs, trying to bring him ahead for the finish of the heat.

Crafts's whip, plied vigorously on flanks, haunches, and belly, cut poor Eclipse sorely, and Colden saw the striving, punished horse flirt his tail as though in token of pain or weariness. "Eclipse is done," Buckley groaned at Colden's elbow, but, under that cruel flogging, Eclipse managed to recover some of the lost distance until he was but a length behind. Walden, using neither whip nor spur, kept Henry at a flying gallop and glanced back only once to assure himself that he was staying well in the lead. They thundered into the final turn before the finish.

"Good God, look at Billy!" wailed John Buckley.

Billy Crafts, too light and frail to control Eclipse at such a headlong speed, had braced his feet in the stirrups and flung his little body back against the cantle. He fairly rocked and swayed in the saddle as he poured the whip into his wretched mount. Eclipse outdid himself to gain a few feet more, but it was too late. Henry shot across the line, winner by a length.

Loud the jubilation of the Southerners, who now offered six to four on Henry; doleful the manner of the Northern sportsmen as they declined to wager.

Eclipse looked fagged and blown. Blood from the cuts dealt by Crafts's whip trickled down the insides of his hind legs, staining the white rear foot a brighter crimson than the Van Ranst colors. Henry, on the other hand, seemed fairly strong and fresh after his tremendous feat. The judges were comparing those split-second chronometers. They announced the official time at seven minutes and thirty-seven and a half seconds—no such four-mile heat had ever been run on an American track. Even if some unofficial timekeepers were correct in clocking the heat at seven minutes and forty seconds, that still beat the previous record of seven minutes and forty-two seconds set by Sir Hal in Virginia. What price Eclipse now?

Stevens huddled his friends for a quick, serious conference, while grooms tried to sponge and soothe the punished Northern horse into some sort of condition to attempt the second heat thirty short minutes away.

Billy Crafts should ride Eclipse no more; all agreed on that. The kindest word to be spoken for Crafts was that, at a scant hundred pounds, he was too light for so much horse as Eclipse. As to the merciless flogging he had administered, no turfman, no human being, could endure to think of it without shocked fury. Who, then?

Colden urged Buckley to volunteer, but an even better substitute was at hand.

That was Samuel Purdy. He and Van Ranst had made up their quarrel, whatever it was. Some said that Purdy had sought out his old patron, and pleaded tearfully to be forgiven and put in Crafts's place for the second heat. A less dramatic rumor held that Purdy had been sought out by members of the board of strategy for Eclipse, had at first demurred when begged to ride, and had been argued at last into the saddle against his own wishes. Somewhere between those two stories must have lain the truth. In any case, insisted still others, Purdy had only to fling off his coat to show himself dressed for the ride in boots, breeches, and crimson silk jacket.

He was heavier than Crafts, and that twenty-six pounds could be taken from the saddle. All the weight Eclipse would carry in the second heat was alive and vital, and full of wise method. Up came the horses to the post.

Henry looked cool and ready, with no discernible ill effects from his record-breaking performance in the first heat. Eclipse, for his part, had made a swift and heartening recovery from Billy Crafts's mistreatment. The blood had been sponged away and the wounds skilfully salved. The brave old horse fairly danced up to the starting post, manifestly eager to try a mending of his fortunes, but still the New Yorkers shied away from those odds offered on Henry.

The four-year-old from the South took the inside position. A moment of breathless silence, all around the great packed course. Then the thump of the drum, and "Go!"

Henry flung himself forward to speed along the poles, grabbing the lead as before. Purdy hurled Eclipse after him, determined to press Henry, to make him run swiftly and exhaustingly without a moment's respite. At top speed Henry led the way around, again opening a gap between himself and Eclipse until it showed fully twenty feet of distance. For two miles the little Southern horse held this advantage, for nearly three. Again and again, amid storms of

He Glories in His Children

cheers from New York's brigades of watchers, Eclipse sought to catch up. Those in the stands could hear the fife-shrill voice of John Randolph of Roanoke rising above the whole uproar. Randolph had wagered heavily on Henry, in hopes of financing a voyage to Europe with his winnings.

"You can't do it, Mr. Purdy!" squealed out Randolph. "You can't do it, Mr. Purdy! You can't do it, Mr. Purdy!"

Purdy thought otherwise. Carefully, tensely, he coaxed ounces more of effort from Eclipse. Up came the splendid old horse, and up. At the end of the third mile, his nose was almost at Henry's tail. Into the last mile they whirled, Henry grimly intent on winning in straight heats, Eclipse toiling to pull ahead, win a heat for himself, and leave the final issue to a third trial of speed and grit.

Colden and Buckley shoved their horses through the press inside the oval and gained the center. There they sat looking over the heads of the mob. They watched as the two rivals sped around the track like two scampering beetles on the rim of a great platter.

It was a gallant contest. Starting into the first turn of the final mile, Eclipse had moved so close behind Henry that no light showed between them. Shouts and cries rent the blue sky overhead.

"See Eclipse! Look at Purdy!" roared Buckley in Colden's ear. "By heaven, on the inside!"

It was true. At the center of the turn, Purdy twitched the reins and fairly crammed Eclipse's head leftward and inside of Henry's rear quarters, next to the line of flying poles that fenced off the interior of the oval. Watching, Colden felt a chill of apprehension crawl through his blood. If Walden should rein Henry suddenly to the left, Eclipse would be dashed against those poles, perhaps would be forced to run between two of them and off the track, out of the race and into disaster.

But Eclipse struggled perilously forward, inch by grim inch, and now the two were running neck and neck, Eclipse on the inside. Almost at the end of the turn, Eclipse wore his way to the front, his

Sir Archie

hind quarters drawing opposite Henry's head and neck. They sprang into the straightaway of the rear stretch, and Eclipse, frantically refusing defeat, came at last into the clear ahead of Henry.

Purdy drove in his spurs. Eclipse responded valiantly, and Henry, for all his striving, could not overtake him. The noise of the crowd, great before, became a deafening hubbub. As Eclipse fairly spun around the second turn and came home, a winner by two glorious lengths, the whole mass of thousands seemed to be shouting, yelling, and clapping their hands. To the enthralled Colden it sounded like the chorused war shout of armies rushing into battle.

The time of the heat was announced as seven minutes and forty-nine seconds, and again the two horses were seized upon by their crews of handlers, who stripped away saddles and bridles to sponge and curry and rub.

Northern enthusiasts, their despair suddenly banished, eagerly dug out money by wads and handfuls, but the Henry backers who at the end of the first heat had offered six to four now refused to bet. As Stevens had held council after that first heat, the Southerners conferred in troubled voices after the second.

It was their turn to call for a change of riders. Walden had handled Henry well in the first heat, but he was no genius, and a genius was badly needed if Henry was to win in the third. Otway Hare, who had watched the race from his saddle, rode quickly along the front of the grandstand and leaned toward the box where Arthur Taylor sat.

"You must ride in the next heat," he harangued the veteran. "There are hundreds of thousands of Southern dollars depending on it. That boy don't know how to ride; he don't keep his horse's mouth open!"

Taylor shook his head. "I haven't been in the saddle for months," he demurred.

John Randolph, one of those heavy wagerers on Henry, pushed close to Taylor and added his own shrill-voiced arguments. They were eloquent and conclusive. Taylor rose and hurried from the stand; he found and put on boots, breeches, and a jacket and cap of the William Johnson blue. When the horses came forth for the deciding heat, Taylor was up on Henry.

He weighed 110 pounds as he put his booted feet into the stirrups, only two pounds more than Walden. He was thirty-five years old, a sober man of family and substance, and he had not ridden a race for more than a decade, but his seasoned brilliance was a heartening hope to the Henry faction as the drum boomed for the third time.

Both horses were weary from the hard galloping they had done already, but Purdy managed to get a slight head start and took the lead. Once fairly in front of Henry, Purdy whipped and spurred Eclipse almost as Crafts had done, but to better result. Plainly he meant to make it a sustained hard run all the way, letting Henry have the difficulty of catching up, if indeed Henry could catch up.

Three miles they finished, and three-quarters of the fourth. Henry was five yards behind when Taylor, on the last turn, put him to a supreme effort. Up came Henry, using his last atom of young strength, his last gasp of wind, to bring his head alongside Eclipse's sorrel haunch. But he held that threatening position for moments only. Then he fell back because he must, lost ground again, and saw Eclipse come in three lengths ahead of him.

The time for that final heat was eight minutes and twenty-four seconds, and both horses were exhausted almost to the point of collapse.

The outnumbering Northerners cheered so loudly as to make all their earlier noise seem a whisper by comparison. Happy hands caught Eclipse's bridle and led him up to the judge's stand, shaky but victorious. Somewhere a band burst brassily into *See the Conquering Hero Comes.*

The bets Eclipse had won for his supporters were estimated at $200,000.

Swift riders spurred swiftly back to New York with the news.

Sir Archie

One of them, sent by Michael Burnham, carried a hurriedly scribbled dispatch which the *Evening Post* published for what may well have been the first sports extra in newspaper history. Another galloper did not rein in until he reached to door of William Niblo's Coffee House. At his shouted word, a white flag was hoisted to a staff on the roof—it would have been tragic black had Henry won. When members of the rival committees assembled at the coffee house that evening, Judge Van Ness of New York presided at a dinner as sumptuous as that which had laid William Johnson low.

After the food came the wine. Rising, Judge Van Ness began with a toast that sounded jauntily defiant in the ears of listening Southerners. "Eclipse," proposed His Honor, "still the best courser of his day."

All present drank to that, North and South. Mr. R. Emmett of the visitors rose in his turn, glass lifted. "Henry," he announced sturdily, "the best four-year-old horse in the country."

No argument on that score, and no heeltaps, either. General Barnum of New York attempted courteous diplomacy. "Our opponents of the South," he offered, "gentlemen in prosperity and adversity." And Stevens, generous in victory, was on his feet next, with: "The better health of William R. Johnson, a trainer of a four-year-old to run a four-mile heat in seven thirty-seven."

That added up to four glasses of wine apiece, no more than a starter for revellers such as these. Theophilus Feild poured his fifth. "The spirit and emulation and magnanimity of our rivals of the North," he toasted.

"Eclipse and his dam," was the clarion response of Commodore Rogers, "neither improvable by foreign crosses."

"Southern pluck and Northern bottom," was the toast of A. Hascock, nicely straddling the fence between the sections.

Dr. Wyche of North Carolina became eloquent over the eighth toast. "The State of New York," he intoned, "unrivalled in her population and in her enterprise for internal improvement—so far victorious on the course."

"The State of Virginia," wound up a Northerner for the ninth round of drinks, "ambitious of being distinguished in all things useful to our common country."

By the morning of the following day, Johnson was on his feet once again but squirming with chagrin over the defeat of Henry. He wrote at once to John C. Stevens:

"Sir—I will run the horse Henry against the horse Eclipse at Washington City, next fall, the day before the jockey club purse is run for, for any sum from twenty to fifty thousand dollars; forfeit ten thousand dollars. The forfeit and stake to be deposited in the Branch Bank of the United States at Washington, at any nameable time, to be appointed by you.

"Although this is addressed to you individually, it is intended for all the betters on Eclipse, and if agreeable to you and them, you may have the liberty of substituting for Eclipse, any horse, mare or gelding foaled and owned on the northern and eastern side of the North River; provided, I have the liberty of substituting in the place of Henry, any horse, mare or gelding foaled on the south side of the Potomac...."

That same day, Betsey Richards raced against Eclipse's full brother, Cock of the Rock, at four-mile heats, and decisively vanquished him. In the evening, Johnson received at his Long Island hotel Stevens' candid and sensible reply:

"... The bet just decided was made under circumstances of excitement, which might in some measure apologize for its rashness, but would scarcely justify it as an example; and I trust the part I took in it, will not be considered as a proof of my intention to become a patron of sporting on so extensive a scale. For myself, then, I must decline the offer. For the gentlemen who with me backed Eclipse, their confidence in his superiority, I may safely say, is not in the least impaired. But even they do not hesitate to believe, that old age and hard service may one day accomplish, what strength and fleetness, directed by consummate skill, has hitherto failed to accomplish.

"For Mr. Van Ranst I answer, that he owes it to the association who have so confidently supported him, to the state at large, who have felt and expressed so much interest in his success, and to himself as a man, not totally divested of feeling, never, on any consideration, to risk the life or reputation of the noble animal, whose generous, and almost incredible exertions, have gained for the north so signal a victory, and for himself such unfailing renown...."

That meant no return match between Eclipse and Henry.

Southerners managed to derive some cold comfort from assurance to one another that the Northern turfmen were afraid to try again. Indeed, the consideration extended itself, those Yankees were mighty lucky to have won the race at all. Had Johnson only been present on the Union Course with all his Napoleonic powers of management, direction, and inspiration—"A plate of lobsters," quoth the mournfully sententious John Randolph of Roanoke, "cost the South the championship of the turf." Or had John Richards been able to run instead of Henry, or had Purdy ridden for the South instead of the North—the atmosphere of discussion among the Virginians and Carolinians buzzed with ifs and almosts.

On the fourth day of the Union Course meet, Thursday the twenty-ninth, Childers vanquished a Duroc mare by the embarrassing name of Slow and Easy. Rain forced cancellation of the Friday event. On Saturday, Henry returned. He was enough recovered from his mighty exertions to take two-mile heats from Jane of the Green.

Eclipse ran no more after his supreme exhibition of speed and sustained courage. He was retired to stud, this time permanently, while Henry headed for other races and victories. In later years, fate chose to swap these horses from North to South; Eclipse eventually became the property of William Johnson, while Henry, after a

BOSTON, THE GRANDSON

From a portrait by Edwin Troye, by courtesy of the New York Jockey Club. Son of Timoleon and grandson of Sir Archie, Boston won more than forty races from the best opposition of his time, and he retired from the track to an equally distinguished career at stud.

glorious career as a four-miler, was sold as a stallion to a New Yorker named Ludlow.

Sir Archie was at the happy height of his 1823 season at stud, even as his son ran thus so narrowly short of an immortal turf triumph.

Mowfield was beseiged by horse breeders who wanted Sir Archie foals from their mares, for nobody disputed Sir Archie's claim to be the greatest stallion America had ever produced. Every effort was made to secure offspring rich with his blood, and not even the Egyptian Pharaohs, striving to keep as pure as possible their legendary descent from the gods above, mated more often with their near relatives than did Sir Archie. Not only his sisters but his daughters were presented to him, and their produce by him again and again showed brilliance, strength, speed, beauty, and fertility. Sir Archie began to convince the gravest of observers that he was a phenomenon of a sire who had no weak traits to be doubled by such close inbreeding.

His sons became sires, too, with heritage of his own vigor and success. Both Director and Tecumseh, colts of his first season at stud, had got their own good progeny. Timoleon's swift son Washington was followed by others of promise quickly fulfilled. And, lest any of this success be attributed to the choice of blue-ribbon Thoroughbred mares as mates for Sir Archie, let people look to the western South. There the self-made champion, crossbred Walk-in-the-Water, continued to conquer blood horses in races at four-mile heats.

William Amis of Mowfield had reached his sixties. He began to show signs of infirmity. His letters, even to friends, were dictated to acquaintances with steadier hands. His son John and his overseer John Bell supervised his business affairs. Susan Amis had died, and William Amis was an aged but not inconsolable widower. He contrived to divert himself with a young woman of the Gumberry District and by her had a daughter.

Affairs prevailed more normally at White House, the home of

Sir Archie

John Amis. Thomas Sully was a guest there at about the time of the Eclipse–Henry race to paint a portrait of John's only daughter Mary, and during his stay Sully made a visit to Mowfield, where he painted Sir Archie as well. Another artist was on his way to Northampton County; Alvan Fisher of Massachusetts, the Amises were told, had been commissioned to paint Sir Archie for the private gallery of Charles Henry Hall of New York.

Uncle Hardy was the name of the Negro groom whose congenial task it was to curry, water, feed, and care for Sir Archie. The two achieved a splendid companionship. William Amis appeared less and less frequently at the stables. For William Amis weakened daily until, early in 1824, he died.

His will had been drawn the previous October, and it disposed of nearly a hundred slaves; two big plantations and other tracts of land; numerous horses, cattle, hogs, and sheep; and more than $20,000 in securities.

John Amis already had received at his father's hands the White House property and other valuable gifts, but a special bequest settled a somewhat vexing family question:

"... I give and bequeath to my son, John D. Amis, my stallion 'Sir Archie' and all debts or claims which I have against him for advances or otherwise."

William Amis did not recognize the daughter of his old-age amour in any official manner, but he left her a considerable inheritance, bleakly limited by its terms. The child was to receive $10,000 in stock in the Tarboro branch of the State Bank of North Carolina, and for administration of this bequest William Amis appointed his old friend William B. Lockhart as trustee. Lockhart was given power to furnish money to the little girl's mother "as may be necessary to support [the child] in a comfortable and genteel manner." Then, when the girl reached the age of five, she was to be taken from her mother "and educated in a suitable manner." Should the mother

He Glories in His Children

refuse to give up her daughter, the legacy of bank stock would be divided among Amis' grandchildren, share and share alike.

A third special bequest awarded $500 to faithful John Bell, with the proviso that Bell attend to the settlement of William Amis' affairs.

The bulk of the estate went to the grandchildren. The five children of Lemuel and Mary Long inherited fifty slaves, $10,000 in the form of bonds against their father, and whatever money might be realized from the sale of all livestock on the Mowfield plantation other than Sir Archie. John's three sons, William, Thomas, and Junius, were left Mowfield and the rest of their grandfather's broad lands, more Negroes, and a share of money from the sale of personal property. John Amis' daughter Mary was not mentioned. She may have received gifts from her grandfather before his death. A codicil provided that John Amis administer the property left to his sons until the youngest of them, Junius, had reached the age of twenty-one years.

The will was certified and placed on record in March of 1824. John Amis moved his family to Mowfield and assumed charge of the beautiful mansion, the outbuildings, the race track, and the fields. To Sir Archie, lounging in the stable with Uncle Hardy, the new head of the Amis family presented greetings as to a loved and respected associate.

❦ VII ❦

SIR ARCHIE
Gets into Politics

THE spring of 1824 was, like all springs of that period, a happy one for Sir Archie, and it was an important one as well. His nineteenth birthday was noted, and quite probably it was celebrated in some way. He began his fifteenth season at stud, and his seventh year as an honored and welcome resident of the Mowfield stables.

At about that springtime, Alvan Fisher completed his painting of Sir Archie with the devoted Uncle Hardy standing at the halter rope. The picture survives, and is spirited if not brilliant in its presentation of the figure of a dark bay horse with a white blaze on the right hind foot, grown solid with maturity but sleek, powerful, and splendidly proportioned as to legs and barrel. The neck is vigorously arched, and the proud, shapely head displays a brilliant eye and a finely flared nostril.

Contemporaries who saw the portrait felt that it was a good likeness. Indeed, said one, Sir Archie's "figure is correctly drawn by Fisher; he has even presented a correct likeness of the way in which he stood, from lameness in his left stifle, from an accidental injury

Sir Archie Gets into Politics

soon after he became the property of Mr. Amis." Some of this apparent accuracy may have lain in the eye of the beholder. Fisher executed a portrait of Sir Hal, a great winner in William Johnson's hands and by 1824 a successful sire, and this surviving portrait, groom and all, can be distinguished from that of Sir Archie only after a study of minor details.

Sir Archie's sons and daughters continued to bring celebrity to their sire. Flirtilla, now owned by Racing Billy Wynn, was perhaps swiftest of the newer ones. By May of 1824 she won at four-mile heats at Baltimore, then up at the Union Course. Henry scotched a rumor that he had broken down in the race with Eclipse by beating Betsey Richards for the Newmarket Proprietor's Purse. Meanwhile, older Sir Archies stood up well. Blucher, son of the first season, still ran sturdily and successfully at thirteen years of age. Walk-in-the-Water, at nine, continued to embarrass his pedigreed contemporaries on Western tracks. Director, Harwood, and Tecumseh, all foaled in 1811, gained note as stallions. So did Sir Charles, whose first sons and daughters, foaled in 1824, were destined for greatness. Timoleon, in Alabama, served mares not wholly worthy, perhaps, of so splendid a consort. Many other Sir Archies shone both on the turf and as progenitors, and to Sir Archie himself, healthy and potent and nineteen, a glorious troop of sleek Thoroughbred mares were enticingly displayed.

John Dillard Amis was about forty years old that spring, an age which at the time and in the region was considered respectable and ripe. He had begun to put on flesh and wore spectacles. A man of position and property, he was a man of family as well. His three sons developed their own distinct individualities. William, the eldest, was a strapping and handsome youth of sixteen who rode well, spoke boldly, and began to consider himself somewhat of a blade. Mary, now thirteen, was a beautiful child who would be a beautiful woman.

The question of who owned Sir Archie had not quite been settled by the bequest of the elder William Amis that gave him to John; for that bequest also assigned to John "all debts or claims which I have against him for advances or otherwise." John Amis continued to feel that Sir Archie had belonged to him all the time, while John's sister, Mary Amis Long, felt herself obliged to bring suit for an accounting of the receipts from Sir Archie's recent seasons and a share in the profits. But this lawsuit did not cause any lasting coolness between William Amis' son and daughter. They and their households continued to visit back and forth on the most affectionate of terms.

Indeed, Mowfield saw many more visitors and entertained them in more lavish manner than in the days of the rather thrifty William Amis. John liked company, and it is remembered of him that he kept a dignified black house servant on post where his private road joined the highway, there to survey passers-by and invite any who seemed genteel to come and call on the new master of Mowfield. He gave big dinners, took an important part in all social life of the neighborhood, and began to gain a reputation by helping, with loans or outright gifts, friends who were in financial straits. Meanwhile, he raced several promising Sir Archies of his own, generally under the colors of his old friend William Johnson. In the mind of John Amis grew the determination to contribute importantly to the American racing world; he planned for the writing and publication of that American stud book similar to the master work of England.

William Johnson came often to see him. So did John Randolph of Roanoke. But of all guests and companions, John Amis liked his own kinsmen best. In particular he was glad to welcome his young brother-in-law Jesse Atherton Bynum at Mowfield.

Jesse Bynum was twenty-seven years old in 1824 and unmarried. He had attended Princeton for two years, had studied law, and was a rising light of the bar in neighboring Halifax County. The Bynum property in Northampton remained in the hands of Jesse's widowed

He Gets into Politics

mother, under management of her older son Wade. Jesse boarded at the tavern of the Fenners in the town of Halifax.

Almost since his first coming to manhood, Jesse Bynum had shown energy and ability in political matters, and with his numerous relatives in the community he was in a position to command a snug block of votes. In 1823 he was elected to the North Carolina House of Commons from the town of Halifax, which was one of the several communities, specifically designated as boroughs, then empowered to elect their own representatives separately from the counties. Little Halifax could muster only fifty or sixty white and colored freemen qualified, by their ownership of property and payment of taxes thereon, to vote for legislators; but these voters were proud, lively, and individual. They did not forget that at Halifax the State Constitution had been drawn up and that at Halifax, too, the Declaration of Independence had been endorsed before any other North Carolina town cared or dared to take such action. The men of Halifax, of high degree and low, considered themselves company and example for the best.

As Halifax's representative in the House of Commons, Jesse Bynum headed a political fellowship that opposed the faction of another attorney, Thomas Burges. Burges was older than Bynum and a lawyer of recognized ability who had held several public offices, but in 1824 he seemed to be losing his grip. Bynum enjoyed the friendship and support of Sheriff Pettway of Halifax County, and his young cousin John Reeves Jones Daniel, a lawyer and bachelor like Bynum, was the town's inspector of elections and at the brink of a brilliant career. Other family connections of Bynum included the influential Dawsons and Barneses.

Jesse Bynum's election to the House of Commons in 1823 had seemed to threaten the very existence of the Burges party and to promise for Bynum higher honors in the future. Bynum gloried in his office. In his twenties he was a man of rather nervous manner and movement, a ready smiler and scowler, quick to warm friendship or bitter enmity. He was frequently at Mowfield where John Amis, some dozen years his senior, was glad to see him and may once or twice have lent him money. Young William Amis, for his part, rode again and again to the Roanoke Ferry and beyond into Halifax where society was gay. There the lad associated happily with his admired uncles, Jesse and Wade Bynum, and with Cousin John Daniel.

Of the defeated Burges, relatively little was thought, and less feared, by either Jesse Bynum or William Amis in the spring of 1824; but, at about the time that Sir Archie turned nineteen years of age, Burges added to himself a fantastically formidable ally, one who was destined to give bitter trouble to the Bynums, the Amises, and all their circle; nor would he ignore respectable old Sir Archie in his pleasant paddock.

Robert Potter was born in June of 1800 on a small farm near Williamsboro in Granville County. If no comet ripped the sky that night, perhaps comets suddenly had become timorous. The tiny son of rustic parents was fated to a career of political demagoguery and incandescent personal violence that at times would verge on the incredible.

His father and mother were poor and of ordinary attainments, and opportunities for their son's education and advancement had been meager. But from his days as a toddler, Robert Potter displayed intelligence, energy, daring, and an utter and disdainful lack of any restraint whatever.

Somewhere he found friends and funds to gain him a midshipman's berth in the United States Navy in 1815—just too late to fight, and surely he would have fought excellently, in the second war with Great Britain. He sailed far, studied for a naval commission, and improved a keen appetite for books. Juvenal, Alexander Pope, and Richard Steele were among his favorites. So, inevitably, was Shakespeare, and so was Lord Byron, just then at the height of his poetic and heart-smashing career and exactly the personality to

He Gets into Politics

inspire in young Midshipman Potter dreams of emulation. Potter looked into American and European history, and he knew about the Italian poet-orator Rienzi long before Bulwer-Lytton wrote his novel or Richard Wagner his opera.

He could wield weapons before he could well wield a razor. For lack of military enemies, he quarrelled with shipmates and fought at least one duel while yet in his teens. Life at sea, to judge by his later self-romanticizing accounts, was a dramatic wonder to him.

As a midshipman he grew to young manhood, dark-haired and dark-skinned. He was of only medium height and figure, but well-knit, muscular, and sure of movement. His finest feature was a pair of burning, expressive black eyes. A portrait of him, painted at about his twentieth year, shows an intelligent but rather truculent face with a broad short nose, a heavy jaw, full firm lips, and a mop of shaggy hair. His presence and manner could not but attract notice.

He resigned, for no stated reason, as of March 26, 1821, some months before his twenty-first birthday. His writings suggest that he left the service because his parents died, leaving younger children who needed support and rearing. It may be that he had grown tired of waiting for the commission he had sought. Returning to land, he lived for a while in Granville County. He visited several other North Carolina communities during the next two years and finally, about the end of 1823, arrived in the town of Halifax.

There he was for some months a guest at the Grove, the beautiful home built by Willie Jones and presided over by Jones's widow.

Mary Montford Jones had been an arrestingly beautiful young woman, and in her old age she maintained a charming individuality. Her reputation for courageously pungent wit extended back to the days of the Revolutionary War. Potter's manners and talents must have interested her, and his need for help aroused her generosity. While living at the Grove, Potter read law with Thomas Burges. In a short time he was able to pass an examination for admittance to the bar, not an exhaustive ordeal at that period, and early in 1824 he became Burges' partner, with quarters in Burges' home. He may not have achieved a profound grasp of the finer points of jurisprudence, but almost at once he proved an able and successful arguer to juries.

That summer Bynum was a candidate to succeed himself in the House of Commons, and he expected scant opposition from Burges' creaky organization at the town election which was set for August 11. He relaxed his stiffness toward the Burges faction sufficiently to accept from Robert A. Jones, a kinsman of Willie Jones and a friend of Burges, an invitation to an Independence Day dinner. Potter, too, was invited. These and others sat together on July 5 at the Mansion House, the largest and finest tavern in Halifax, to eat heartily and probably to drink heartily as well.

Bynum took exception to something Jones said and began suddenly to quarrel with his host. Potter shoved between the two, and Bynum struck at Jones across Potter's interposed arm. Others separated the wranglers, and Jones retired to a private room. Bynum then turned on Potter, scolding him loudly, and Potter interrupted with a string of sailorly oaths. More intervention by the other guests, or blood might have been shed then and there.

It may have been that very night that the supporters of Burges helped Potter to make up his mind to announce as a candidate for Bynum's seat in the House of Commons.

This was audacious in a comparative stranger to Halifax, but audacity was a characteristic which Potter possessed in the highest degree. He began a zealous campaign. Bynum plainly was worried and addressed the town's scanty electorate in rather peculiar terms.

"It is true I have not given universal satisfaction," he said, "but Christ, the only son of God, failed when upon earth to please everybody, and was sacrificed by those He came to serve." Querulously he added: "I had offered under the expectation that there would be no opposition, and that the people would continue in harmony and friendship, but the demon of discord has come."

The first of these pronouncements was characterized by Potter

He Gets into Politics

and his friends as utter blasphemy, and the second as evidence that Bynum claimed a lifelong title to his seat in the legislature. Some voters rallied to Potter, and the town looked for vigorous happenings on election day.

Those qualified to vote assembled at the courthouse on August 11 with a relishable air of expectancy. John Daniel, as inspector, stood with Sheriff Pettway to hear challenges of voters by the rival candidates.

Bynum questioned the ballot of a youth named Alsobrook, who had just turned twenty-one and was not registered as a property-owning voter. Potter angrily protested that Alsobrook was of legal age and, as proprietor of a store, had paid town taxes that would qualify him. This plea both sheriff and inspector disallowed, and Alsobrook was turned voteless away. Another Potter adherent approached, a young man who had not lived long in Halifax. As proof of his rights, he exhibited a deed by Burges to a plot of land within the town's limits.

Bynum charged that the man was of foreign birth and not yet naturalized. "How old are you?" he demanded sharply.

"I don't know," was the reply.

"Where were you born?"

"I don't know," the young man repeated.

Bynum pointed accusingly at the deed. "Is there any agreement between yourself and the grantor to re-convey the lot?"

"There is not," said the young man, definite at last.

But Bynum insisted that, at the time of previous elections, the same piece of land had been deeded to others to enable them to vote and that it had been re-deeded to Burges after each election. Sheriff Pettway and Daniel rejected this vote also. Two other men stood near by, one of them a free Negro. They had brought similar deeds to offer as proof of their rights, but now they walked away as though daunted.

Potter and Bynum came face to face and fairly lathered each

other with fighting words, but again they were separated. Bynum, some felt, had had rather the better of this verbal skirmish, and he plumed himself accordingly. "Potter attempted to dictate to me," he told a friend, "and I put him down."

When the votes were counted, they showed that Bynum had been reelected by a decisive majority. If this was enough for Halifax, it was not enough for Potter. Next morning he wrote a letter to Bynum, first evidence in the locality of his flavorous prose style:

"SIR: I forebore to chastise your insolence at the polls yesterday, because I was unwilling to involve my brave and devoted friends in the consequence of a quarrel with you. I understand you have renewed your vaporing today; indeed, you appear to have a wonderful itching to riot in the van of mobs. This is to invite you to the field of combat, I cannot say of honor, your presence would deprive any spot of that character. You can choose your own weapon and distance. My friend, Mr. Burges, will make the necessary arrangements with any person you think proper to appoint for that purpose."

Burges, older and more calm of nature, did not want to carry this inflammatory missive. "There is no cause," he tried to persuade his bloodthirsty young colleague, but Potter was sternly insistent, and Burges sought out Bynum at Fenner's Tavern.

Bynum read the challenge without comment and left Halifax that same day to cross the Roanoke and seek John Amis at Mowfield. With him he took a case of duelling pistols, and he may have fired several shots, for the sake of practice, within hearing of Sir Archie's stall.

But if Bynum thought of fighting, his brother Wade soberly advised him against it. Amis, too, very probably urged Bynum to ignore a challenge offered in such insulting terms. Bynum yielded, as regarded Potter's invitation, but it occurred to him that here was a splendid opportunity to deal decisively with his old political adver-

He Gets into Politics

sary Burges. After several days he returned to Halifax, where on August 17 he wrote to Burges in language not greatly dissimilar to Potter's own mock-formal savagery:

"SIR: I received the other day by your hands, a communication from Mr. Potter, inviting me to 'the field of combat', not 'that of honor'. Of Mr. Potter I know nothing. Judging from his conduct, however, during his residence in this place, I do not think him entitled to the standing of a gentleman, and shall therefore take no further notice of his insolence. But, sir, I believe you to have the standing of a gentleman, and I consider you to have insulted me, by being the bearer of such a communication from such a person; I therefore demand satisfaction of you. You will choose your weapon and distance, and meet me upon the field of honor. My friend, Mr. Dawson, will make such further arrangements as will be necessary, with any gentleman you may think proper to appoint."

Bynum's cousin, Jesse A. Dawson, bore this counter-proposal to poor Burges, who was no man of violence and who must have begun to wish he had never met either Potter or Bynum. He shrank from fighting anyone, but he, too, found himself unable to resist the opportunity to be valiant with his pen. That same evening he addressed a letter to Dawson:

"SIR: Out of respect to *you*, I send this reply to Mr. Bynum's communication of this date. From a perfect knowledge that Mr. Potter has always been considered, and as I am fully satisfied ever will be, a *gentleman*, and supposing that Mr. Bynum had, *at least*, some pretensions to that character, I was, as I shall always be, disposed to serve Mr. Potter in an honorable way.

"The communication of Mr. Bynum is of a character which I *cannot*, with propriety, *consent* any further to notice; for were I, *for the reason assigned by him*, to accept his invitation I should exhibit to the world the appearance of acquiescing in the opinion expressed by Mr. Bynum of Mr. Potter. I must, therefore, decline

Sir Archie

any further notice of the note which you handed me, considering it unworthy of my attention, and intend this as a final answer."

He finished his outraged underscorings and handed the letter to Potter, who brought it to Dawson. That gentleman said, with the stuffiest of dignity, that Bynum had instructed him to receive no communication through Potter's hands.

"It is directed to you, and not to Mr. Bynum," reminded Potter.

Dawson then read Burges' letter. He appeared embarrassed.

"I regret having participated in the affair at all," he said, thereby identifying himself as one of the very few sensible men on either side of the dispute.

Potter replied with one of the painfully rare expressions of courtesy he ever addressed to a supporter of Bynum and took his leave. But if both Bynum and Burges were too proud to fight, Potter was not. Two days later he nailed a placard to the front door of the courthouse:

Halifax, Aug. 19, 1824

JESSE A. BYNUM having been called to atone for his ungentlemanly conduct, and having refused satisfaction I publish him as a poltroon and a coward.

ROB. POTTER

Lest some of the townsfolk might not come to the courthouse and so miss this stigmatizing declaration, Potter affixed a duplicate to the signpost of the Mansion House, to which popular place of refreshment most male Halifaxians could be expected to resort at least once a day. A week after the posting of his enemy, Potter distributed throughout the town copies of an eleven-page pamphlet, with a bleak title:

A STATEMENT

By ROB. POTTER of the circumstances connected with the affair between JESSE A. BYNUM and himself.

He Gets into Politics

Under that appeared a quotation from Lord Byron: "Fools are my theme, let satire be my song."

The text reads entertainingly even at this distance of time and space, and, hot off the press in Halifax so soon after those election-day bickerings, it must have been considered fascinating.

Potter sketched in highly partisan fashion the details of the quarrel at the Mansion House on July 5, describing Bynum as a brawler, a would-be assassin, and "a ranting demagogue, the butt and jeer of the legislature." He set forth in full his challenge, in language of which he was manifestly proud, and the subsequent letters of Bynum and Burges with acid comments. Further, he charged Sheriff Pettway and John Daniel with "a vile and dishonest combination" to secure Bynum's reelection to the legislature; "... for had not the rights of the people been basely betrayed by those whom the law trusted with the protection of them," he accused, "my election must have been proclaimed." He concluded, not with full consistency: "The facts are before the public, and I submit them without a single comment."

From some source Bynum drew the patience to endure these barbs without protest by word or deed, and the quarrel seemed to sag in the bright heat of the late Carolina summer.

John Amis, undoubtedly glad to think that Bynum had restrained himself from further feuding, continued to make him welcome at Mowfield. Amis' attention turned ever to horseflesh. His cherished project of an American stud book had growing support among turfmen, and he conferred with Theophilus Feild of Brunswick County. Feild and Amis continued to gather material and now proposed to underwrite publication. On December 15, Amis wrote to Richard Singleton of the High Hills of Santee, a frequent sender of mares to Sir Archie:

"With a view to put a period (as much as lies in our power) to the numerous inaccurate pedigrees given to public blood-horses and mares: a friend and myself have it in contemplation (in the course

Sir Archie

of the ensuing spring) to publish a general Stud Book after the manner of the general Stud Book of England.

"Will you do us the particular favor to furnish us with the full pedigree of all the Blood Stock you have had for many years past, also those you will be able to procure in your neighborhood or in the remote parts of South Carolina."

Finishing his letter, Amis may have glanced from his window to see Sir Archie frisking happily in the paddock. He added a postscript: "Old Sir Archie is in high order, and as lively as a colt."

Amis hoped for similar assistance from Feild's neighbor, James J. Harrison, and from George Washington Jeffreys, of Caswell County, North Carolina, who had begun to write bits of racing history for various papers.

As for Bynum, though he had endured the insults of Potter's placard and pamphlet, he could not hear with any great calmness the report that Potter again would oppose him in the coming year's election and that the faction of Burges rallied more strongly to Potter than ever.

Christmas was celebrated with varying types of gaiety at Mowfield, at the home of the Bynums, at the house where Potter and Burges lived, and elsewhere. The New Year came, and unlucky stars twinkled down upon the town of Halifax a wry prophecy of greater strife in 1825.

One Dr. Wilson, remarkable in that small but lively community for having no enemies and playing no political favorites, invited almost everybody who was anybody to a dancing party on the evening of January 26. Young William Amis had ridden over from Mowfield to visit his uncle Jesse at Fenner's Tavern, and he attended Dr. Wilson's party with Jesse and Wade Bynum and John Daniel. Robert Potter and Thomas Burges appeared, and a host of ladies and gentlemen besides.

Despite the presence of the political rivals, the affair began merrily. The belle of the occasion was lovely Miss Lavinia Barnes, a kinswoman of the Bynums. Jesse Bynum and Potter avoided each other with elaborate, cold silence. But after a while, Benjamin S. Long drew Bynum aside to whisper that Potter had come carrying a dirk—a straight dagger meant for combat, perhaps the same that Potter once had worn as a naval midshipman. Long asked if Bynum, too, were armed.

Bynum was not and quickly sent John W. Simmons to bring him a dirk of his own, also a pair of pistols. To a friend of Potter, Bynum darkly observed that if a quarrel rose, somebody might be killed. Wade Bynum also hurried a messenger to Sheriff Pettway's house to fetch him back a sword cane.

Before the armaments arrived at Dr. Wilson's door, the fiddles tuned, and Potter asked Miss Lavinia Barnes to dance with him. She replied that she was already engaged, but Potter detained her and said something else. Abruptly Bynum bustled across the room, seized Potter by the arm, and leaned to whisper in his cousin's pretty ear. Then he wheeled and walked out into a passage.

"Did Mr. Bynum's observations have any reference to me?" Potter demanded of the girl.

"I do not recollect," she replied, both nervously and implausibly.

Potter hastened into the passage after Bynum. A moment later, loud, angry voices drowned out the music of the fiddles.

Several guests made speed to the passage and pulled the two apart. Burges was one of these interposers, and he persuaded Potter to leave the Wilson home. The two emerged togther into the winter night. By that time, Wade Bynum had his sword cane. Jesse snatched it from his brother's hand and charged out of the door in the wake of Burges and Potter. Behind him came Wade, John Daniel, and the excited and eager young William Amis.

Potter spun around and truculently faced this quartet of pursuers. "If you are disposed to meet danger like a man," he addressed Bynum, "appoint some friend and I will appoint another, and we will retire together to a private apartment."

Sir Archie

"You are too damned a rascal to notice in that way," snarled back Bynum.

Wade Bynum spoke reasonably, saying that a fight of four against two would not be fair. Brushing aside what sounded like an attempt at peacemaking, Potter challenged Wade to combat.

What Wade might have replied was drowned out by Burges and Jesse Bynum, who began to thunder accusations at each other. Jesse struck at his rival with Wade's cane. Burges caught it by the shank, which came away in his hand as Jesse wrenched free the sharp blade concealed inside. William Amis, also spoiling for a fight, ripped a branch from a tree to use as a club.

Potter flung himself at Jesse Bynum, who stabbed him in the muscles beneath his right armpit. Outnumbered, Potter and Burges retreated, and a servant ran from the Burges home with a pistol to help them to safety. Potter examined his wound, found it a slight one, and then saw some of his friends arriving. To them he said that considerably more blood would be spilled the very next morning.

Strong in the determination to fulfill this prophecy, Potter arose on the twenty-seventh, belted himself with his dirk, and put two small pistols into his pockets. Lest these be not enough, he cut a stout cudgel. Then he tramped down the street toward Fenner's Tavern.

Jesse Bynum stood on the tavern piazza as Potter approached. From the door behind Bynum, looked out the faces of John Daniel and William Amis. Bounding up the steps, Potter brandished his club over Bynum's head.

"Last night you had me in your power," he roared. "I now have you in mine. Draw your dirk, for I intend to kill you."

With that, he flung down the cudgel. Out flashed his blade. He struck furiously at Bynum's face. Bynum partially blocked the slashing blow with his upflung arms, but the point dug Bynum's forehead and cheek and sent him staggering back. Recovering,

He Gets into Politics

Bynum drew a pistol. Potter turned and ran. Bynum sprinted after him, bloody-faced and howling with rage.

Near at hand was a store, belonging to a man named Holliday, with two doors. Potter rushed through one of these, slamming it shut behind him. Bynum found the other entrance, which brought him into a room with an inner door separating him from Potter. As Daniel and William Amis followed their kinsman into the store building, Potter looked through the half-open inner door, thrust a pocket pistol almost against Bynum's chest, and fired.

The pistol was little more than a toy. The bullet barely penetrated Bynum's flesh, then plowed off along a rib and flew away under Bynum's left arm. Potter then slammed the door between them, and Bynum, undaunted and uncalmed by blood-letting, shoved and kicked until he forced it open again. Potter tried his other pistol full in his enemy's face, but it failed to go off. A crowd gathered in the street outside, jostling and shouting. Potter retreated up a flight of stairs, again drawing his dirk.

Supporters of both political factions ran into the lower rooms. Bynum found himself at close quarters with the unlucky Thomas Burges and clubbed him heavily in the face with his pistol. Then Wade Bynum appeared, grappled his brother, and dragged him outside. Pulling free, Jesse Bynum fairly danced in the street, loudly and profanely daring Potter to come out and fight to a finish.

That was exactly what Potter wished to do, with no interference from Bynum's family connections. He came down the stairs. One of his friends handed him a double-barrelled gun and a pair of loaded pistols, larger than those footling little pocket pieces. Thus replenished for war, Potter made for the outer door and a renewal of combat, but Sheriff Pettway met him on the threshold and disarmed him. Leading his prisoner into the street, Pettway informed Jesse Bynum and John Daniel that they, too, were under arrest. He marched all three to the courthouse, where they were charged with rioting and placed under bond to keep the peace.

Sir Archie

Potter made bail, pledged himself to circumspection, and returned to his own quarters. Again sympathetic friends gathered, and again Potter felt his anger rise. He spoke bitterly of Daniel in particular and vowed to drink that young gentleman's blood at an early opportunity.

These words were promptly repeated, and perhaps exaggerated, throughout the town. On the following morning, Friday, January 28, Daniel's cousin Judge J. J. Daniel appeared at Potter's law office to demand an explanation. Potter had grown cooler again overnight and replied that he recognized his bonded obligation to keep the peace; he would not be the first to start a battle.

"I hope," he added, with a plausible air of candor, "that you have a better opinion of me than to suppose I would do an act of the kind."

Judge Daniel was relieved to hear such assurances, and went to repeat them at Fenner's Tavern, but Jesse Bynum growled pessimistically that Potter was not a man to be trusted.

William Amis still lingered in Halifax, plainly hoping to witness, and perhaps to take an active part in, further diverting violence. He accompanied his two uncles on a social visit to some ladies, walking past Potter's gate to do so. Later in the day the Bynums, John Daniel, and William all stood on Fenner's piazza when Potter swaggered into view. In his pockets Potter carried the two small pistols which had availed him so fatuously little on the previous day.

John Reeves Jones Daniel was a sensitive, quiet man, with a record of studious distinction at the State University. Thus far he had been no more than a witness, possibly a would-be peacemaker, at the clashes between Potter and Jesse Bynum. But he was as brave, if not as loud, as any man in Halifax. As Potter approached, Daniel stepped down into the street and spoke.

"Sir," said Daniel evenly, "I wish you to tell me whether you have ever threatened to take my life, and at what time you intend putting your threats into execution."

He Gets into Politics

Potter glared at him. "I will give you timely notice when I deem it necessary to attack you," he retorted.

People paused to stare and listen; these squabbles had become a recognized diversion in Halifax. Daniel repeated his question as to whether Potter had threatened to kill him.

"If the company will withdraw," announced Potter suddenly, "I will be very happy in answering you."

That sounded like fight, especially from Potter. "Let us withdraw," suggested someone, undoubtedly the most prudent man on the scene. The press of onlookers shrank away, some entering Fenner's bar, others pausing on the far side of the street. Sheriff Pettway came running from somewhere toward the two men who bristled at each other.

As he ran, he shouted to remind them of their bonds to keep the peace. Then, as he reached them: "Don't shoot!" he cried warningly.

For Daniel had whipped out a pistol. No dainty pocket piece this, nor was it a graceful duelling weapon. It was a big, ugly, practical horse pistol, something like a foot long and an inch across the bore, such an instrument as could slap a leaden slug all the way through a man.

Pettway stepped in front of Potter, shielding him with his body. A countryman named Robert Perkins snatched Daniel's big pistol away and handed it to someone else, then raced across to seize Potter's elbow and lead him away. The rest of the crowd closed in again, jabbering. Jesse Bynum's voice rang above all the others, cursing Potter roundly and blackly.

Some there were in Halifax who by this time had become tired of such extravagances. Another social gathering had been announced, with both Bynum and Potter invited, and folks hoped they might dance without an accompaniment of discordant war cries and rattling weapons. Solemnly public-spirited, therefore, was the demeanor of Benjamin C. Eaton when, on January 29, he entered the shop of L. Clanton. Eaton was of Burges' political following,

Clanton voted with Bynum, but both wished alike for less knife and pistol play around them.

"I will pledge my honor," said Eaton, "that Potter will molest neither Bynum nor his friends, unless compelled to do so in self defense."

"From what Bynum has said to me," replied Clanton weightily, "neither he nor his friends are disposed to attack Mr. Potter if they can be convinced of that fact."

The two volunteer men of peace sought out and pleaded with their respective friends, with more success than had attended the efforts of Judge Daniel. A meeting was arranged at the Mansion House, where, in the presence of Clanton, Eaton, and several other witnesses, Bynum and Potter icily agreed to lay aside the weapons they now wore as habitually as they wore their trousers. Nobody heard the faintest hint of a proposal that the two shake hands.

Further dampers were put on the spirits of both brawlers when North Carolina's attorney-general William Drew indicted them, with Burges and Dawson, for the sending and bearing of challenges to duels. Halifax gratefully passed a tame spring, and in June the four defendants appeared in court, where charges against them were dropped.

But the passing of months had not sweetened Potter's disposition. On June 24 he wrote to John Daniel the sort of note one might have expected:

"Sir: The expiration of our recognisances at the last Superior court has restored us to the freedom of action, which before they had withdrawn; and but for the restriction imposed by them, I should long since have called on you for the satisfaction I now demand. Your interference in the affray in which I was engaged on the 26th, 27th and 28th of January last, is an injury not to be passed over in silence, and I now require redress of it at your hand. I say nothing of apology and explanation, they are altogether inadmissable; it can

He Gets into Politics

be adjusted in one mode and that is unnecessary for me to designate."

By this time, Daniel had married. The Bynums and others persuaded him to ignore, for his bride's sake, Potter's challenge. By the end of the month, Potter comforted himself and staggered the community by issuing another pamphlet more bitterly vituperative than the first.

This was of thirty-five pages, and the title it bore was long but not really tedious:

AN ACCOUNT

OF THE ATTEMPT MADE BY JESSE A. BYNUM, ATTENDED BY SEVERAL ARMED ASSOCIATES, TO MURDER *ROBERT POTTER* AT MIDNIGHT ON THE 6TH [*sic*] OF JANUARY LAST: AND OF THE AFFRAY AND RENCONTRE WHICH AFTERWARDS ENSUED, IN WHICH *POTTER* WAS ENGAGED ON ONE SIDE, AND *JESSE A. BYNUM, WADE BYNUM, WILLIAM AMIS*, AND LAST AND LEAST, *JOHN REEVES JONES DANIEL* WERE LEAGUED ON THE OTHER.

Again he began with a quotation, this time from Shakespeare's *King John*, and inaccurately remembered: "Doff that lion's hide, and put a calfskin on those recreant limbs." His first paragraph rang out like a volley of muskets:

"All who know the character of John Reeves Jones Daniel, a name of stupid length and trifling sound, will at once perceive the propriety of the motto, under which I propose to recount to the public, the knightly achievements of that 'young son of Chivalry' in a late affray in which I was engaged. To furnish a clue to the motives of his participation, in that nefarious and dishonorable transaction, it is only necessary to state, that he is the same individual, who acted as an Inspector of the Polls at the last election for the town of Halifax; and whose corrupt and dishonest conduct on that occasion, made it my duty to expose and degrade him."

Sir Archie

Potter amplified these accusations in an ill-tempered account of that series of fights which began outside Dr. Wilson's home and continued at Fenner's Tavern and in Holliday's store. He accused Daniel of trying to shoot him in the back, boasted that he had knocked Jesse Bynum down with a blow, and branded both Wade Bynum and William Amis as supplementary bravos who had drawn swords and guns against him. All these passages of arms, Potter continued, resulted from what he chose to consider his own gallant and public-spirited exposure of Jesse Bynum and his kinsmen as brutal, dishonest, and licentious.

In his account of each incident, Potter described himself as infinitely superior in deportment, repartee, and fighting skill to his enemies. He felt that nobody on Bynum's side was greatly to be feared. He compared Daniel to "a gibbering ghost," Bynum he pictured as "ranting like an idle maniac in the street," while William Amis he dismissed as "a thoughtless and misguided youth."

He represented the succession of scuffles as the single-handed strife of a brave and honest man against a horde of vicious but woefully inept persecutors, and he wrote with circumstantiality, suspense, and color. He garnished his narrative with further quotations from Shakespeare, more or less apt, and a sizeable slice of Byron's *Childe Harold*. In addition to "cowardice and villainy, unparalleled in the annals of any civilized community," he declared his foes guilty of a whole docket of trespasses against law and good taste, ranging from spiteful envy to ballot-box stuffing.

Daniel, according to Potter, took refuge behind the skirts of his new-wed wife when he refused to fight a duel. "As to Jesse Bynum in particular," Potter dismissed that adversary, "the print of my steel upon his forehead, the impression of my ball upon his breast, have left him evidences that my *path* is only to be crossed at peril." Wade Bynum he was willing to recognize "as a superior man in every respect to his brother," which, from Potter's viewpoint, was faint praise indeed. He added: "I am tired of challenging men, who

He Gets into Politics

upon frivolous and unfounded pretensions, refuse to fight me; but if Wade Bynum is aggrieved at aught in this publication, he has only to signify it to me, and I will cheerfully attend to any communication he may make."

New enemies he singled out, charging them with malicious slander. One of these was John Amis of Mowfield, and into his indictment he brought mention of Sir Archie. Amis, said Potter, "is known abroad as the proprietor of a celebrated *horse*, and owes his chief distinction to his connection with that animal."

Of himself he had much to say, and that in a Byronically romantic vein:

"I have led an obscure and undistinguished life, and from the earliest dawn of my youth, had to stand up against the most embarrassing and torturing difficulties, that ever beset the path of any man. I have borne in silence and without complaint, shocks that would have crushed and broken down, such craven souls as theirs. Scarce fifteen years old, I was thrown by the misfortune of my family, without education and destitute of resources upon the current of life.... it was my lot to face the wrath of tempests; my only music the rage and roar of the ocean; driven down the tide of fortune, like a shattered bark before the gale, unable to shape her course or control her evolutions, my life has been a perpetual convulsion of all the moral elements of nature. But amidst all the oppressive turns of fate, I have kept unspotted my 'sacred honor.'"

His only fear, he took care to explain, was of being ambushed: "The idea of annihilation in the abstract, raises no emotion in me: Life wearing no blandishments for me, death has no terrors; and whenever he presents himself in the shape of honor, like the son of Altnomak, I shall meet him 'as a friend that comes to relieve me from pain.' But prompt as I should be to offer my bosom to his shaft, where honor or service of my country might require it, I confess that I feel some aversion at the thought of falling in an obscure and despicable brawl, beneath the hands of a set of miscreants, who are incapable of one elevated or manly sentiment...."

And he wound up in a frenzy of heroics: "I stand here an isolated man, the defense of my fame resting on my pen, as that of my person does upon my arm alone. Let none whosoever suppose me so weak, as to mention this as an appeal to the sympathy of my fellow-citizens; I spurn the thought; I ask and will receive from the public, *no other verdict*, than that which may be *accorded* from the *sternest rules* of honor. *Disdaining* the *compassion* of the world, I *demand* its *justice*."

This incendiary publication, its style the more intriguing, perhaps, for Potter's prodigal overuse of commas and italics, entertained Halifax during July. August would bring a new election, and at the beginning of that month appeared yet another pamphlet, "A SERIES OF POLITICAL LETTERS Addressed to a PARTICULAR FRIEND by Pliny." The letters were dull reading in comparison to Potter's efforts. They included fawning praise of Potter: "Mr. Potter has the most decided advantage in every respect.... His knowledge of jurisprudence will ever raise him to a level high above his opponent in legal qualifications.... There is not a young man at the bar in this part of the state who possesses a greater weight of character...." Bynum was charged afresh with trying to assassinate Potter and with slandering the family of Willie Jones.

Even as Pliny's sheaf of political letters came off the press, Jesse Bynum was finishing and sending to the printers a work of his own.

This was longer than all three of the attacks upon himself and bore a heading more temperate than did any of them:

AN EXPOSITION
Of the misrepresentations contained in a publication issued by ROBERT POTTER, against JESSE A. BYNUM and others

Bynum's essay resembled the plea to a jury by a defense attorney in refutation of charges made. It was almost as flavory as Potter's efforts, but somewhat less extravagant in its assault, and it included a number of sworn affidavits by citizens. Several of these were in denial of Potter's boast that he had knocked Bynum down, a story that seemed greatly to grieve Bynum. Bynum sought further to explain why he refused Potter's challenge to a duel and defended his own friends, notably John Daniel. He replied at length to Potter's scornful description of John Amis and the back-handed compliment to Sir Archie:

"The name of John D. Amis, which has also been introduced by the author of that publication, is too well known throughout this state, to be affected by any thing that could be put forth against him by his defamer. Mr. Amis is a gentleman of wealth and of unblemished character, and has retired far beyond the scene of political bickerings; whose hospitality is rivalled only by his indiscriminate politeness to the honest and the upright. Indeed, his residence exhibits a continual scene of generosity, from the coming in of the year, to the going out thereof; whose greatest ambition, is to relieve the wants of the poor and unfortunate, and administer comforts of life to his oppressed fellow men. Yet we have been told, that this man too, owes his respectability and standing, to the standing of a horse! If shame and confusion do not await the libeller of such a man, in the eyes of a just public, what protection does a virtuous life have from calumny?"

He called Potter a bully imported by Burges to cause trouble and assured his readers: "I cannot, I will not consent to sport away my life with any *fussey-boy*, or *understrapper* which may be set on me, while the principals remain shielded, both from censure and from danger."

The author of the *Political Letters* Bynum addressed directly: "Doct. Pliny, are you, or are you not, the person who resided some years since, a short time in Raleigh, and whom public execration compelled to leave there? Are you not, Doct. Pliny, the same, who resided in Petersburg some years since, and whom, your salacity and scandalizing *tongue* compelled, (after committing some other offences,) to fly that place? Are you not the same *Doct. Pliny*, who resided in Portsmouth and was there cow-hided, as report says, for your scandal and defamation? Are you not the same person, Pliny, whom these evil geniuses followed into Bertie, and from thence into Martin, each of which places you fled with the curses of an insulted public at your heels? Are you not the same Doct. Pliny, who within the last fifteen months have located yourself in Halifax, and have acted alternately, the parts of debauchee, priest, politician and bully?"

Deplorably from the standpoint of the historian, no public answer was made to this series of questions, which probably were meant to be rhetorical. The town election of 1825 exploded in Halifax like a powder magazine.

Partisans of Bynum and Potter made of the occasion a pitched battle. Guns, knives, and clubs were employed on both sides, and the election officials left their duties to throw themselves into the fight. When the noise had died down and the smoke was cleared away, one man had been killed and several others badly wounded. State officials very properly declared the election as no election at all, and stormy Halifax went without borough representation in that year's House of Commons.

During all this violence, John Amis stayed at Mowfield. So did his son William, who had been in trouble enough the previous January. Amis had other preoccupations than the embattled political adventures of his brother-in-law.

On September 15 Theophilus Feild, his partner in the stud book project, printed a sheaf of announcements of the publication plan for circulation to those who might subscribe or help with pedigrees. It began: "This work has engaged much attention for several years—considerable matter has been collected, and it is now

He Gets into Politics

advancing to maturity." It included a form for the pedigrees of horses and mares, and it gave, as an example of the latter, a carelessly inaccurate outline of Castianira's pedigree and progeny:

CASTIANIRA

A brown Mare, folded [*sic*] 1776 [an error for 1797], bred by John Tayloe, Esq., of ——— County, Va., imported 1799, got by Rockingham, he by Highflyer—dam Tabitha, by Trentham —Bosphorus, &c.

    1805, b. c. *Sir Archy*, by Diomed.
    1807, s. c. *Hephestion*, by Buzzard.
    1808, br. f. *Castiania*, by ArchDuke.
    1809,   missed, to ———

The book would go to press, thought Feild, not long after February of 1826. But he fell ill and did not recover, and publication was delayed.

Brilliant John Randolph of Roanoke talked of writing a stud book of his own, one which might be published before the Feild-Amis compilation. James J. Harrison, too, planned a similar work, and sent Patrick Nisbett Edgar, an Irish journalist-adventurer, to collect pedigrees. Edgar was a colorful character whose talent for making enemies, though nothing to approach Potter's, made him unwelcome at Mowfield.

Theophilus Feild had intended to lease Sir Archie's services for the 1826 stud season, but his illness and other matters made this impracticable. Amis, advertising Sir Archie again, raised the fee for his service to $75, or $100 to insure. That spring and early summer, Sir Archie was mated with more than eighty-three mares. His get from those matings would include no less than eight distinguished sons and daughters.

Sir Archie

August of 1826 saw the death of Feild and the shelving of the stud book project. It saw also another election in Halifax.

Bynum, perhaps eyeing chances of higher office, did not offer for the House of Commons but gave his support to Dixie C. Fenner, of the family that operated Bynum's favorite tavern. Potter was back on the ballot, and his friends spread, with consummate success, a report that Fenner had withdrawn his candidacy at the last moment. Very few of Bynum's followers turned out. Potter was elected by a vote of twenty-eight to eight—it did not take long to count—and in the legislature he made a prompt bid for notice and leadership.

He introduced a bill for establishment of a "Political College" for the education of needy and intelligent young men who would learn the arts, agriculture, and military science. In his melodramatic speech on the measure, Potter blackly reviled North Carolina's State University as available only to the sons of rich, deplored at the top of his voice the decay of the state's education and culture, and called the political leaders of North Carolina ignorant and libertine. He did not scruple to offer, as handy examples of such unworthy men, the names of Congressman Daniel L. Barringer, Willis Alston, and Lemuel Sawyer. His bill was defeated by a narrow margin of votes, and his execration of men in high places brought him angry opposition. Even his old friend and patron Thomas Burges deserted him. In 1827 Bynum ran once again for the House of Commons from the town of Halifax and defeated Potter as in 1824.

Bitterly disappointed and angry, Potter made ready to leave Halifax, but first he wrote and published one more indictment of his enemies, beside which his earlier efforts appeared comparatively subdued.

It is said that the proprietor of the Halifax *Free Press* refused with horror to set up the type for this work and that Potter bribed apprentices to sneak into the shop, in the late night hours, to produce

He Gets into Politics

it. The slipshod appearance of the pamphlet would seem to give strength to this legend. Its title was a promise of extravagances within:

THE HEAD OF MEDUSA
a Mock-Heroic
POEM
Founded on fact—in which "the word is suited to the phrase, and the phrase to the action."

by

RIENZI

"In hoc est hoax, cum quiz and jokesez,
Et smokum toastem, roastem, folksez,
Fee, faw, fum, Psalmanazar."

He began with what he rather inconsistently called an apology, in which he named as his models Juvenal and Steele; but plainly he was more influenced by Byron's angry *English Bards and Scotch Reviewers*. His dedication read: "To the Village, once distinguished for 'wit and wisdom, gaiety and grace,' but notorious now, as the haunt of swindlers, liars and assassins, this Poem, descriptive of their manners, practices, sentiments and principles, is dedicated, with all imaginable contempt...."

Followed seventeen pages of verse, occasionally witty, often pedestrian, and distinguished with a degree of bad taste that amounted to a certain perverse genius. He included a prefatory essay on "Plan and Character of the Poem," to make clear some of his allusions, and several pages of notes.

Daniel and Bynum he attacked with all the old charges of political dishonesty, bad manners, clumsy terrorism, and cowardice, and to these he added new indictments for stupidity, swindling, and the keeping of slave concubines. He singled out John D. Amis, as a notable target, first in his preface:

Sir Archie

"... deriving less credit from his alliance with [Jesse Bynum] than from the *more honorable* connexion he has formed with a celebrated *horse*—whose company is only interesting as the groom of that *nobler* animal, whose praises form the *chief* theme of his conversation.... Has put on *spectacles*, either to enhance his *dignity*, or *conceal* the *chicanery* and *dishonesty*, otherwise so *expressive* in his *eyes* and always so *legible* in his *acts*.... That whereas in England, Pope justly thought and boldly declared, that the *best blood* of the '*iron barons of the Magna Charta*' could not enoble 'sots or fools or cowards,' *here*, the blood of a *horse* was found sufficient to atone for the defects in the blood of a *man*—to *enoble* a *rascal* and make a *gentleman* of a Jack Ass—or, marvellous coincidence of initials, of a Jack A- - -, and the *money* arising from the services of his horse, to place him at the head of the *wealth-adoring* fools among whom he lives...."

This was preparation for Potter's rhymed attack on Amis:

>Gumberry's chieftain of ignoble name,
>Who from Sir A- - -'s loins draws bread and fame;
>A *stud-horse* gentleman, whom nature's God
>Meant to revolve and break the stubborn clod;
>Whose soul proud science only taught to stray,
>Far as a *slave* can plough, or mule can bray;
>Whose hands were formed to *hold* the whip and lines,
>And drive the *coach*, in which he now *reclines*....

Of Bynum, accusing him of depending for support on Amis:

>*He*, a *parishoner* on A- - -'s bread,
>*How* will *he* live when old Sir A- - -'s dead?
>Without one ray of genius or of worth,
>In mind a fool, a *cut-throat* by his birth....

He Gets into Politics

Of himself, as the poem's hero Rienzi, Potter spoke with much more admiration and in the Caesarian third person:

> Long had he toil'd upon the *waste* of life—
> Gone were the parents whom his childhood lov'd;
> And he stood friendless in this world of strife,
> Yet still, with heart *unshaken* he had roved—
> His *early youth* was spent among the brave,
> The high, the generous, and the lofty soul'd,
> Who bore Columbia's thunder o'er the wave,
> Where fear'd, and shun'd before, the Lion rul'd....

Burges he also blamed, in verse, for turning from him; but a footnote made one exception to Potter's wholesale indictments of the Halifaxians: "the honored family of the Grove—who dwell in this moral morass, like an oasis in a desert."

By the time this wordy belaboring of Halifax and the surrounding region was distributed, Potter had gone, but not far. He returned to his native Granville County, where he contrived to marry Isabella Taylor, daughter of an influential family noted for church work.

Granville elected Potter to the legislature, and he almost achieved passage of a preposterous bill for the suspending of charters of the state's banks. The publicity sufficed to send him to Congress, but his lifelong habit of extravagant violence impelled him to mutilate two men he charged with seducing his wife, and he went to prison for three years.

Emerging, he was able to secure reelection to the legislature, which body expelled him when he took back, at pistol point, some money he had lost at cards to a fellow-member.

He emigrated to Texas, just then on the eve of revolution against Mexico and a splendid natural field for his quarrelsome talents. He was one of the convention that signed the Texas Constitution. Thereafter he served with some success as the new Republic's

Sir Archie Gets into Politics

secretary of the navy. Later, as Senator in the fifth Texas Congress, he did not hesitate to offer savage criticism, in public debate and in print as well, of the policies and behavior of the dangerous Sam Houston. Somewhere he found time to steal another man's wife and to try to murder a neighbor. One evening several enemies dragged him from bed in his nightshirt, gave him a fifty-yard start, and shot him as he tried to swim across a lake.

Charles Dickens commented disparagingly in *American Notes* upon Potter's violent death, which he offered as an example of America's lawless ways. The Texas Senate wore crepe for Potter. Back in North Carolina, old acquaintances were bound to remember that Potter had insulted and blackguarded almost everyone he had ever known, with only two notable exceptions.

He had never failed to admire the Jones family of the Grove. And, though he had unrestrainedly slandered John Amis, he had always spoken well of Sir Archie of Mowfield.

It remained for one of higher fame and reputation than Potter to voice malicious gossip about Sir Archie.

• VIII •

SIR ARCHIE
Is Assailed by Scandal

JOHN RANDOLPH of Roanoke was greatly renowned during his lifetime for incisive wit, political power, and eccentricity that bordered on the grotesque. Of all major figures in American history, his is very likely the most vivid and comprehensive illustration of the aphorism that to be brilliant is not necessarily to be wise.

Descended from both English gentry and Indian chiefs, he had been born in 1773 and could remember fleeing with his mother from the British invaders of rebel Virginia. At twenty-six he was elected to the House of Representatives and later to the United States Senate. On the floors of both houses he gained fame. Some colleagues he fascinated, others he terrified. Extravagantly emotional in upholding states' rights and class distinctions, yet he was remarkable among political leaders in maintaining a high order of personal honesty. His appearance was strange; he seemed never to mature beyond a slender, beardless, high-voiced boyhood. Yet he did not impress his acquaintances as ludicrous, and, when he wished, he could be marvellously ingratiating. His manners were cosmically agreeable, his repartee sparkled as though written expressly for him by Richard Brinsley Sheridan. He attracted many women, and several attracted him. Indeed, a whispered tradition in North Carolina attempts to name him as the rival who played cards with Nathaniel Macon for the lovely hand of Hannah Plummer. But he never married.

Horses were early his great and successful enthusiasm. From boyhood he attended races, developed a fine critical opinion, and on several occasions rode as a gentleman jockey. Inheriting a considerable property, he made of his Roanoke estate in Charlotte County, Virginia, a famous stud and training ground. His horses scored on a number of tracks, and from the first he kept good stud records of them. His library was full of publications on the breeding and racing of Thoroughbreds. He himself gathered and clarified pedigrees, and he wrote with readable authority, under the pseudonym of Philip, for the early American turf publications.

He was fond of travel. Frequently he voyaged to England, and in his own country he made great journeys by coach or on horseback accompanied by numbers of favorite dogs. He visited the homes of other famous horsemen. Among those who were glad to have him as a guest were William Johnson and the Amises. Sir Archie commanded John Randolph's respect as much as any living American, whether with two legs or four.

By 1824 Randolph had bred at least nine sons and daughters of Sir Archie in his Roanoke stables, and quite probably he had known Sir Archie from that notable stallion's foalhood at the Ben Lomond estate of John Randolph's kinsman, Captain Archibald Randolph. Certainly he had seen Sir Archie race, as he was to explain during the summer of 1824.

At that season, about the time that John Amis was making complete his regime of authority over Mowfield Plantation and Sir Archie, and Jesse Bynum and Robert Potter began circling for trouble in Halifax County, a group of wealthy turfmen assembled

He Is Assailed by Scandal

at the Virginia Hot Springs for relief from the sultry weather of the state's lower altitudes. The center of this group was John Randolph of Roanoke. As usual with such men, the conversation turned upon Thoroughbreds, and, also as usual, Randolph did his generous share of the talking.

He dredged from his memory stories of the great racers of past years. All listened, with respect and interest, as Randolph rehearsed Sir Archie's phenomenal adventures of failure and success on Virginia tracks, with final recognition as champion in his day. Randolph spoke, too, of Ridgeley's Postboy and Ogle's Oscar, both great in their own time but eclipsed by the mightier deeds of Sir Archie who followed them. Postboy and Oscar, the sportsmen there gathered were all aware, had been sired by Gabriel, the splendid English racer who had been imported by John Tayloe III of Mount Airy, in the same year that Tayloe fetched Castianira into the country.

Gabriel had been bay in color, reminded Randolph. So, too, had been his swift sons, Postboy and Oscar. That was usually the way with horse heredity; a sire passed on his color to his get. And Sir Archie was another bay, pursued Randolph, while his reputed sire, Diomed, was a chestnut, as were most of Diomed's sons and daughters. What did all this prove?

Randolph answered his own question, while his audience gaped and stared. He, Randolph, had the tale from a certain white groom who had tended Diomed when Miles Selden stood that high-priced animal at Tree Hill outside Petersburg. The groom vowed that Sir Archie was not Diomed's son, but Gabriel's.

And the groom, as Randolph quoted him, had elaborated that Gabriel, too, was at Tree Hill in 1804, serving as a teaser for Diomed; that when Castianira had been sent there by Captain Archie Randolph, Gabriel had been able to consummate a courtship of her that should have been held to the preliminaries. Sir Archie's bay color bore this story out, was the opinion of the master of Roanoke.

John Stuart Skinner, Randolph's close friend and editor of the *American Farmer* which frequently printed Randolph's letters and essays on racing matters, was to remember that Randolph spoke as though he completely believed the story and that he went on to argue that William Greenfield, the London philologist and Bible scholar, was the author of the Waverly Novels attributed to Scott, into which works Randolph and his fellow-horsemen liked to dip for names to give their favorite colts.

Another rapt hearer of this discourse on equine paternity was Archibald Harrison of Clifton in the Virginia Piedmont, nephew and partial heir of Captain Archie Randolph, and, as was Sir Archie, the Captain's namesake. On Harrison the story made a considerable effect. When he returned to Clifton, he told it to several acquaintances.

One of these was James M. Selden, the son of Miles Selden who had once been a partner in Diomed. The younger Selden was a guest at Harrison's home, and as he heard the tale, he protested at once, speaking as one having authority.

For it happened, he assured Harrison, that he, Selden, had been a boy at Tree Hill on that spring day of 1804 when Castianira was brought. He had been allowed to watch the mating of her with Diomed, the first time he had ever witnessed that dramatic aspect of turfmanship. It had impressed his young mind—so vividly, indeed, that he felt he could go, even though a score of years had passed, to within ten feet of the spot where it had happened.

Specifically he challenged any story from a white groom who claimed to have tended Diomed. James Selden remembered that Diomed, while in Miles Selden's hands, had been the sole and special care of a trusted slave, Charles. Further, Castianira had been led into Diomed's presence by another slave, Captain Archie

He Is Assailed by Scandal

Randolph's Nat. If Nat survived and could be found, surely he would remember all about the matter.

By one of those amazing coincidences that would make a fictitious account unconvincing, Nat was easy to find. He had been one of the bequests of Archie Randolph to Harrison, and at that very moment he was in the house. Harrison sent for the faithful old family servant, who respectfully but plainly said that Selden's story was true in every detail. He, Nat, had been Castianira's attendant during her entire stay at Tree Hill. She had been mated with Diomed and with no other stallion.

This appeared to be quite enough evidence for Harrison, who circulated his distinguished relative's tale no more. Selden, for his own part, searched through his father's correspondence and found a letter from Archie Randolph that concerned the mating of Castianira. This included some statement that ascribed Sir Archie directly to Diomed's siring. Selden handed the letter personally to Theophilus Feild, who, as Selden was aware, intended to collaborate with John Amis on an American stud book. Feild assured Selden that he would employ Captain Randolph's statement to correct any rumor of Gabriel's alleged getting of Sir Archie.

Feild sickened and died, and the letter given him by Selden was not found in the great mass of his papers. Meanwhile, the Sir Archie scandal persisted in other mouths than Harrison's and grew with each telling.

Circumstantiality was added to what John Randolph appears to have said at the Virginia Hot Springs. Some details were counterbranded over from ancient stable gossip about English champions.

There was, of course, that romantic legend of how the Godolphin Arabian had fought and driven away his owner's prize stallion Hobgoblin in order to win the affections of Roxana and sire upon her the celebrated Lath. The soberer version, that Hobgoblin, far from seeking Roxana's favors, had disdained her and forced her owners to avail themselves of the second-choice Godolphin

Arabian, seems also to have been well remembered in America. A scandal hung around the name of English Eclipse, some saying that his sire was not Marske of the Darley Arabian line but Shakespeare, descended from Hobgoblin. As for Diomed himself, a libellous snigger persisted that a mare, after being sent to him, was in time delivered of a mule colt; and that a groom confessed that, to save excessive trouble in mating the mare to Diomed, he had bestowed her high-pedigreed affections upon a jack in a nearby stall.

General T. M. Forman of Maryland heard what must have been a quaint combination of these various prattlings. As the General had it, Diomed in 1804 was so aged and hypercritical as to refuse utterly to notice poor blind Castianira, who then found consolation in the attentions of the more vigorous and less discriminate Gabriel.

All this excitement was by no means as fatuous as it might appear to observers without an intelligent interest in horses. After all, Sir Archie had won recognition as the foremost sire in America, as he had been the foremost racer. So frequently and thoroughly had his get vanquished rivals of all other paternity that there seemed to be no contest, save in notable exceptions like that of American Eclipse's outrunning of Henry in 1823. All turfmen wanted to breed their mares to Sir Archie or his sons, and very few wanted to breed them to stallions of any other line. It would repay the world of the Thoroughbred to make sure of Sir Archie's descent, the value of claimants thereto, and of the value of their respective progenies.

Gabriel, if he were to be given official credit for Sir Archie's getting, would be no unworthy sire. His was an excellent record. Foaled in 1790, he had begun racing at the age of four. Out of twenty-two starts he had won fifteen against the finest competition England afforded in his day. Among Gabriel's prizes had been no less than four King's Plates, one of which had been presented to him after he had walked around a course on which no rivals dared step with him. He had been retired to stud in 1797 and in 1799 came to

MANSION OF A TURFMAN

This is a lithograph by Pendleton of Boston of Mount Airy in Richmond County, Virginia, home of John Tayloe III who was one of the breeders of Sir Archie. It represents the mansion before the damaging fire of 1844. Here Tayloe maintained a magnificent stable and stud, and bred and trained some of the great winners of his time; but somehow he never appreciated Sir Archie, who lived at Mount Airy only a few weeks before he was sold to Ralph Wormeley.

THE CO-BREEDERS: TAYLOE AND RANDOLPH

Handsome, turf-wise John Tayloe III (*above*) owned Castianira, Sir Archie's dam. The graceful, ineffectual Captain Archie Randolph (*left*) partnered with Tayloe in the breeding of the colt later named Sir Archie. Tayloe's singular short-sightedness and Captain Randolph's financial difficulties lost them the peerless horse before he had run his first race. (Tayloe's portrait is from the Cook Collection, Richmond, Virginia; Captain Randolph's is from a silhouette belonging to Dr. A. C. Randolph of Upperville, Virginia.)

He Is Assailed by Scandal

America as the property of John Tayloe III. His sons, Postboy and Oscar, deserved the praise given them by John Randolph in his conversation at the Virginia Hot Springs. Almost equally successful had been their brother Harlequin. All three of these Gabriels had been good racers, and by the 1820's had won reputation as fine stallions.

If, therefore, Sir Archie was demonstrably the son of Gabriel, how much more important and worthy would be considered the descendants of Postboy, Oscar, and Harlequin—the more so because no Diomed colt save Sir Archie had risen to any particular distinction as a foal getter. The story continued to spread, as accepted or questioned, throughout the whole racing fraternity of America.

John Randolph himself grew to regret his part in furthering the scandal. In 1825 two more Sir Archie colts were foaled at his Roanoke stables, and he valued both of them. That December the importance of Sir Archie's get was stressed in another fashion in the Warrenton *Reporter*, where a letter appeared titled VIRGINIA RACE HORSES and signed, "A Bit of a Jockey."

"... The best Virginia racers have been for many years raised in North Carolina, and a few counties of Virginia lying between James River and Roanoke. Most of the capital race horses which within the last thirty years figured on the turf as Virginia racers, were actually foaled and raised in North Carolina...."

Thirty-nine horses considered to come under this curious category were then listed, and no less than thirteen of them were Sir Archies. The commentator finished drily:

"... *Our* cotton, *our* tobacco, and *our* race horses are called by the name of Virginia; while our *ague and fever*, our *bad roads*, and our *bars and shoals*, are admitted, even by the Virginians themselves, to belong to North Carolina."

More reason, John Randolph must have reflected as he read, to clarify pedigrees and records by an official American Stud Book. Feild's illness delayed and endangered the Feild-Amis collaboration project, and so Randolph announced a hope of his own in a letter of February 14 to the *American Farmer:*

"A gentleman of the South of Virginia has many years employed, at vacant hours, in compiling, for his own use and amusement, a Stud Book.... Profit is no object to him, but, believing such a work to be a desideratum to breeders, sportsmen and amateurs, he wishes to form a tolerably correct estimate of copies which he may order to be struck off, without incurring loss.

"Such persons, therefore, as feel a disposition to have the work, are respectfully requested to indicate the same (as promptly as possible) to the Editor of the *American Farmer....*"

On that same Valentine's Day, Randolph drew up a handbill to advertise that his stallion Roanoke would stand at twenty-five dollars. Perhaps hoping to quiet the buzz of gossip that had arisen after the idle story he had told, he included in the announcement:

PEDIGREE

Roanoke was got by Sir Archy, which was bred by Archibald Randolph of Benlomond, esqr., and got by Sir Charles Bunbury's Diomed....

This statement, over Randolph's signature, naturally was widely circulated and read; but it was not enough, or nearly enough, to put an end to the scandal. Edmund Irby, Jr., of Nottaway County, Randolph's friend and neighbor, was happy that spring when his Bellair mare Calypso produced a chestnut filly by Sir Archie. Irby named her Gabriella, for the stallion he accepted as her grandsire.

If Randolph intended further active disavowal of his earlier statement, he must have forgotten it in the grim adventure that befell him in April. President John Quincy Adams proposed admission to Panama, and Randolph chose to criticize it on the floor of the Senate in terms of sleek invective that infuriated Secretary of State Henry Clay. There was an exchange of notes, then a challenge to fight.

The resulting duel, comfortingly bloodless, was conducted in a manner to make it a far loftier example of such formal violences than the brawlings of Robert Potter and Jesse Bynum in Halifax. Senator Thomas Hart Benton, present as one of Randolph's seconds, called the meeting "high-toned," and Benton's personal experience and taste qualified him to speak with complete authority about the tone of duels. Randolph was reconciled with Clay, but not with other political opponents. Summer brought him an awareness of preparations to drive him from the Senate at about the same time that the Sir Archie scandal got into print.

The coolly intelligent Skinner, who had heard Randolph name Gabriel as the sire of Sir Archie, wondered but did not wholly believe. He wrote to John Tayloe, who sent back a statement of emphatic sobriety:

"To your inquiry relative to the sireship of Sir Archy, I have to observe in reply, that I sold one half of Castianira, the dam of Sir Archy, to Mr. Archibald Randolph before Sir Archy was foaled on the south side of James River in the spring of 1805 the joint property of Mr. Randolph and myself. I believe that Gabriel was alive in 1804, but I am very confident he never covered at the stand with [Diomed]. Gabriel and Sir Archy are something alike in form, but not in color, Gabriel being brown—can't speak positively as to marks, but have no hesitation in saying there can be no doubt of Sir Archy's being got by Diomed. Castianira was a dark brown, almost a black mare."

Skinner inserted this letter in the *American Farmer* for August 11, 1826, as a footnote to an instalment of George Washington Jeffrey's *Annals of the Turf*, which Skinner reprinted from the Petersburg *Intelligencer*. Skinner, Tayloe, and others who did not

Sir Archie

believe in the story of Gabriel's mating with Castianira probably felt that this was sufficient for any interested person.

John Amis, at Mowfield, was not noticed as commenting on either side of the argument. That August saw the election at Halifax where Robert Potter defeated Jesse Bynum's candidate for the North Carolina Assembly, and Amis must have been actively interested in Bynum's plans for the next political campaign and also in keeping his own reckless son William from further clashes with the Potter faction. In any case, there had been no loss of patronage for Sir Archie during the 1826 season.

For, whatever stallion had got Sir Archie, his human admirers wanted him to get colts for them. The 1826 season was a banner one, and a busy one as well, for the monarch of Mowfield. In addition to the mares from Southern estates, one at least came from as far away as Pennsylvania. She was Sir Archie's daughter Coquette, now the property of John Craig of Bristol, and as a result of her visit she would produce Virginia Taylor, great as a racer at one and two miles. Amis, too, bred that year for a colt to train.

The following January brought disaster to John Randolph of Roanoke; he was defeated for the United States Senate by John Tyler. As for Sir Archie, though his paternity was still clouded in some opinions, his fame increased by spring.

His descendants began another of their habitual sweeps of tracks near and far, and an elaborate intersectional event, planned for three years ahead, was dominated by still others of his blood.

This would be a Colt Sweepstakes, mile heats at the Union Course of Long Island, to be run in May, 1830, by colts and fillies foaled and entered that spring of 1827. Northern and Southern nabobs of the turf posted their forfeits, half of the $500 entrance fee each, and named the fifteen newborn racers who were promised to be there three years in the future.

Six of these were sons and daughters of Sir Archie, among them John Amis' fine bay colt out of a Gallatin mare. Henry had sired

He Is Assailed by Scandal

four others, Sir Charles another, out of Sir Archie's daughter Reality. John Richards, now a stallion, had got another, and Sir Archie's son Arab yet another—a total of thirteen of the patriarch's blood. The only rival paternities were represented by a colt by Eclipse and a hermaphrodite by Duroc.

This overwhelming Sir Archie majority helped to drive heavy nails of despair into the souls of those who still sought to uphold other Thoroughbred strains. News of it penetrated the Western frontiers along the Mississippi together with the talk about Sir Archie's questioned descent.

In those more remote regions, Sir Archie's unique son Walk-in-the-Water continued to be successful after more than a decade of races. Ignored by those who insisted on the bluest of equine blood, unmentioned in the stacks of pedigrees gathered here and there for various proposed American Stud Books, yet he thrashed one Thoroughbred after another on tracks in Mississippi, Tennessee, and Louisiana. In 1827 he was fourteen years old and a pet possession of a horseman as rough-hewn and successful as Walk-in-the-Water himself.

This was Green Berry Williams, familiarly called Uncle Berry, while his rugged old gelding four-miler often heard his own name shortened to Walk. The same year of the entry of infant four-footed princelings in the future Union Course Colt Stake, Williams came to a Natchez meeting after a toilsome journey along wild, swampy trails, and so exhausted were the horses of his string that they lost in several early races of the week. In the feature race, the Natchez Jockey Club's four-mile heats, competitors stood off in gingerly fashion from Sir Archie's Thoroughbred son, the gelding Blucher, sixteen years old but still a fine and long-winded four-miler and much feared on the American frontier. Somewhat desperately, Williams matched Walk-in-the-Water against Blucher.

The Natchez club's rules reduced to 100 pounds the weight that must be carried by horses of fifteen years or older, while those below fifteen would carry 124 pounds, with three pounds less for mares or geldings. Walk, still short of his fifteenth birthday, thus would carry a handicap of twenty-one pounds more than Blucher. Williams' frantic plea that the weights be made equal was coldly disallowed.

Despite that considerable extra burden, Walk-in-the-Water won the first heat, coming home half a length ahead. The second heat found Blucher sternly contesting Walk's lead every stride of the way. Green Berry Williams, peering down the home stretch of the last mile, saw Walk's honest chestnut face a trifle forward of his kinsman's.

"Come home, Walk, come home!" screamed Uncle Berry. "Your master wants money, and that badly!"

Walk seemed to hear him, to understand him, and summoned what was left of the power of his youth to drag himself more inches forward of the equally determined Blucher. Walk won. During that entire heat, swore an observer, a single horse-blanket could have covered both racers from start to finish.

Williams went to the judges' stand with his winner, and in pungent language expressed his low opinion of the club officials who had obliged Walk-in-the-Water to carry those twenty-one extra pounds for eight killing miles. Then he stamped off to the row of stalls where the horses of his string were quartered. He stopped to glower at a colt that had lagged and lost the stake posted for him.

"Joe," Uncle Berry scolded, "you won't do to tie to. I've always done a good part by you. I've salted you out of my hand while you sucked your mammy; you know what you promised me before we left home, and now you have thrown me off among strangers."

He moved along, visiting other members of his troop in turn. Equally ill-tempered were his remarks to each loser. Finally he came to the stall where Walk-in-the-Water stood with a groom sponging down the weary, victorious old legs.

He Is Assailed by Scandal

Williams paused a moment in silence. Horse and man looked into each other's eyes. Then Uncle Berry burst into unabashed tears and flung his arms around Walk's neck.

"Here's a poor man's friend in a strange land!" he sobbed.

In June of that year of 1827, while Robert Potter was polishing the intriguingly scurrilous rhymed address that would celebrate his departure from the vexed political life of Halifax, everyone's memory of the story about Gabriel usurping Diomed's place with Castianira had further refreshment.

General Forman wrote to Skinner on June 4. The sustained warmth of the dispute made the General somewhat cautious, but he was determined to get at the truth somehow:

"... It is whispered among sportsmen that the justly celebrated horse Sir Archy was *not* got by the imported horse Diomed. The story goes, that the dam of Sir Archy was offered to Diomede [*sic*], who from age or dislike, refused to mate with her. Upon the suggestion that the mare ought not to lose her season, when so fine a horse as Gabriel was convenient, she was offered to and mated with Gabriel, who thus became the real sire of Sir Archy. I repeat that such a report is in circulation, but do not vouch for its truth, neither is it any use to name my authority. Sportsmen interested in the Sir Archy stock will no doubt investigate this report, and through the medium of your valuable journal, confute or confirm it."

This letter, rather timidly signed only with the initial "F," was published by Skinner in the *American Farmer* for June 22.

Colonel Tayloe had already offered his written word, a year earlier. He repeated it, with something more of emphasis than before, in a letter dated July 11, which nine days later appeared in the *American Farmer:*

"Having perceived in one of your late papers some doubts manifested respecting the pedigree of Sir Archy, and a request for information, I send you the pedigree of him in full (extracted from my Stud Book). I can assure you that he was begotten by Old Diomed as Captain Archibald Randolph (who bred him in partnership with me) often assured me of the fact. Therefore, any doubts concerning his pedigree are out of the question. You will find his pedigree upon the opposite side."

The conclusion of Tayloe's message, in particular, carried something of truculence. Discussion in the correspondence columns of the *American Farmer* died down once again. In any case, other matters had risen to perplex and preoccupy turfmen.

In late August, the Washington Jockey Club completed a reorganization of its affairs in the District of Columbia and announced a schedule of three days of races to start October 24. Southern horse owners scowled over a qualifying phrase in the announcement: "Free for any horse, mare or gelding, *bona fide* owned and trained for six months previous to the races, North of the York or Pamunkey Rivers."

That parochial limitation would bar the championship blood of Sir Archie from competition at the nation's capitol, save where it had trickled northward here and there. A few days later, the Maryland Association announced its own four-day meeting to begin on October 17 at Baltimore. The first and second days' races could be entered by any horse from anywhere; but the third day was open only to entries owned in Maryland or the District of Columbia for at least sixty days prior to the race, and the race of the fourth day was restricted to animals actually raised in Maryland or the District.

Feeling snubbed and outraged, the Virginia and North Carolina horsemen registered strong protests. The *Reporter* in Warrenton, North Carolina, previously a voice for the Roanoke center of Thoroughbred racing and published among plantations where squadrons of Sir Archie colts and fillies trained, spoke for the rejected owners:

"*Sporting Intelligence—the Union Divided.*—The Baltimore Races commence on the 17th of October, and are *half* free for the sportsmen and horses of the South. The City of Washington Races com-

He Is Assailed by Scandal

mence on the 24th, and are free only for the sportsmen and horses *North* of the Pamunkey or York River."

Up in Washington, the urbane editor of the *National Intelligencer* strove to assuage Southern wrath by the frankest confession of defeat:

"We are afraid that our friends in North Carolina are *displeased* at our Jockey Clubs having excluded the Roanoke racers, but surely without reason. Do they not perceive that, in so doing, our Clubs pay them the compliment of considering them invincible? Our breeders acknowledge themselves beaten to their heart's content— they give up: What more would our friends in the South ask of them? Whenever we can produce animals that are able to compete, with any chance of success, with those South of the Pamunkey, our friends may be assured that they will be welcome. Of late, the associations here and at Baltimore have had all the pleasure of making up purses, for the Roanokers to come and take for asking. This was not only an expensive amusement, but it also defeated the object of these 'trials of speed,' as our friends at Boston call them, which is, to hold out inducements to emulations in the improvement of the breed of horses."

Horses able to compete with those south of the Pamunkey—what could such horses be, if not Sir Archies? Earlier that year, mares had been sent to Mowfield by Dr. Duval of Maryland, Edward Parker of Pennsylvania, and Commodore R. F. Stockton of New Jersey. Other Northerners eagerly bargained for Sir Archie colts and fillies from Virginia and North Carolina.

All this flattering attention was paid to a stallion not wholly cleared, in some opinions, of the suspicion of doubtful pedigree. In spite of Skinner, Tayloe, and Selden, the story continued to go its rounds, among stable crews, at race meetings, and over tables and bars in taverns where men of the turf gathered.

Randolph himself was very little to be heard from on the subject. His health had failed alarmingly following his departure from the

Sir Archie

Senate, but he sought and won election to the national House of Representatives for a term of two years. He also served as an extremely vocal member of the 1829 convention to amend the Virginia State Constitution and was an earnest upholder of Andrew Jackson's candidacy for president. Gratefully, Jackson appointed him minister to Russia.

But Randolph had the time and inclination to notice the activity of his friend Skinner on behalf of turf publication. Skinner had sold the *American Farmer* and had founded in Baltimore the *American Turf Register and Sporting Magazine*, which issued its first number in September of 1829. The fourth number, in December, was headed with a long and laudatory memoir of Sir Archie, illustrated with an engraved portrait based on the Alvan Fisher painting.

This essay did not choose to ignore the scandal, and it had its emphatic opinion thereon:

"... What stallion, then, so worthy to be the sire of Sir Archy as Diomed? Yet a report has been in circulation a dozen years or more, calculating to rob Diomed of this honor, and to confer it on another stallion called Gabriel, sire of Postboy, Harlequin and Oscar.

"This report first originated among grooms, who, of all others, are best calculated to give currency to reports without foundation. Col. Tayloe, who jointly with Col. [sic] Randolph, bred Sir Archy, confidently avers the fact that Diomed was the sire of Sir Archy...."

A footnote referred to Tayloe's correspondence previously published in the *American Farmer*. Another footnote, at the end of an article about Diomed in the same issue of the new magazine, said: "It has been stated, but I believe on no good ground, that the imported Gabriel by Dorimant (a very distinguished horse, and sire of those excellent horses, Post Boy, Oscar and Harlequin) was sire of Sir Archy."

Randolph was booked to sail for Europe and the court of the Czar in June of 1830. However, he found time to write, under his pseudonymn of Philip, for the *American Turf Register,* and on April 17, 1830, added a postscript to one of his letters to the editor:

"As to the absurd report, set afloat from interested motives, that Sir Archy was got by Gabriel—no faith is due to it. Capt. Archibald Randolph's faithful and confidential servant Nat told me that 'he had held the Rockingham mare when Diomed covered her & that Sir Archy was the produce.' Some years ago I met with Larkin, the noted trainer, at Neabsco, & asked him what horse got Sir Archy. He answered, 'Diomed, sure,' & told me that he also was present when the mare was covered. Yet so bold & artful a story was put in circulation, the author of which could never be found, that for a short time I was persuaded that to Gabriel was due the honor of getting the first of our racers & stallions."

More than that, Randolph could hardly say or write in redress of the idle gossip he had repeated at the Virginia Hot Springs and had by his emphatic tone made loud throughout the land. Even such handsome amends, however, did not quite make all things as before. Randolph's part in the noising of the scandal may have been one reason for the failure of his stud book to come to publication, and here and there remained those who still wondered about Gabriel and Diomed and Castianira.

As late as April 1834, the *American Turf Register* published evidence of the hard-dying suspicion.

A correspondent who signed himself "Fair Play," at Columbia, South Carolina, wrote comments on horse breeding in Virginia and the Carolinas, and he stirred up the scandal once again:

"... By the way, it is not extraordinary that Diomed never had a son distinguished as a foal getter except Sir Archy—*if Sir Archy be his?*

"I do not know much of his other sons; but it has always struck me as a remarkable fact, that among all the fine racers of Diomed's get, *not one* should have turned out a good stallion, and has gone far to make me doubt the fact of *his* being the *sire* of Sir Archie. If, as has been stated, with *no authority* but that of the groom, Castianira was covered by Gabriel—it matters not if she went to Diomed after—I must believe that he is the *son* of Gabriel...."

James Selden was manager of the Central Course at Baltimore in 1834, and quite probably he read that issue of the *American Turf Register* almost as it came fresh from the press. The reiteration of the old question made him lose his temper. On April 6 he wrote to Skinner:

"A correspondent signed 'Fair Play' in your last number, seems somewhat impressed with belief in a silly, and most certainly false rumor, and may I add, scandalous report, of Sir Archy's being sired by Gabriel, (instead of Diomed), and being possessed personally, of as much information on the subject as any living person, I have deemed it my duty to give the public what information I have on the subject."

The information Selden proceeded to give to the public was the same he had offered to Archibald Harrison a decade earlier. Carefully, like a man making a legal disposition, he wrote of his own presence at the mating of Diomed and Castianira, named his father's Negro servant Charles as the only groom of Diomed, and quoted Nat, trusted personal retainer of Archibald Randolph and later of Harrison, as another witness who had spoken to the facts. About Gabriel as a reputed teaser for Diomed, he waxed scornfully furious again:

"... which statement out of itself, at once to have stamped it as a falsehood, for in the first place, I do not think Gabriel ever was in the neighborhood of Tree Hill, and in the next, [he] certainly could never have been used as a teaser to any horse, being a horse of high and deserved reputation...."

Selden concluded with a stern repetition: "I have felt it my duty to correct this idle rumor."

That should have done it. Selden, Larkin, and the servant Nat were all on record as having witnessed the mating of Castianira to

He Is Assailed by Scandal

Diomed. Skinner added his own wry memory of John Randolph's narrative at the Virginia Hot Springs, noticing Randolph's assurance that Greenfield had authored the Waverly Novels.

This latter feat of literary accomplishment, if true, would have marked Greenfield as brilliantly precocious, since he had been born in 1799, only fifteen years before the publication of *Waverly*, first of Scott's popular series. As to the Sir Archie controversy, another date, completely ignored by all the disputants, badly demonstrated a downright impossibility of Gabriel's claim.

Gabriel, the records show, died in 1800, full four years previous to Castianira's blind journey from Ben Lomond to Tree Hill. He could never have sired Sir Archie.

But by the time Selden was summing up the irrefutable facts of the matter, Sir Archie, too, was dead.

• IX •

SIR ARCHIE
Fulfills His Destiny

THE spring of 1830 was Sir Archie's twenty-first at stud. Mares were sent him from Virginia, North Carolina, Tennessee, Alabama, Maryland, and New York. Nor did he neglect a mare of the Mowfield stables, the daughter of imported Saladin, who would produce his colt there at home.

He did not seem so active in his attentions to these mates as in other years, but his supreme vigor abode in his scores and hundreds of descendants wherever they stood or ran.

They were running most famously that spring at the Union Course on Long Island, where the National Colt Stake, so elaborately organized three years earlier, was set for Monday, May 24, at 1 P.M.

New York was in as great turmoil as on the occasion of the Eclipse-Henry race in 1823. Hotels and taverns again swarmed with race lovers from the Deep South, New England, the western frontiers, and all turf centers between and among these points. John Amis had come with his colt Pilot, son of Sir Archie and Maria, the daughter of imported Bedford and also a dweller in the Mowfield

Sir Archie Fulfills His Destiny

stables. J. J. Harrison was present to manage Pilot's race. Present also was white-haired William Johnson, fifty-eight years old but as handsome and masterful as ever. He escorted the gray filly Bonnets of Blue, daughter of Sir Charles and Reality and thus an inbred double granddaughter of Sir Archie. Again a journey over jammed roads to the enclosure of the course, again a thronging of the grandstand, the outer edge of the oval, the inner enclosure. Then entries were called up.

Of the fifteen colts for which stakes had been posted in May of 1827, eight did not appear. Their sponsors forfeited $250 apiece, which with the $500 each from owners of entries present, made a purse of $5,500. Besides Pilot and Bonnets of Blue there were other Sir Archies coming to post. Walter Livingston of New York sent in Sir Kirkland, by Sir Archie's son Arab. Other New York aspirants of the Sir Archie blood were John Van Mater's General Jackson and the entries of R. L. and John C. Stevens, Henry's chestnut daughter Celeste and an unnamed gray son of Sir Archie.

Van Ranst's Eclipse colt had been withdrawn, and the sole entry of the line other than that of Sir Archie was Price's Hermaphrodite, by Duroc out of a Figure mare. Some question was raised as to whether this sexual anomaly should carry the ninety pounds specified for a colt or the eighty-seven pounds for a filly. The judges considered, then ordered full colt weight.

Pilot had suffered slightly from a cold a few days earlier. He was pronounced recovered, but his nostrils still dripped, and the report of his ailment had its effect when he and Bonnets of Blue were declared the favorites, even money for either against the other. A little more backing appeared for Bonnets of Blue than for Pilot. The price on any other entry was four to five against.

A bugle blew melodiously, the seven glossy entries approached the post, and the riders heard the usual admonition from the judges' stand concerning observance of course rules. The immense crowd cheered and applauded.

Sir Archie

"Mount!" bawled the paddock judge.

The jockeys swung into their saddles.

"Are you ready? Come up!"

The grooms led the colts and fillies to the starting line, set them in their places, and hurried away to the side of the track.

The great starting drum boomed like a cannon. The first heat started in a frantic dash.

Price's Hermaphrodite, contending against six Sir Archies, achieved a burst of swiftness that momentarily captured the lead. Around the turn he sped, with Bonnets of Blue, a gray cannonball, running second and gaining. In the rear stretch she locked herself at Hermaphrodite's side. John Amis' bay Pilot drew close behind these leaders, and the others trailed in his wake.

At the half-mile post, Bonnets of Blue passed Hermaphrodite, and shortly afterward Pilot, too, came from behind to give Bonnets of Blue a fight for the rest of the way.

The approach to the second turn found Pilot and Bonnets of Blue sweeping furiously along, almost together. Cadwallader Colden, as eagerly watching as when Eclipse and Henry raced in 1823, felt his sympathy flow to the miraculous gray filly. He would write his emotions down within short days after the race, a vivid recording of a fine expert's stream of consciousness and his mental appeal to Bonnets of Blue and her sweating jockey:

"... Look to yourself my filly Bonnets of Blue—Pilot is at you—pull to him, my boy, round the sweep. He is upon you—be cool—don't lay out of your ground—be careful how you make the last turn—lay well for it—take off a little—pull to him again—don't be alarmed...."

They were straining and struggling for the lead as they swung at full speed around the turn. Colden wished he could cry aloud to the rider of Bonnets of Blue. His thoughts were the thoughts of a master trainer of fine racers:

"... take care you don't swerve. Well done, my boy—you are

SOME OF THE AMIS FAMILY

Amis family portraits are scarce, as several were lost in a steamboat disaster that destroyed a number of treasures. At the upper left is Mrs. William Amis, wife of the founder of the family fortunes who purchased Sir Archie from Allen Jones Davie. At the upper right is the younger William Amis, son of John Dillard Amis, remembered in Northampton County, North Carolina, as handsome, dashing, and violent. At the lower right is a childhood portrait by Thomas Sully of John Dillard Amis' daughter Mary Emily, which hints strongly of the reigning beauty she became. All three of these dwellers at Mowfield knew Sir Archie and loved him dearly.

WILLIAM RANSOM JOHNSON (*upper left*), the far-seeing "Napoleon of the Turf" who first recognized Sir Archie's great championship qualities. (From an engraving of Henry Inman's portrait for the *Spirit of the Times*.) ALLAN JONES DAVIE (*upper right*), lucky in owning Sir Archie, ill-starred in losing him to another. (From the copy of a family portrait by Herman Niemeier, now in the North Carolina Collection of the Louis R. Wilson Library at the University of North Carolina.) ROBERT POTTER (*lower left*) the demagogue who quarreled with almost every human being he ever knew, but who praised Sir Archie. (From a portrait at the State House in Raleigh, North Carolina.) JOHN RANDOLPH OF ROANOKE (*lower right*), brilliant, eccentric, opinionated, who started an ugly story about Sir Archie that was hard to stop. (Courtesy of the National Gallery of Art, Washington, D.C.)

He Fulfills His Destiny

round, nothing to fear—hold her steady and let her come best pace home—pilot is up—he challenges. Bravo, Pilot! Well met my filly, that's the pace...."

Colden joined the tempest of thundering applause as Bonnets of Blue won by the meager half of a length. Time for that mile, a minute and fifty-one seconds—swift, but not a record. Price's Hermaphrodite came in no better than a fair third. Livingston's Sir Kirkland was fourth, General Jackson fifth. Celeste and the unnamed Sir Archie colt were distanced.

All that appeared for the second heat were Bonnets of Blue, Pilot, and the stubborn Hermaphrodite.

At the signal, the filly managed a quick start and a slight lead that lasted all the way around the first turn. Then Pilot came up and alongside. In the back stretch, poor Hermaphrodite began to fall back and back, farther out of the running with every vain stride. Halfway around, Pilot and his gray niece were neck and neck—"head and head," Colden called it. Into the second turn they galloped as though it were a dead heat, Pilot on the outside but keeping his position. He strove to better it. Colden imagined Pilot speaking to Bonnets of Blue, courteous as any human gentleman of the turf: "Can you live, Madam, through this rally home?" The home stretch found them still together, without an inch of advantage to be discerned for either as they dashed for the winning line.

"Pilot has it!" yelled a chorus of his backers.

"The filly Bonnets of Blue leads!" came back a counter-cry.

They were at the wire, and under.

"Pilot has it!" rang out again, and so it was. The judges called him winner by no more than half the length of his outthrust bay neck. Time by the watches in the stand, one minute and forty-eight seconds. Hermaphrodite had been distanced, and for the third heat only Pilot and Bonnets of Blue came out together. Each had won a heat; Pilot's time had been the better by three seconds.

Pilot was given the inside position for the start, and Johnson's

Sir Archie

groom led Bonnets of Blue to a stand fifty feet to Pilot's right. He brought her upon the track at something of an angle, and when he took his hand from her bridle she remained facing a few degrees to the leftward.

Again the ringing thud of the signal drum, and Pilot seemed to spring out first.

But his hoof fell falsely. He seemed to slip with his very first stride, almost to flounder. Recovering on the instant, he was away, while Bonnets of Blue, who had started without fault, snatched the lead by a length.

Darting diagonally across the track rather than straight down it, she grappled for the lead before they had gone twenty yards. Pilot's head was almost against her as she closed in, between her haunch and the line of poles at the inner rim of the track. For an instant there was dire danger of a collision, perhaps a fall for one or both of the horses.

Sandy, the rider of Pilot, showed good presence of mind. He reined his mount's head high and swung it to the right and outside, above the filly's buttocks. From the left of Bonnets of Blue, Pilot now ran to strive at her right. Thus close together, they stormed around the first turn.

Pilot was racing on the outside now, but he did not lose ground as they flew into the back stretch. Colden could see that Pilot had gained by inches, by a foot, by more. His head advanced from opposite the filly's gray haunch to opposite her gray shoulder. Past the half-mile post they battled, and toward the second turn. Colden's silent applause shifted to Pilot and Sandy:

"... Well done, Pilot—well attempted, my boy Sandy. But it won't do—the filly, Bonnets of Blue has it—you can't help it—keep her going—it is life or death with you, game and stoutness is your salvation...."

On that final turn, Sandy brought Pilot close to Bonnets of Blue, crowding her narrowly as she ran, until she slid along close to the

He Fulfills His Destiny

string of poles that seemed to gallop backward past her and Pilot. Sandy still forbore to force Pilot to his utmost. His sure hand on the reins kept Pilot ready to profit by any swerve or misstep of William Johnson's filly. Close-locked, the two made the turn, and Sandy dashed in his spurs to hurl Pilot to the top of his speed.

Ears laid back against her head like the ears of a coursing hound, Bonnets of Blue also gave her best. Neither whip nor spur could get another ounce out of her. The thrilled heart of Colden was pleading as though Sandy and Pilot could hear him:

"... Look well to her—give her no respite. Well done, Pilot! Now, boy, take a light pull at him—do not let him get abroad—*give and take in your pull—keep his mouth alive*, and be sure to catch his stride with the motion of your hands and body. *Lift him a little, and give another stab*. Bravo! my boy!—Well done, Pilot!—well done, filly, Bonnets of Blue! Anybody's race yet...."

Together, under incessant whip and spur, Pilot and Bonnets of Blue were at the finish line. Seemingly together still, they darted across it.

Bonnets of Blue was the winner, decided the judges, by the very slimmest of margins; Pilot had "run her up to the eyebrows," as Colden phrased it. The third heat had been completed in a minute and fifty-three seconds.

But what about that near-collision at the very start of the second heat, when Bonnets of Blue had crossed over so abruptly, had thrust herself into the lead before she was properly clear of her opponent? The judges, however sharp-eyed concerning that close finish, had taken no notice of the manifest foul, though others had. The rules of the Union Course were specific enough on the matter. Here, jabbered horsemen to each other, look here at Section 16:

"Every horse that shall fail running on the outside of every pole, or whose rider shall cross, jostle, strike or use any other foul play ... or who shall take the track before he is clear of every other horse, shall be deemed distanced, and the next best horse declared winner."

Sir Archie

All right, would not John Amis and his associate Harrison protest and claim the third heat on a foul by Bonnets of Blue?

No doubt but that Amis was disappointed and chagrined, but he did not plead a foul cross. He and William Johnson loved each other as brothers. Often in the past, Amis's horses had raced under the colors of Johnson, nor did Amis or others charge that Johnson himself was to blame. The fault, wise heads agreed when they grew cool, rested with the groom who had led Bonnets of Blue to her starting position and left her faced at an oblique across the track. However, Colden had something unpleasant to say about the silence of the officials who had given Bonnets of Blue the deciding heat:

"Although the purity of intention on the part of those who, in this case, acted as judges cannot be in the slightest degree questioned, yet it is to be regretted that gentlemen, not thoroughly versed in turf matters, should, by overzeal, even be induced to enter upon a duty for which they are not qualified.... The ordering or judging of a race ought to be delegated solely to men of actual practice and long experience in racing;—not such as keep and train horses in imagination, and start them round the festive board...."

Whichever racer had the right to win, the glory was to Southern Thoroughbreds of the Sir Archie descent. Still maintaining patient silence about the way in which that third heat had been won, Amis and Harrison offered to match Pilot against Bonnets of Blue in another trial for the following Monday, but Johnson courteously declined. Pilot journeyed back to Mowfield and eventually was sold to Johnson, who raced him with great success. Later he came into the hands of Thomas Watson, and his name was changed to Wild-Bill-of-the-Woods, under which title he triumphed in Virginia, the Carolinas, and Tennessee.

The first completed attempt at a published record of American Thoroughbreds appeared in 1830. Peter Cottom, owner of a Richmond printing shop, reissued the *Gentleman's New Pocket Farrier* by Dr. Richard Mason of Surry County, Virginia. This recog-

He Fulfills His Destiny

nizedly standard work on the ailments of horses was augmented by Cottom, who added brief essays on the training of racers and other matters and an appendix, which he entitled *American Stud Book*.

This latter item included, among more than a thousand others, the pedigree of Sir Archie, with Diomed recorded as his sire. Undoubtedly John Amis had contributed this information, and Cottom must have drawn upon the collections of pedigrees made by Feild, Amis, and George Washington Jeffries. Anyway, so much for that Gabriel whisper! By then, John Randolph had written the frank disavowal of his own idle repetition of the gossip by that mysterious "white groom."

Sir Archie grew feeble at Mowfield. More and more he kept to his stall, a mahogany-lined compartment as tastefully built as a room in the big white mansion itself. Uncle Hardy had died, and Sir Archie's faithful new attendant and companion was Hall Summeral, a towering Negro with large feet, a larger heart, and a still larger understanding of the distinguished animal that was now his charge.

In 1831, while his sons and grandsons continued to manifest their superiority everywhere, Sir Archie creakily emerged from his stall to begin his twenty-second season as a stallion. Mares were offered, in herds, to the sire of two whole generations of racing champions. One of these was his granddaughter, Camilla by Timoleon, the property of Robert A. Jones of Halifax.

This was the sunset of Sir Archie's active usefulness, but he merited proper care as he approached retirement, and the Amises saw that he received it.

A critic of Thoroughbreds who signed his writings "Observator" travelled through the Roanoke region during the spring and summer of 1831, visiting the great estates where top stallions and younger racers were on show. He admired, among others, Sir Archie's prolific sons, Timoleon, Sir Charles, and Gohanna, and wrote about them to the editor of the *American Turf Register*.

Sir Archie

"I saw old Sir Archy," he added, with respect and sympathy. "He is very infirm, complains of rheumatism and the other ills of age. May it be your happy lot to attain the one without the other."

This letter appeared in the August issue, and the following number brought something of a protest from a correspondent who signed himself "Senex": "I can perceive no fault in the American Turf Register except the term *old* to imply *veritable*, as Old Sir Archy. Why not copy the English in this particular also, and drop the Americanism?"

Whether or not the point was well taken, it meant little to Sir Archie himself. He was veritable—no doubt in the world about that—but he was old, too. Nobody could dilute either actuality by altering the terms. Even the sons and daughters of Sir Archie had begun, in some cases, to feel the chill advance of age.

Of all his early get, perhaps Walk-in-the-Water had longest defied the weakening inroads of time and hard work. After Walk's victory at Natchez in 1827, Green Berry Williams was sustainedly grateful and admiring, and he felt that the old gelding should retire to an easy old age. He presented Walk to Thomas Foxhall of Sumner County, Tennessee, on Foxhall's assurance that the veteran would neither train nor race again.

Foxhall was a British emigrant who had married the wealthy widow of a Tennessee horse breeder. He was accused of treating her badly. Her son by the first marriage was a minister, but his devout calling did not prevent him from administering to his stepfather a public flogging with a horsewhip.

Old Walk, eighteen years old, still liked to gallop at the Sumner County farm, and Foxhall allowed him to take the exercise track as a companion to certain colts on their training runs. In October of 1831, Foxhall brought him with several younger horses to a meet in Nashville.

The high point of the Nashville acres would be four-mile heats on Monday, October 10, for a purse of $600. The high favorite in this event was five-year-old Polly Pavell, daughter of Sir Archie's son Virginian. All who dared enter against her were two four-year-old grandsons of Sir Archie—Marshall Ney by Stockholder and Larry O'Gaff by Archy Junior, both of them relatively untried at four miles and both considered poor competition for Polly Pavell. The proprietor of the course induced Foxhall to enter Walk-in-the-Water as an attraction to draw spectators.

Foxhall's agreement to do so was in blatant repudiation of his promise to Green Berry Williams, but nobody protested save Williams himself. Uncle Berry was at the Nashville meeting, and he expressed concern for Walk-in-the-Water and angry disdain of Foxhall's bad faith and the proprietor's heartlessness. Walk was called for with the other entries. Decrepit, poorly conditioned, the venerable winner of full forty races through the years made his way to the starting post.

Uncle Berry turned his back and tramped out of the crowd. Balie Peyton, Tennessee's great analyst of horse racing, followed him away and came upon him sitting disconsolately on a log in a grove outside the enclosure.

"Are you not going up to see old Walk run?" inquired Peyton, but Uncle Berry shook his craggy head in mournful refusal.

"No," he grumbled, "I would as soon see a fight between my grandfather and a boy of twenty."

It did not go quite as badly as that with Walk-in-the-Water, while all but Uncle Berry watched and cheered.

In the first heat Polly Pavell forged ahead, but Walk kept close to her, forcing her to do her considerable best. She won, with Walk a good second and his two younger kinsmen third and fourth. The call for the second heat found Larry O'Gaff withdrawn, Marshall Ney timidly hopeful, and Walk understandably weary but game. Polly Pavell, however, showed a temperamental sulkiness. Several heifers were grazing close to the gate that led to the track, and twice, passing in view of them, Polly slowed her pace as though in protest of their presence. On the third round she actually bucked, but her jockey kept his saddle and managed to spur her into a final straining gallop that brought her in ahead of Walk for the second time. Marshal Ney was a poor third.

That performance, not without its grace and gallantry, was the final turf venture of phenomenal Walk-in-the-Water. Unlike his sire, he could not hope for sons and daughters to inherit his courage, speed, and endurance, and to keep his name in the mouths of race watchers. Retired, he vanished from the attention of horsemen, but not wholly from their memory.

Back at Mowfield, meanwhile, John Amis ministered to Sir Archie's comfort and viewed with a variety of emotions the approach of his own children to maturity.

Young William Amis had celebrated his twenty-first birthday in 1830. He was tall, vigorous, handsome, and recognized in Northampton County as a champion footracer and a fine rider. Too, he had hopes of a political career. The raffish promise of those adventures with Jesse Bynum and Robert Potter on the streets of Halifax also seemed to develop. William Amis was a powerful wrestler, more than six feet in height and weighing 175 pounds, all of it solid bone and hard muscle. Frequently he tussled with his young neighbors, not always good-humoredly for he was quick and violent of temper. His second brother, Thomas, seemed more quiet and conventional, and Mary, at fourteen in 1831, was at the threshold of beauty and belledom. But Junius, the seventeen-year-old third brother, gave his father more trouble than all the other children together.

Junius was extravagant and wilful, fond of fine clothes, and ardently gallant, even in his teens, to the ladies. His adolescent affections centred on pretty Celeste Hawkins, daughter of the late Governor William Hawkins of Warren County.

Celeste's widowed mother had been married a second time to R. J. Boyd, a relative by marriage of the Amises. The Boyds lived

He Fulfills His Destiny

at Shocco Springs, a flourishing health resort near Warrenton, and apparently they treated Junius' courtship of Celeste with good humor, even with approval.

But John Amis felt concern over so serious a romance for his young son. Junius rebelled and swore that he would marry Celeste. His father swore the contrary, and in October, somewhere about the time that Walk-in-the-Water ran his last race at Nashville, John Amis found it necessary to lock the defiant Junius in an upstairs room at Mowfield to prevent him from eloping with Celeste Hawkins.

According to surviving family tradition, John Amis sought further to keep his rebellious son immobilized by taking away his entire wardrobe of modish suits and beautifully-cut pantaloons. But Junius had won the stealthy loyalty of his Negro valet. The servant cunningly smuggled back one or two of the confiscated suits, and Junius, clothed and determined, crept out of his prison by night, managed to saddle a horse, and rode away.

Not far from Mowfield, he met a party of his friends, mounted and determined. They had come, announced their spokesmen, from Warren County, where poor lovely Celeste Hawkins bewailed Junius' imprisonment and absence. Their melodramatic intention had been to surround Mowfield, storm it like knights around the castle of an ogre, and set Junius free, by violence if necessary, to take him to his wedding.

Junius galloped with these merrily faithful hearts to Shocco Springs, and there he was welcomed with affectionate joy by his sweetheart and with friendly courtesy and sympathy by Mr. Boyd and Celeste's mother. Later John Amis read, and had to accept as final, a marriage notice published in the Halifax *Roanoke Advocate* for November 3: "At Shocco Springs, in Warren County, on Saturday, the 29th ultimo, Mr. Junius Amis of Northampton County to Miss Celeste Hawkins, daughter of the late Governor Hawkins...."

Sir Archie

This runaway romance culminated in tragedy. Celeste Hawkins Amis died within months of the elopement. Junius, sullenly defiant, did not return to Mowfield.

That same autumn of 1831, another Sir Archie began a brilliant and dramatic racing career. This was little Trifle, daughter of Sir Charles out of a mare that was the daughter of Cicero and the granddaughter of Sir Archie. Trifle was a bright chestnut with a white left rear leg, and she stood barely fourteen hands and three inches, with slender lines even for such low stature. She looked fast, but small and frail, and, like Sir Archie himself, had several times been sold or traded before she began running.

Nor was her debut more auspicious that than of her famous progenitor. She lost two races at mile heats, then at Broad Rock, Virginia, she won at two-mile heats from William Johnson's Mary Dismal. This was followed by two more disappointing losses at Tree Hill, and she went to Baltimore without much confidence expressed in her for the close of the fall season.

Somewhere she had gained style and stamina. In a $1,000 match race with Screamer, a double Sir Archie filly by great Henry out of great Lady Lightfoot, Trifle breezed home a winner, and three days later won the Jockey Club Purse from a field headed by the much-admired Black Maria, daughter of Lady Lightfoot by Eclipse, who had been a two to one favorite. Johnson, seeing Trifle's potentialities as he had seen those of her grandsire, prevailed on his friend John Craig to buy her and he himself undertook her training for four-mile heats.

On January 10, 1832, she won the Jockey Club Purse at Columbia, South Carolina. Later, at Charleston, she won the Jockey Club Purse on the Washington course, lost three days later to Little Venus, but on the same day beat Mary Francis in a $500 match race. She returned to Virginia for a summer's rest, while, in North Carolina, Sir Archie's last recorded foal was born.

This was a bay filly out of Robert Jones' Camilla, at once

He Fulfills His Destiny

daughter and great granddaughter of Sir Archie, named by her owner Lady Wilkinson. Her relatives, with degrees of kinship hard to compute, continued to assail records on race tracks throughout the nation.

Sir Archie greeted no mares that season. He faced the approaching night toward which all living creatures at last must turn their steps. He lived in an open stall in which Hall Summeral had set himself up a cot so as to be with his charge day and night. Sir Archie went uncurried—probably the dragging scrape of comb and brush irritated his ancient hide—and the bay hair grew long and shaggy upon his flanks. John Amis visited him often and ordered that he be fed and tended with the gentlest care. A visitor to Mowfield wrote a description:

"... of all animals he is the worst looking and would be the last taken for the most celebrated horse of his age. His owner treats him with all possible kindness, as it would be unpardonable indeed if he did not. Provender without stint, at rack and manger, and a soft and delicate bed, proclaim the proprietor's gratitude...."

Sir Archie did not wear a halter, and he could leave his stall and stable at pleasure, but seldom did he venture into the open except to drink from the outside tank. His thirst assuaged, he tottered back at once.

There was no tottering, however, among his descendants on the race courses. Trifle began the autumn campaign of 1832 by winning at Lancaster, Pennsylvania, then headed for the Union Course on Long Island, where she was one of a field of four to run four-mile heats on October 13 for the Jockey Club Purse of $600.

Two of her three rivals were relatives. Her old adversary Black Maria was there, six years old, with 111 pounds up. Slim, a four-year-old bay filly by Flying Childers, would carry only ninety pounds like Trifle. Lady Relief was remarkable, in that company and indeed throughout the world of crack racing animals, for having no Sir Archie blood; she was the five-year-old daughter of

Sir Archie

American Eclipse out of a First Council mare, and she came to the post with 104 pounds. The track was soft from rain, and Trifle was the favorite—five to four against the field, five to three against Black Maria.

But Black Maria brilliantly won the first heat. In the second, she was well ahead as they galloped into the final mile. Trifle, striving gallantly, came up and alongside, and the judges called it a dead heat for the second. In the third, with both Black Maria and Trifle somewhat wearied, Lady Relief seemed to be winning until her jockey pulled her up, and Trifle fought to the front and won.

The fourth heat was run with equally resolute rivalry, and this time Lady Relief came in first, a neck ahead of Black Maria. In the fifth heat, Trifle battled bravely for three miles with Lady Relief but slowed down in utter exhaustion, while Black Maria came from behind to win at last, having raced twenty miles to do so.

It had been a cruelly tiring ordeal. Black Maria, the winner, had weighed in at 900 pounds and came off the track at last to weigh 800, a loss of an even hundred pounds in a single afternoon's racing. Trifle, almost broken down by her efforts, was ordered a full year's rest by the gravely concerned Johnson.

Concern for another reason was felt by the human dwellers at Mowfield. Junius Amis, after the death of Celeste, lived at Silver Heels, another of the family plantations, and resumed his lavish expenditures. In particular he was a frequent patron of tailors' establishments. Still without his grandfather's bequest before he came of age, he found himself as embarrassed by debt as once had been Allan Jones Davie. He became forced to insert an advertisement in the *Roanoke Advocate* of November 22, 1832, its language at once sheepish and defiant:

NOTICE

is hereby given to all those to whom I may be indebted that for all the debts contracted prior to October, 1831, application need not be made, as those debts were contracted upon the authority of my father's credit, such as for clothing and other necessary articles. It is well known to all of you that it is entirely out of my power to pay those debts at present and most of you I have promised to pay when I arrive at the age of 21 years, but for the more certain satisfaction I do (once for all) assure you that for debts contracted as far back as 3 or 4 years, such as clothing, the making of clothes, and other necessary articles for which I do not deem myself in honor bound to pay, Application need never be made.

JUNIUS D. AMIS

November 18, 1832

Such embarrassing behavior on Junius's part, as well as William's proud and hot-tempered escapades, helped certain neighbors who disliked the folks at Mowfield to coin a phrase to their discredit: "A drop of Amis blood would poison the Atlantic ocean." The saying persists today and is rather relished by descendants of the Amises as evidence of the flavory individuality of their ante-bellum kinsmen.

Nobody, however, spoke of Sir Archie except in admiring terms, even the die-hards who clung to the theory that he had been irregularly sired by Gabriel. He passed a fairly comfortable winter in middle Northampton County. John Amis's daughter Mary, sixteen years old in 1833, began to figure as a queen of beauty in North Carolina society and at points more distant, but she was by no means the most admired member of the family at Mowfield. At the Virginia Hot Springs she was chosen to open a ball on the arm of her impressively stalwart young cousin John, son of Lemuel and Mary Amis Long.

"Oh!" exclaimed a tourist from the North. "What a beautiful girl, and what a handsome man. A most distinguished couple. Who are they?"

Sir Archie

"Why, don't you know?" laughed a Southerner. "They are the Sir Archie blood."

At the beginning of the year 1833, John Amis computed that Sir Archie's stud fees, after deduction of purchase money and all expenses of keep, had profited him $76,000. He declared as much, and it was published in the *American Turf Register* of February. This impressive figure did not include, of course, Sir Archie's winnings on the race track or his earlier profits as a stallion belonging to Allan Jones Davie. Davie still scowlingly regretted the loss of those profits.

From Lansford, South Carolina, Davie sent Skinner an article entitled *The Race Horse Region*, in which he upheld the benefits of environment as a factor in producing good runners:

"My opinion is that the southern part of Virginia, and perhaps an equal portion of the northern border of North Carolina, are most favorable to the perfection of that animal (the thoroughbred) and that, with less of what we term blood or pedigree, a superior horse will be produced, if the stock have been in that district sufficiently long to become thoroughly acclimated. And I come to this conclusion because less blood will there produce a race-horse of the first class...."

This was but a prologue to a sly assault upon the memory of William Amis, once Davie's creditor and the man who had taken Sir Archie from him:

"... Betsey Abner was a mare of fine game—won all her colt races, opposed to some of the best colts of her day. She sold at a high price and was sent off young. She was bred by the late William Amis. She was got by Sir Archie; her dam by Peeble's Ratler [*sic*]— a horse of no reputation; her granddam one of Mr. Amis' work mares. I knew the late Mr. Amis well—his way of breeding horses, and many, if not most of his stock. He was a man who never dealt in retail. It was his habit, every spring, to engage some owners of a stallion to visit his plantations regularly every week—he paying a moderate price (generally about $4) for each colt. And, as he was a man of large fortune, his custom, even at this low price, was an object to those who had common stallions. Mr. Amis seldom bought a horse; on the contrary, he had always some for sale. I mention this circumstance to show that Betsey Abner could have had but little racing blood, yet in good hands, she would have been a respectable race nag on any turf...."

He then noticed the career of Walk-in-the-Water with back-handed compliment: "... Old Walk-in-the-Water has perhaps won as many races, at all distances, as any nag in the country. On the side of his dam, he had almost no blood. She was by **Dongolah**, yet he was a four mile horse of the first class...."

These judgments, published with the initial "D" as signature in the Turf Register for February, drew immediate fierce response from William Williams, a Virginian who had become a circuit judge in Tennessee and secretary of the Nashville Jockey Club which had sponsored Walk-in-the-Water's last brave race, who signed himself "Panton": "... Amis' plough mares, if equal to the generality in the country, are blooded. If D will trace any distinguished Roanoke Racer to a known dray mare, within four or five crosses, I will succomb. Till then, P will think absence of pedigree and absence of blood are not synonymous in the racing region."

Williams' sharp rebuke to Davie was published in May. At nearly the same time, a new effort to clarify questioned pedigrees was published.

This was Patrick Nisbett Edgar's compilation of materials gathered under direction of J. J. Harrison, and it bore an imposing title, *The American Turf Register, Sportsmen's Herald and General Stud Book*. Fully six hundred pages long, it was a valuable work, but mistakes and omissions were noticed by those who read. Sir Archie, for instance, was not there—some wondered if this was because of the last whispers of the scandal—though his name appeared in the pedigrees of his get. Davie was to attack the pedigrees

Sir Archie

of Sir Charles and his descent and to evoke quarrelling responses for a decade to come.

John Randolph of Roanoke, whose glib chatter about the wrong sire for Sir Archie may have spoiled his own chances of publishing a better stud book than Edgar's, died on May 24 in Philadelphia, where he had gone to await ship for England. He had handed Skinner, for publication in the *American Turf Register*, a list of 130 Randolph Thoroughbreds, including eleven of Sir Archie's get and seventy-six of Sir Archie's sons Janus and Roanoke. Also to Skinner, a correspondent had protested an anonymous report that William Johnson had called Reality the finest racer he had ever known:

"... Until I see the written opinion of Col. William Johnson revoked that 'Sir Archie was the best racehorse he ever saw,' or one of equal weight in support of the one that he has been surpassed or equalled by any of his descendants, I cannot adopt that of our anonymous writer, especially one who appears to have erred more than once...."

That was included in the June number of Skinner's magazine, along with a brief word on Sir Archie's condition that wound up: "Except those of the finny tribe, it is conjectured that Sir Archie's posterity outnumbers that of any living animal."

But on June 7, before the new *American Turf Register* had come to the hands of most of its subscribers, Hall Summeral came sadly to tell John Amis that Sir Archie lay motionless in his stall and would not rouse.

Stiff and soundless his great bulk sprawled there. He was a legend of his own creation.

Twenty-eight years had passed since, a clumsy-legged little colt, he had gained his feet to nuzzle the flank of his blind dam Castianira; twenty-six years since short-sighted John Tayloe III had sold him for a ridiculous price to Ralph Wormeley; twenty-five since he had shown promise in early training, and had suffered from

He Fulfills His Destiny

distemper; twenty-four since William Johnson and Arthur Taylor had schooled and managed him to his golden triumphs after his earlier defeats; twenty-three since he had first covered a mare; nineteen since his children had begun to win as he had won; ten since his son Henry had challenged the whole nation for supremacy on the turf; two since he had retired for a brief twilight of life, before life departed from him as a race horse departs from the post at signal.

At almost the same hour, at William Johnson's Virginia estate, Sir Charles had died.

John and Elizabeth Amis and their children were stricken with grief, as at the passing of a near and beloved relative. The slaves at Mowfield bowed their heads in mourning. Horsemen everywhere were saddened as the news was brought to them.

Skinner editorialized on Sir Archie and his great son, enclosing his announcement in the broad lines of black that usually distinguished the death notices of statesmen:

"... Peace to their ashes; Theirs was an enviable destiny. They felt not the misery of dependence; for all their wants were supplied. They experienced not the machinations of the envious, had not occasion to sicken with disgust at the baseness which leads some 'lords of creation' to slander and supplant their friends and benefactors. How few of us can boast of having so honestly acted well our parts as did these two noble animals. And well were they rewarded by the humanity of their owners, and the pleasures procured for themselves by the glory of their achievements...."

John Amis cut dark hair from Sir Archie's tail to keep as a cherished relic. One of Sir Archie's hoofs was requested by Skinner for display in his editorial office. The Amises buried Sir Archie under quiet summer trees, not far from the house and race track, within sound of the stables.

X

SIR ARCHIE
Lives in His Descendants

STILL his blood lived on, flowing hot and fast, and continued its fleet course to applause and triumph as though by peculiar family custom. Various records showed that Sir Archie had sired at least 164 sons and 225 daughters. The sons, in their turn, were to sire 4,162 recorded colts and fillies; the daughters would produce 491. Many of these were racers, and afterward progenitors. Racing was their life work, and some of them seemed to know more by inherited aptitude than many human preceptors could teach them.

In the autumn of 1833, at Springfield, Alabama, a horseman named Duke wagered $100 on his promising chestnut gelding for a mile race against the aged but sturdily active Pelham, by Sir Archie's son Kosciusko, the possession of Duke's neighbor Wizer. Weights were left to the pleasure of the owners. Duke's gelding came to the post with a trusted jockey up; Wizer's groom led forth Pelham, saddled and bridled but without a rider.

They were off at the beat of the drum. Unguided, Pelham on his own judgment tried, and at first failed, to steal an early lead from his younger adversary. When the gelding drew ahead, Pelham

Sir Archie Lives in His Descendants

sagely reduced his pace to round the first turn on his very heels. Again Pelham speeded up, pulled ahead in the back stretch, and on the second turn ran his veteran best to secure the advantage. Far ahead in the home stretch, he slowed his pace as though judiciously reined, and came across the line in the tidy time of one minute and fifty-five seconds. He then stopped, turned, and trotted toward the judges' stand as though to report his own triumph. "Old Pelham forever!" rang the cheers of the onlookers for his feat.

Completely impromptu, with no rider at all for any of the three entries, was another race reported at Kendall's training track near Baltimore that December. Three of Sir Archie's grandchildren were let out of their stalls to play as they wished—Industry's son Camsidel, Spring Hill's daughter Mary McHenry, and the filly Mary Granville by Sir Charles. Together they came upon the exercise track. Suddenly, as though at the boom of a spectral drum, they dashed off at full speed. Mary Granville outran her cousins in that mile dash, and a correspondent of the *American Turf Register* wrote of the "very pleasant affair."

More formal and far more sensational was the career of Trifle in the autumn of 1833. The despairing judgment that she might have broken down in those twenty miles against Black Maria and the others in 1832 had to be set completely aside. She raced again, and from that time forward she won in a blaze of glory. She started first at Broad Rock, triumphing in three-mile heats. From there she went to Baltimore, to win four-mile heats. Next at the Union Course, where just a year before Black Maria had vanquished her, she took a happy revenge by beating both Black Maria and the vaunted Alice Gray for the $1,000 Jockey Club Purse. She finished at Tree Hill with yet another victory at four miles.

In the spring of 1834 she won all of her four races, and in the autumn four more—all of them at four-mile heats, and not one of them saw her lose a single heat. Nobody dared enter a horse against her after that; and she would be seven years old in 1835, obliged to carry 123 pounds. That would be a heavy burden for her small, dainty frame, and she was retired from the track. Her record was nineteen victories in twenty-five races, and this included winning her last twelve races, ten of them at four-mile heats. In five of the six races she did not win, she was second. Her winnings totalled $14,380. She became a brood mare, and her sons and daughters were winners only less great than herself.

Meanwhile, Sir Archie lay at peace in his grave at Mowfield, but his human friends had worries to vex them.

William Amis, twenty-four years old in the summer of 1834, announced on the Whig ticket for a seat in the North Carolina State Senate. His popular and influential Democratic opponent was Colonel William B. Lockhart, for years clerk of the Superior Court for Northampton County. The campaign was waged in a manner only less lively than those notable canvasses by Potter and Bynum. One of Lockhart's supporters, young Dick Mason, was especially outspoken to the discredit of William Amis's manners and morals. On election day that August, he and William met at White's Hotel in Jackson, and William undertook to punish Mason in the fine florid manner he had achieved by example from his Uncle Jesse down in Halifax eight or nine years earlier.

William struck at Mason with a hickory cane. Mason, who appears also to have followed local political tradition, had walked out that day with two pistols, ready cocked, in the pockets of his pantaloons. He dived his hands after these, but the hammers of both of them caught in the cloth of his pockets. As he struggled to draw, one pistol went off, inflicting a flesh wound in Mason's thigh.

William struck again and again, staggering Mason and cutting open his scalp and cheek. Herod Faison, a Whig leader of the community and as muscular as William, grappled the cane-wielder and dragged him away from his victim. Mason ran, bleeding. The votes were counted, and Lockhart was declared winner. The clatter of

LEXINGTON, THE INCOMPARABLE

From the portrait in the collection of the late Harry Worcester Smith. Lexington was Sir Archie's grandson, with Boston as his sire and Timoleon as his grandsire. In seven races he proved himself the foremost race horse of his time and then became a mighty sire in his own right. With Lexington the outstanding line of Sir Archie sires came to an end, but Lexington's many and brilliantly fruitful daughters spread the Sir Archie blood widely through the world of Thoroughbreds. Man-o'-War descends from Sir Archie through a daughter of Lexington.

disapproving tongues helped to decide John Amis in a plan to emigrate to Mississippi.

Thomas had married Sarah, the daughter of Dr. Stephen Davis of Warrenton, and would accompany his parents. Mary, too, left North Carolina, to the despair of her battalions of admirers. The lands once owned by the elder William Amis were divided; Junius, still youthfully defiant, kept Silver Heels, and the rest of the property was sold and the money divided between William and Thomas.

The Amises narrowly escaped death aboard the steamer *Lucy Walker*, which burned to the water's edge on the Ohio River on October 25, 1834. They saved themselves but lost much of their luggage and nearly all of their family records. Undaunted, they journeyed on to Mississippi where they prospered. William followed them to their new home, and so, eventually, did the reconciled Junius.

But while the Amises bade farewell to North Carolina, with strangers possessing Mowfield and ignoring the grave of Sir Archie, grooms on John Wickham's farm in Henrico County, Virginia, commented on the sprightly action and high temper of a certain bay colt.

This was a son of Timoleon out of a Florizel mare, and he had been foaled in the spring of 1833, not far from the time of his grandfather's death. He was temperamental, sometimes even vicious. Wickham did not order him broken to the saddle until he was two years old. At three, owned and trained by William Johnson and the Washington sportsman James Long, he became a race horse that overwhelmed every thing, everywhere. He was given the name of Boston—not for the city, but for the card game.

Boston had no great length of stride but ran close to the ground like a scurrying beetle, usually far ahead of all competition. Race after race he won, in the North and South, at all distances, until he came to the top of the four-mile aristocracy. He assumed the

Sir Archie

habit, common among Sir Archies, of winning purses by lonely walks upon race courses from which his contemporaries had been banished by the mere mention of his terrible name.

James Long gloried in him, offering $50,000 and more as a side bet for a match at four-mile heats with any horse in the world whose owner was weak-minded enough to bring him to the post. When that challenge went unaccepted, Long offered $20,000 on Boston against any two horses—Boston to run four-mile heats in succession, while the two challengers ran a heat apiece. Should a third heat be required, a contingency which Long considered highly improbable, Boston would run it against whichever of the two against him would be thought best able to give him any trouble. Another $5,000 of Long's money said loudly that Boston would outrun both such opponents in straight heats. Nor did anyone seriously argue the contrary; this offer, too, went without takers.

Out of forty-five races in five years, Boston won forty, was second in two, third in one, and distanced twice. His turf winnings totalled $51,000 when, nine years old in 1842, he was retired to stud.

He was a prolific sire, as he had been a supreme race horse. In 1850 he died, but in that year his greatest son, Lexington, was foaled in Kentucky, out of Alice Carneal by imported Sarpedon.

In May of 1853, Lexington won two important stake races in a single week. He went from those triumphs to New Orleans, which had become a center distinguished by big purses and tremendous race gatherings. He beat another Sir Archie descendant, Sally Waters, in straight four-mile heats to take a purse of $8,500. In April of 1854, as Kentucky's entry in the State Stakes that also mustered the carefully chosen best from Mississippi, Alabama, and Louisiana, he won again in straight heats. The following week, his half-brother Lecomte beat him in a $20,000 match, setting a new four-mile record of seven minutes and twenty-six seconds.

In 1885 Lexington raced against time in New Orleans, alone on

He Lives in His Descendants

the track, with only split-second chronometers to oppose him. A single heat of four miles, from a running start, he accomplished in seven minutes and nineteen and three-fourths seconds. A final match with Lecomte that year saw him utterly distance his former conqueror in seven minutes and twenty-one seconds. After that there was no profit or reason in looking for anything to come to the same starting post with Lexington.

He lived for a quarter of a century beyond this final victory, a great stallion after a great racing career, in the tradition of his father and grandfather and great-grandfather. The tracks still swarmed with his kinsmen of the Sir Archie blood in the thousands, seeking to outrun each other for the highest fame and reward of the turf.

With Lexington, the Sir Archie line of male champions came to an end. But Lexington's daughter Aerolite was a fruitful progenetrix, and her descendant was Man o' War, who was true to the blood—supreme on the track and supreme as a sire.

Today, no Thoroughbred of American descent but can trace back a century and a half to Sir Archie. Surely his blood will exist as long as Thoroughbreds exist; perhaps even until the last horse has died and is one with Eohippus.

Appendix A

The Spelling of "Sir Archie" and "Mowfield"

AMERICA'S horse of horses was much discussed in writing. As with various of his notable human contemporaries, his name was spelled in several ways.

Both "Sir Archie" and "Sir Archy" are common in various surviving documents. The *American Farmer* and the *American Turf Register* used "Sir Archy" and may have altered other spellings to this form when editing letters and articles for publication. "Sir Archy" was also used by John Randolph of Roanoke and by Sir Archie's early co-owner John Tayloe III, as shown by their manuscripts. Cottom and Edgar, the two American stud records that were published during Sir Archie's lifetime, both have "Sir Archy." Several persons wrote the name "Sir Archer," and some so write it today.

But he was named for Captain Archibald Randolph, who wrote his own nickname as "Archie." Allan Jones Davie advertised him as "Sir Archie," as did William and John Amis. Today's descendants of the Amises insist upon this spelling, and letters and family memoranda of their forbears support them. Therefore, it was "Sir

Appendices

Archie" for the greatest part of his life with those who were closest to him.

The plantation in Northampton County, North Carolina, where Sir Archie lived from 1817 to 1833 has its own various spellings. Mrs. Blanchard and several descendants of Mary Amis Long accepted "Moorfield," which spelling is accepted by the recent turf authorities John Lewis Hervey and Fairfax Harrison. Most residents of Northampton County, including a number of Amis family connections, insist on "Mowfield," as it was sometimes written by both William and John D. Amis. William Amis also wrote "Mofield," and Northampton County records of the early nineteenth century have "Mowfield," "Moefield," and "Mofield." On several maps, both of Sir Archie's time and of more recent years, the name is "Mowfield," which is generally accepted today as the official spelling.

APPENDIX B

The Ancestry of Sir Archie

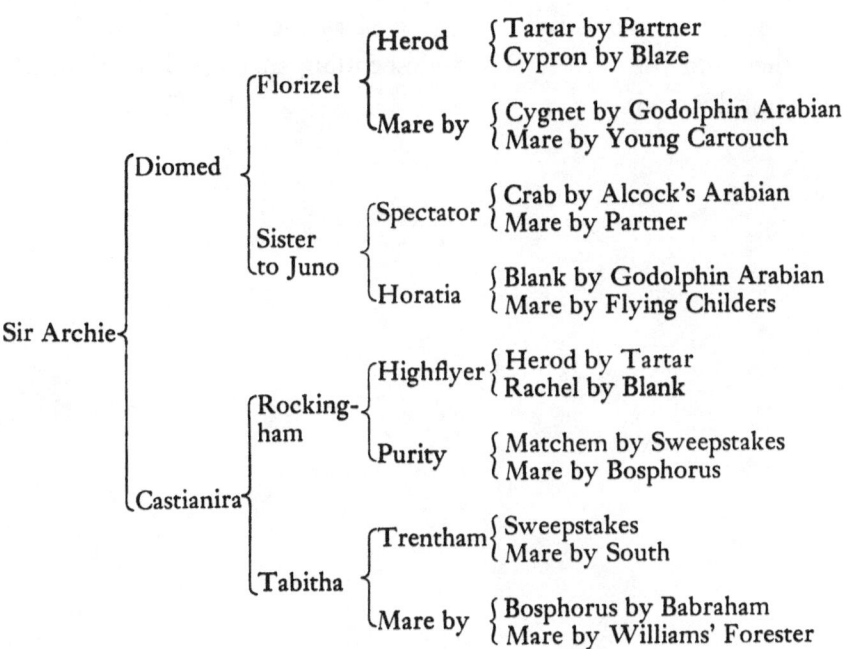

Appendices

Several claims that Sir Archie's sire and dam were nearly related came into print toward the end of Sir Archie's life, and were stoutly denied. Their closest kinship was in the Herod line, Diomed being the grandson and Castianira the great-granddaughter of that sterling English race horse and progenitor. In terms of human genealogy, Diomed and Castianira were first cousins once removed.

Diomed descended in tail-mail from Herod, and, through him, from the Byerly Turk. A second Byerly cross came through Partner and Spectator on the side of Diomed's dam. There were also two crosses to the Godolphin Arabian, through Cygnet and Blank, and no less than four to the Darley Arabian in Diomed's descent. The whole pattern as regards Diomed's breeding shows a concentrated and balanced admixture of the blood of the three historic English progenitors.

Castianira's ancestry shows two Godolphin Arabian crosses, by way of Blank and Bosphorus, as well as the blood of the Darley Arabian and the Byerly Turk, descending through Herod, Highflyer, and Rockingham.

Appendix C

The Birthplace and the Grave

FOUR localities, fairly widely separated in Virginia, have offered claim to be the place where Sir Archie was foaled.

Mount Airy, in Essex County in the Tidewater, is still the possession and home of the descendants of John Tayloe III, who remain insistent on the claim for Sir Archie. A tradition not quite so closely argued ascribes his birth to Carter Hall in Clarke County, home of Captain Archibald Randolph's father-in-law Nathaniel Burwell. Some commentators feel that logic supports the theory that Sir Archie was foaled at Miles Selden's Tree Hill estate near Richmond, where Castianira returned in the spring of 1805 to mate a second time with Diomed and where mares in foal often went in time to drop their offspring before mating. Others favor Ben Lomond, the vanished Cumberland County estate of Captain Randolph.

The Mount Airy claim probably is founded upon Tayloe's splendidly kept stud book which records the purchase of Castianira and includes a note on the foaling of Robert Burns, later Sir Archie. But that particular record does not take note of the fact that

Appendices

Castianira was sent to Captain Randolph at Ben Lomond in 1803 and that Captain Randolph had full charge of her as a brood mare.

Sir Archie was at Carter Hall by the autumn of 1805, but hardly went there until Captain Randolph left Ben Lomond to live with his father-in-law, and Captain Randolph's letter to Tayloe in the spring of 1807 dates fairly exactly the transfer of Sir Archie to Mount Airy at that time.

All of these matters would remain more or less in the realm of conjecture, but for Tayloe's unequivocal statement, published in the *American Farmer* for August 11, 1826, to refute the gossip about Sir Archie's paternity. In that letter, Tayloe said that Sir Archie "was foaled on the south side of the James River," which disposes at once of the claims of Carter Hall, Tree Hill, and Mount Airy, all of which estates lay to the north of that stream.

John Lewis Hervey accepts Ben Lomond as the birthplace. It would not be hazardous or even extraordinary for a vigorous young colt to accomplish the forty miles or so of travel from Ben Lomond to Tree Hill in 1805, and that Sir Archie made the trip seems to be made certain by Tayloe's flat assurance.

Difference of opinion as to Sir Archie's place of burial is limited to Mount Airy and Mowfield. Tayloe's descendants speak of "Sir Archie's grave" at Mount Airy, and in recent years this supposed grave has been shown to visitors, but evidence is overwhelmingly on the side of Mowfield. Sir Archie lived at Mount Airy but a few weeks during his second year; he lived at Mowfield for the last seventeen years of his life, and he died there. Not only all Amis family traditions but opinion of members of every old Northampton County family agree that he was buried on the Amis plantation.

Exact location of his grave is virtually impossible. Three spots, two close to the house and another some five hundred yards distant, have recently been suggested. None of these are marked, nor are the burial places of William Amis, his wife, and a number of family

Appendices

servants. Mrs. Blanchard employed digging crews to search the various spots but found no remains.

Sir Archie's bones, if discovered, probably would lack two or more hoofs, since Amis traditions are to the effect that these were kept as relics and that one was given to John S. Skinner for display in the editorial office of the *American Turf Register*. In the October, 1832, number, a note says: "We have bespoken one of [Sir Archie's] hoofs...," which bears out the story. Mrs. Blanchard's search for this relic was painstaking but uncovered no trace beyond a rumor that for a while it was in a museum at Philadelphia.

In any case, all likelihood is that Sir Archie was buried where he died and that his body was not shipped from North Carolina to Tidewater Virginia for burial at Mount Airy.

Appendix D

The Racing Record of Sir Archie's Sons and Daughters

by Alexander Mackay-Smith

IN THE YEAR 1867 there appeared simultaneously in New York and London a sumptuous two-volume work entitled *Frank Forester's Horse and Horsemanship of the United States and British Provinces of North America* by Henry William Herbert, the first comprehensive book devoted to the horse in this hemisphere. Among its many interesting features was a history of racing in this country from the earliest times to the date of issue, also the first attempt in this field. By way of appendix there appeared at the end of Volume I a "Table of Stock of Foreign and Native Sires." This consisted of tables for each year, beginning with August, 1829, and ending with December, 1865, listing each sire with winning offspring during that year and including the number of winners, the number of races won, the number of heats won, and the number of miles run. No figures were included for the amount of money won, the factor now used to rank stallions (average earnings index). In those far-off days, when racing was conducted as a sport rather than as a business, the success of a sire was measured according to the number of races won by his get.

Appendices

Although Herbert's history of American racing went back to the seventeenth century, his tables did not begin until August of 1829, and for a very good reason. This was the month which marked the first issue of *The American Turf Register and Sporting Magazine*, founded, edited, and published by John Stuart Skinner of Baltimore. It was not until the advent of the *Turf Register* that any comprehensive lists of races in this country appeared in print. Herbert's figures have ranked as standard ever since the date of their publication.

Also in 1829 in the *Turf Register* appeared a "Memoir of Sir Archy" (reprinted by Herbert *in toto*) which contains the statement: "... he stands upon higher ground than any other horse that has covered in America.... He has done as much for the turf stock of this country as the Godolphin Arabian, King Herod, or Highflyer, for that of Great Britain. Most of the best stock at present [1829] in this country are either immediately from the loins of Sir Archy, or have been produced from his sons and daughters."

This statement has been taken at face value ever since it was printed and has never seriously been questioned. It is, however, a statement of opinion. Until Mrs. Blanchard undertook her monumental work no figures were available to prove it. To assemble them proved to be a most arduous task. Except for a few racing notes published in the column "Sporting Olio," a feature which began in Skinner's earlier publication the *American Farmer* in 1825, the only sources were original letters and documents and local newspapers.

It was from the latter that Mrs. Blanchard succeeded in assembling the great wealth of data on Sir Archie's offspring with which she filled over a thousand typewritten pages, thus making him the best "documented" sire of his era. In the spacious days of the early nineteenth century it was the custom of Thoroughbred breeders to advertise their stallions in the local newspapers and to

Appendices

advertise them at considerable length. Not only was the racing and breeding record of the horse himself set out in detail, but also the records of his colts and fillies. Mrs. Blanchard was assiduous in combing contemporary local newspapers for stud advertisements and for accounts of race meetings. Under the guidance of the late Harry Worcester Smith, who personally conducted her on two extended tours of the states, particularly in the South where Sir Archie and his get had been most active, and with the cooperation of the authorities of the American Antiquarian Society at Worcester, Massachusetts, and other institutions with outstanding collections of early newspapers, she copied and had photographed literally thousands of such stud advertisements. She and Mr. Smith spent a week visiting the writer in Virginia in the course of which she occupied eight or nine hours each day going over his collection of stud advertisements from newspapers published in the Lower Shenandoah Valley.

Having assembled this source material she made an alphabetical list of Sir Archie's offspring, adding to the name of each everything in her notes pertaining to the individual animal. All this made a most impressive array, but it was still impossible to appreciate its actual significance without further arrangement and analysis. Unfortunately at this point Mrs. Blanchard, then an old lady, found that she did not have sufficient strength to go on and entrusted her manuscript to the writer.

With the invaluable assistance of Mrs. Howard Adams of West Point, New York, each of Sir Archie's offspring was listed according to the year in which it was foaled. Considering the way in which it was compiled, it is obvious that Mrs. Blanchard's data could include only the more successful of his get. Of the 366 colts and fillies listed the foaling dates were recorded for 298, and were unrecorded for 68. As we know that at the height of his popularity Sir Archie was bred to more than 80 mares per year, it is evident that the figure 366, or an average of 16.6 foals per year for the 22

Appendices

seasons in which he stood at stud, represents only a fraction of Sir Archie's total output as a sire.

The foals of each year were listed on graph paper and their records outlined under headings which included their names; the names of their dams and of their dams' sires; their color and sex; the names of the courses on which they raced and the dates of the races; the names of the races and their conditions; where they placed in each heat; the names of the horses against which they raced, their color, sex and age, their sires, and the names of their owners; the total amount of the purses and their distribution; the times and weights carried; and references as to the sources from which the above information was acquired. In subsequent columns were recorded the breeding records of the colts and fillies listed including the racing records of their offspring. The same procedure was followed with the 68 colts and fillies for which no foaling date was recorded. To contain the above information 143 sheets of graph paper were used with 38 columns to the sheet and 50 lateral lines.

From these 143 sheets were compiled a summary table, "The Racing Record of Sir Archie's Sons and Daughters," which is herewith reproduced. The sheets of supporting data were obviously too extensive to publish here, but are available for consultation in the Louis Round Wilson Library of the University of North Carolina.

The table speaks for itself, but a few comments will perhaps give it emphasis. In 1823 the get of Sir Archie won 45 races—a remarkable figure considering the very limited racing opportunities at that time and the distances to be travelled. In the era from 1830 to the Civil War covered by Herbert's list, when the number of races run markedly increased, it was only during two brief "boom" periods (1838-42 and 1852-57) that this figure of 45 races won was exceeded by other stallions. In 1819 his get won 40+ races and in several other years many more races than it took to lead the list in a number of years during the period 1830-65.

Herbert lists Sir Archie as second to his son Sir Charles in 1830,

Appendices

1831, and 1832. It is not possible to compare his figures with Mrs. Blanchard's data in 1830 or in 1832 since they are based on the periods from August, 1829, to December, 1830, and from September, 1831, to September, 1832. The only comparable year is 1831 when both historians cite figures for the twelve calendar months. Herbert gives Sir Charles first place with 19 races and Sir Archie second place with 15 races. Mrs. Blanchard, on the other hand, shows that Sir Archie's get in 1831 won 26 races, which would move him up to first place, ahead of Sir Charles.

Turf historians the world over owe a debt of gratitude to Mrs. Blanchard for the many years of unremitting effort on the basis of which it is now possible to develop figures showing, beyond all doubt, that Sir Archie was in fact, as well as by reputation, the Foundation Sire of the AmericanThoroughbred.

RACING RECORD OF SIR ARCHIE'S SONS AND DAUGHTERS

		LISTED UNDER FOALING YEAR			LISTED UNDER WINNING YEAR		
Year	Number of foals Recorded	Names of Winners and Number of Wins	Total Winners	Total Races Won	Names of Winners and Number of Wins	Total Winners	Total Races Won
1811	15	Brown Bob (3), Director (1), Spring Hill (1), Tecumseh (Few)	4	5+			
1812	6	Reaphook (1), Vanity (1), Lady Lightfoot (More than 31)	3	33+			
1813	15	Blank (3), Buffalo (1), Reality (3), Timoleon (13), Walk-in-the-Water (5+), Warbler (1)	6	26+			
1814	4	Fair Rosamond (2)	1	2	Spring Hill (1)	1	1
1815	15	Beggar Girl (7), Carolinian (4), Contention (20), Kosciusko (4), Napoleon (5), Rarity (1), Virginian (11)	7	52	Lady Lightfoot (3)	1	3

Year					
1816	10	Lottery (1), Henrietta (2), Rattler (17), Sir Charles (20), Sir William (20+)	5	Director (1), Timoleon (4), Reality (2), Walk-in-the-Water (2), Vanity (1)	10
			60+		
1817	7	Childers (6)	1	Brown Bob (3), Buffalo (1), Lady Lightfoot (9), Warbler (1), Timoleon (8)	22
			6		
1818	6	Betsey Richards (15), Muckle John (9)	2	Reaphook (1), Carolinian (2), Lady Lightfoot (4), Fair Rosamond (2), Timoleon (1), Contention (1), Blank (2), Virginian (5), Rattler (5)	23
			24		9
1819	17	Dutchess of Marlborough (5), Elizabeth (1), Henry (6), John Richards (2), Pocahontas (2), Stockholder (3)	6	Beggar Girl (1), Carolinian (1), Blank (1), Contention (10), Lady Lightfoot (2), Lottery (1), Kosciusko (4), Napoleon (2), Rattler (9), Rarity (1), Sir Charles (2), Virginian (6), Sir William (Several)	40+
			19		13
1820	18	Arab (3), Cherokee (1), Bertrand (13), Creeping Kate (1), Flirtilla (13), Iris (3), Janet (6), Marion (3), Platina (1)	9	Beggar Girl (5), Carolinian (1), Contention (7), Napoleon (2), Lady Lightfoot (5), Rattler (2), Reality (1), Sir Charles (9), Sir William (1)	33
			44		9

RACING RECORD OF SIR ARCHIE'S SONS AND DAUGHTERS

Year	Number of foals Recorded	LISTED UNDER FOALING YEAR			LISTED UNDER WINNING YEAR	
		Names of Winners and Number of Wins	Total Winners	Total Races Won	Names of Winners and Number of Wins	Total Winners	Total Races Won
1821	17	Isabella (5), Janus (3), Sir William of Transport (6)	3	14	Beggar Girl (1), Childers (2), Contention (2), Dutchess of Marlborough (3), Lady Lightfoot (1), Rattler (1), Sir Charles (5), Sir William (3), Sambo (1)	9	19
1822	17	Aggy (1), Eliza White (7), Gohanna (4), Janette (7), Lady LaGrange (1), Pacific (5), Sally Hope (22), Sea Gull (1)	8	48	John Richards (1), Betsey Richards (1), Lady Lightfoot (7), Muckle John (4), Napoleon (1), Sir Charles (4), Sir William (4)	7	22
1823	16	Crusader (2), Miss Halifax (3), Mulatto Mary (4), Pirate (2)	4	11	Dutchess of Marlborough (2), Elizabeth (1), Henry (4), John Richards (1), Stockholder (1), Arab (2), Bertrand (1), Flirtilla (2), Janet alias Virginia Lafayette (3), Sir William (12), Childers (4), Betsey Richards (7), Muckle John (5)	13	45

1824	14	Cadmus (1), Giles Scroggins (4), Industry (9), Red Gauntlet (4), Tariff (1)	5	19	Henry (2), Pocahontas (2), Stockholder (1), Arab (1), Bertrand (4), Flirtilla (5), Iris (3), Janet alias Virginia Lafayette (3), Marion (2), Platina (1), Isabella (4), Janus (3), Sir William of Transport (2), Walk-in-the-Water (1), Betsey Richards (2)	15	36
1825	17	Corporal Trim (2), Eliza Splotch (1), Kate Karney (8), Pandora (3), Phenomena (1), Sally Trent (2), Waxy (11)	7	28	Cherokee (1), Stockholder (1), Bertrand (5), Flirtilla (5), Marion (1), Sir William of Transport (2), Aggy (1), Eliza White (2), Gohanna (3), Walk-in-the-Water (1)	10	22
1826	19	Bacchus (1), Charlotte Temple (10), Gabriella (2), Lady Jackson (1), Polly Jones (8)	5	22	Bertrand (3), Creeping Kate (1), Flirtilla (1), Isabella (1), Janette (7), Sally Hope (2), Sea Gull (1), Pirate (1), Gohanna (1), Pacific (4), Eliza White (5), Betsey Richards (5), Miss Halifax (3), Sir William of Transport (1), Lady LaGrange (1)	15	37

RACING RECORD OF SIR ARCHIE'S SONS AND DAUGHTERS

Year	Number of foals Recorded	LISTED UNDER FOALING YEAR			LISTED UNDER WINNING YEAR		
		Names of Winners and Number of Wins	Total Winners	Total Races Won	Names of Winners and Number of Wins	Total Winners	Total Races Won
1827	24	Avarilla (1), Damper (1), Dashall (1), Eliza Riley (3), Hudibras (1), I.C. (2), May Day (6), Mercury (1), Morgiana (2), Snake (1), Jemima Wilkinson (6), Virginia Taylor (9), Wild-Bill-of-the-Woods (5)	13	39	Sir William of Transport (1), Pirate (1), Pacific (1), Sally Hope (9), Mulatto Mary (2), Giles Scroggins (4), Industry (4), Tariff (1), Red Gauntlet (3), Walk-in-the-Water (1)	10	27
1828	20	Delilah (3), Flirtilla Jr. (2), Lancet (1), General Brooke (3), Longwaist (5), Miss Mattie (4), Norfolk (1), Patsey Colbert (1), Roxana (2), Zinganee (2)	10	24	Sally Hope (10), Crusader (2), Cadmus (1), Industry (2), Kate Karney (4), Sally Trent (1), Mulatto Mary (2)	7	22
1829	12	Delila (1), Herr Cline (8), Orange Boy (2), Primrose (1), Whale Bone (1)	5	13	Sally Hope (1), Industry (3), May Day (1), Eliza Splotch (1), Kate Karney (1), Waxy (4), Phenomena (1), Polly Jones (2), Charlotte Temple (4)	9	18

Year				
1830	17	American (1), Charles Kemble (6), Fanny Cline (5), Hibernia (4), Mary Clay (1), Lubly Rose (1), Lauderdale (2), Hebrew (1), Lady Archiana (1)	9	Red Gauntlet (1), Corporal Trim (2), Kate Karney (3), Pandora (1), Sally Trent (1), I.C. (1), Charlotte Temple (5), Gabriella (1), Polly Jones (4), Eliza Riley (2), May Day (3), Mercury (1), Morgiana (2), Snake (1), Virginia Taylor (3), Jemima Wilkinson (3)	16 34
1831	10	Black Heath (7), Nancy Blunt (7), Rushlight (1)	3	Pandora (2), Charlotte Temple (1), I.C. (1), Gabriella (1), Polly Jones (2), Avarilla (1), Damper (1), Dashall (1), Hudibras (1), May Day (1), Jemima Wilkinson (3), Virginia Taylor (2), Roxana (1), Lancet (1), Wild-Bill-of-the-Woods (5), General Brooke (1), Longwaist (1)	17 26

RACING RECORD OF SIR ARCHIE'S SONS AND DAUGHTERS

Year	Number of foals Recorded	LISTED UNDER FOALING YEAR			LISTED UNDER WINNING YEAR		
		Names of Winners and Number of Wins	Total Winners	Total Races Won	Names of Winners and Number of Wins	Total Winners	Total Races Won
1832	2	0			Lady Jackson (1), Eliza Riley (1), Virginia Taylor (4), Delilah (2), Flirtilla Jr. (1), General Brooke (1), Longwaist (1), Miss Mattie (2), Norfolk (1), Roxana (1), Patsey Colbert (1), Zinganee (2), Herr Cline (4), Orange Boy (1), Whale Bone (1)	15	24
1833	0	0			Bacchus (1), May Day (1), Delilah (1), Flirtilla Jr. (1), General Brooke (1), Longwaist (3), Miss Mattie (2), Herr Cline (1), Orange Boy (1), Primrose (1), Charles Kemble (1), Fanny Cline (2), Hibernia (1), Lubly Rose (1), Delila (1)	15	19

1834	Hebrew (1), Herr Cline (2), Hibernia (2), Charles Kemble (2), Fanny Cline (1), Black Heath (3), Nancy Blunt (3)	7	14
1835	Herr Cline (1), American (1), Hibernia (1), Charles Kemble (3), Fanny Cline (2), Lady Archiana (1), Black Heath (4), Nancy Blunt (4), Rushlight (1)	9	18
1836	Mary Clay (1), Lauderdale (2)	2	3
1837	......		
1838	Mohican (1)	1	1
Winning Year Unknown	Henrietta (2), Waxy (7), Tecumseh (Few)	3	9+

❦ SUMMARY ❦

Crops: 22

   Number of Foals:
      Foaling date known   298
      Foaling date unknown   68
      Total recorded   366
      Average per crop   16.6

   Number of Winners:
      Foaling date known   116
      Foaling date unknown   2
      Total recorded winners   118
      Percentage of winners   32.2

   Number of Races Won:
      By horses with known foaling dates   526+
      By horses with unknown foaling dates   2
      Total races won   528+
      Races per winner   4.48
      Races per foal   1.45

   Number of years in which races were won   24

❦ NOTES ❦

CHAPTER ONE

Sir Archie's Ancestors

THE literature of the horse's ancestry and emergence into its present form, with its association with man from early antiquity, is profuse. An informative and readable book for the layman is Arthur Vernon, *The History and Romance of the Horse*. The evolution of the horse in America is noticed scientifically in William B. Scott, *Land Mammals of the Western Hemisphere*, pp. 290-301. A. E. T. Watson, in *Encyclopedia of Sport*, II, 178, offers his bleak complaint about the difficulty of researching ancient horse races and refuses to exploit such research in his essay on breeding and training of race horses.

Mrs. Blanchard consulted a vast number of authorities for the preliminary essay of her seven-volume study of Sir Archie's career (hereinafter cited as *Blanchard*), and in Volume I, pp. 1-53, offers a fairly comprehensive study of early racing, particularly as developed in England. Gervase Markham's oddly-phrased remark on English horses outrunning "Barbaries" is in *The Booke of the English Husbandman*, p. 85, and is quoted, not quite accurately, in *Blanchard*, I, 13-14.

The Byerly Turk, the Darley Arabian, and the Godolphin Arabian are respectfully mentioned in every work on horse breeding, including the more comprehensive general encyclopedias. A good brief essay on the trio, with their chief lines of descent, is in James Douglas Anderson, *Making the American Thoroughbred* (hereinafter cited as *Anderson*), pp. 19-29. *Blanchard*, I, 19-47, employs this work and others in a longer notice of the three foundation sires. The extraordinary legends of the Godolphin Arabian were the subject of a melodramatic tale by Eugene Sue, translated for the London Sunday *Times* as *The Godolphin Arabian; or, the History of a Thoroughbred* and issued as a paperback volume in 1845.

John Lewis Hervey's *Racing in America* (hereinafter cited as *Hervey*), I, 1-108, tells with magnificent and comprehensive authority the rise of breeding and racing of horses in the American colonies. This work was much consulted in a consideration of the same subject in *Blanchard*, I, 54-67.

Quarter racing in Colonial and post-Revolutionary America, with its influence on breeding and racing, is described in *Hervey*, I, 23-25, 156-57, and *Blanchard*, I, 177-86.

The history of imported Diomed, with special notice of Castianira, is made a separate chapter in *Hervey*, I, 167-89. Says Hervey: "Had [John] Hoomes done nothing but import Diomed and [John] Tayloe [III] nothing but import Castianira, they would read their title clear to joint immortality." See also *Blanchard*, IV, 114-22. A report that Castianira failed utterly on American tracks seems false, as the stud book of John Tayloe III says under the date of May 20, 1800: "By a bett won this day in the Richmond sweepstakes, beating Mr. Hoskin's highly thought of filley Celerity for this [bet] $60." Castianira was Tayloe's entry in the race and must have won.

Diomed's career on turf and at stud is summarized in the *American Turf Register and Sportsman's Herald* (hereinafter cited as *ATR*), II, 521-25, and a British certificate of Castianira's ancestry is quoted in *ibid.*, pp. 367-68, as bearing in Tayloe's handwriting on the back: "This filley is in the hands of Archie Randolph Esq., to breed on halves with J. Tayloe, 4 April 1803." An undated note in Tayloe's stud book mentions Castianira as "put to breeding in partnership with Captain Archie Randolph of Cumberland."

Tayloe's note on Castianira's produce in his stud book says: "1805 May 1st. By a bay colt...." This does not necessarily mean that Sir

Notes

Archie was foaled on that specific day; Tayloe dates two more of Castianira's produce, Miss Monroe in 1806 and Hephestion in 1807, as produced on May 1. That was the official birthday for any Thoroughbred of a specific season. Most evidence indicates that Sir Archie was foaled well before May 1, 1805.

CHAPTER TWO

Sir Archie Struggles in His Youth

ARCHIE RANDOLPH is identified with the "weaker strain" of the Randolphs in H. J. Eckenrode, *The Randolphs: the Story of a Virginia Family*, pp. 173-74, 179, where the story of the family scandal is told. Jay and Audrey Walz have made this event and the ensuing trial the plot of their novel, *The Bizarre Sisters*. Little record survives of the rather unhappy Captain Randolph beyond his haphazard connection with the foaling and early training of Sir Archie.

Nathaniel Burwell's career at Carter Hall, where Captain Randolph and Sir Archie moved from Ben Lomond, is from Charles Randolph Hughes, "Old Chapel," *Clarke County, Virginia*, pp. 27-28. The house and stables are still standing. The weird story of Hoomes' death is in *Hervey*, I, 180-81.

Tayloe's stud book includes information on Castianira's foals other than Sir Archie. See also Alexander Mackay-Smith, *Thoroughbred in the Lower Shenandoah Valley, 1785-1842* (hereinafter cited as *Mackay-Smith*), p. 16, and *Hervey*, I, 195.

Blanchard, IV, 124-25, quotes Archie Randolph's letter of May 15, 1807, to Tayloe and carefully gathers all evidence as to Sir Archie's colthood wanderings from plantation to plantation.

The best horses of the early 1800's are noticed in *Hervey*, I, 181ff.

See *Blanchard*, IV, 126, for some notice of Sir Archie's earliest training. The actual regime, as followed by Arthur Taylor, is described in *The Gentleman's New Pocket Farrier, etc.*, as published in 1830, with appendices and pedigrees by Peter Cottom (hereinafter cited as *Cottom*), pp. 366-67.

Distemper and its treatment in Sir Archie's time is described in *Cottom*, pp. 123-24. Preventive inoculations and other modern veterinary care have reduced the danger of this ailment.

Notes

Accounts of Sir Archie's races are few and brief, and these are ably mustered in *Hervey*, I, 196-97, and *Blanchard*, IV, 126-30. Of his first race, *ATR*, I, 283, says briefly that Sir Archie was "utterly distanced" by Bright Phoebus. His second race is well described in a notice of the career of Palafox, signed "J. G. G.," in *ATR*, II, 367-68. The strange inability of Sir Archie's early owners to appreciate him has mystified every commentator, and *Hervey*, I, 195-96, considers the shortsightedness of the otherwise able John Tayloe III fantastic.

William R. Johnson, who saw Sir Archie's wasted talents and developed him into a champion, is skilfully characterized in *Hervey*, II, 77-88. *Mrs. Blanchard*, IV, 130-33, gathers much material on him. He is a vivid memory in his native Warrenton, where data is being assembled for something like a comprehensive memoir.

CHAPTER THREE

Sir Archie Outshines the Racers

THE rise of the Roanoke Region, of which Warren County was the heart, to turf preeminence around the turn of the eighteenth century is summarized in *Hervey*, I, 156-57, with notice of the importance of Marmaduke and William Johnson. Some description of Warren County's golden age is in E. W. Montgomery, *Sketches of Old Warrenton, North Carolina*. Members of the Warren County Historical Society have supplied a number of local traditions.

William Johnson's house, largely rebuilt, still stands in Warrenton and is occupied today. Arthur Taylor is almost as much a legend in Warren County as his employer. *Hervey*, II, 82, tells something of Taylor's early career as a jockey, and *Blanchard*, IV, 138ff., quotes a delightful reminiscence of Taylor in later years, dated August 1, 1832.

Ibid., pp. 135-37, summarizes the triumphant racing career of Sir Archie in 1809 and 1810. *Hervey*, I, 196-97, covers the same subject more briefly. Contemporary records of Sir Archie's races are disappointingly scarce and brief.

Notes

CHAPTER FOUR

Sir Archie Outshines the Sires

A COPY of the 1810 advertisement of Sir Archie's first season at stud, signed by Allen Jones Davie, is among Mrs. Blanchard's papers and includes Johnson's offer to back Sir Archie against any horse in the world at four-mile heats.

Names of mares sent to Sir Archie and colts and fillies got from them are from the three-volume list of Sir Archie's get by Mrs. Blanchard (hereinafter cited as *Sir Archie's Get*). The sons and daughters are listed alphabetically, with reference to a host of stud books, contemporary turf publications, newspapers, and memoirs.

Blanchard, IV, 140-42, tells of Allen Davie's ownership of Sir Archie and several leasings of his services. *Hervey*, I, 198, says that the younger Davie "though a good horseman proved a poor manager and became involved in the financial bog...." Hervey says that Davie gambled much and foolishly, and that Sir Archie was given to William Amis "to pay a debt thus incurred, Davie having borrowed the money to liquidate it from William Amis...." Amis family traditions say that John D. Amis claimed to have won Sir Archie at cards from Davie.

Careers of Sir Archie's racing sons and daughters of the years 1811 and 1812 are from *Sir Archie's Get, passim*. *Hervey*, I, 202-5, lists the most notable winning sons, and 208-9, the daughters most successful as winners and dams. Special attention is paid to the irregular but brilliant tale of Walk-in-the-Water in *Hervey*, I, 206-7; *Blanchard*, IV, 146-52; and the turf reminiscences of Balie Peyton included in *Anderson*, pp. 253-57.

CHAPTER FIVE

Sir Archie Reigns at Mowfield

THE house at Mowfield still stands, unoccupied and bare but otherwise fairly well preserved and impressive. *Blanchard*, IV, traces the family descent as from England, pp. 61, 183-97, 227-32. An Amis

Notes

genealogy in possession of Mr. Willie Jones Long of Longview, Northampton County, North Carolina, traces to French Huguenot ancestors.

William Amis' first handbill advertising Sir Archie is considered an interestingly individual example of such publication by turf experts. Fairfax Harrison called it the best of its kind ever to come to his attention.

The events of the 1817 Charleston Race Week are described in John B. Irving, *The South Carolina Jockey Club*, pp. 31-33, and Irving's *A Day on Cooper River*, pp. 190-91, remembers the elaborate pageantry of such events. See also *Hervey*, I, 160-62.

Lady Lightfoot's career after her 1817 triumphs at Charleston is summarized from all sources in *Sir Archie's Get*, II, 393-99. See also *Hervey*, II, 29-30.

Blanchard, IV, 58, 60-65, describes John D. Amis' ambition to publish an American stud book.

Timoleon's tremendous racing triumphs are in *Sir Archie's Get*, III, 291-300. Johnson's praise of him did not cancel that turfman's belief that Sir Archie was the greatest race horse of all time. See *Hervey*, I, 197.

The phenomenal rise of American Eclipse, with his triumphs that led to the challenge to an intersectional match race, are well told in *Hervey*, I, 260-62.

CHAPTER SIX

Sir Archie Glories in His Children

SEVERAL fine contemporary reportages of the Eclipse–Henry race survive. Of these, by far the best are the narrative of Cadwallader Colden, in *ATR*, II, 4-12, and a story in the New York *National Advocate*, May 23, 1823. *Hervey*, I, 263-69, uses these and others in a consideration of the event, and in *ibid.*, II, 73-74, is quoted an eye-witness account by Josiah Quincy, Jr., interesting for details of the behavior of John Randolph of Roanoke and something of how Arthur Taylor was persuaded to ride Henry in the third heat.

Mrs. Blanchard's painstaking research identified Uncle Hardy, Sir Archie's personal attendant at Mowfield, though this information is to be found only in her notes. See *Blanchard*, IV, 50-51, for details of the

Notes

last days of William Amis. William Amis' will is in the 1824 Will Book at the Northampton County Courthouse, Jackson, North Carolina, and bears the date October 3, 1823, with official probate recorded as of the March term of court, 1824.

CHAPTER SEVEN

Sir Archie Figures in Politics

OF the Alvan Fisher likeness of Sir Archie, Alexander Mackay-Smith writes: "It is unfortunate that the only portrait of Sir Archie painted during his lifetime was executed by an artist who knew so little about portraying horses and their anatomy. The picture is anything but convincing." *Hervey*, I, 210, is somewhat kinder: "Fisher was not a finished artist. However, that he produced a lifelike portrait is conceded...." The original, now in the collection of Mrs. George A. Ellis, Jr., of Hot Springs, Virginia, is the basis for all later pictures of Sir Archie.

A photoduplication of John Amis' letter to Richard Singleton is among Mrs. Blanchard's papers, and is quoted, with comments, in *Blanchard*, IV, 58. The plan for Feild's stud book is discussed in *Mackay-Smith*, pp. 42-43, and a facsimile of his published prospectus is in *ibid.*, p. 41.

The career of Robert Potter, which so curiously affected the life and memory of Sir Archie, is described in Ernest Charles Shearer, *Robert Potter, Remarkable North Carolinian and Texan*, a biography not wholly apologistic. Bishop Joseph Blount Cheshire also wrote about Potter in *Nonnulla: Memories, Stories, Traditions, More or Less Authentic*. But the most revealing record of Potter's adventures and emotions, particularly those he experienced in the town of Halifax just across the Roanoke River from Sir Archie's home, are his own supremely invective pamphlets against Bynum and other Halifaxians, as well as Bynum's only slightly less angry "Exposition," which works are mentioned and quoted in the present account. Bynum's writings may be the more accurate, because the less emotional. Direct quotation of what the various actors said in this lively political melodrama has been difficult to achieve, except where the rivals agreed on what was said by whom.

Notes

In 1903, when Mrs. Blanchard first visited North Carolina in search of family records and material concerning Sir Archie, Bishop Cheshire told her: "Well, yes—Sir Archie was owned by Billy Amis.... Billy Amis was nothing—a nobody." The lady protested, but Bishop Cheshire insisted: "I can't help it. Billy Amis was nothing and a nobody, he got his reputation from the loins of a horse." See *Blanchard*, IV, 2. The Bishop's opinion somewhat echoes Potter's charges in the enchantingly scurrilous *Head of Medusa* and indicates that Potter succeeded in damaging the character of at least one enemy.

CHAPTER EIGHT

Sir Archie Is Assailed by Scandal

FAIRFAX HARRISON, *The Roanoke Stud*, deals with the breeding and racing of horses by John Randolph of Roanoke, and pages 55-58 consider the so-called Sir Archie Scandal.

Contemporary account is fairly extensive in the form of letters in *ATR* and the *American Farmer* (hereinafter referred to as *AF*). Archibald Harrison, in *ATR*, V, 600, remembers Randolph's discussion of the scandal at the Virginia Hot Springs. Another reminiscence of the same event is that of John Stuart Skinner, in *ibid.*, VI, 66, including Randolph's professed belief that Greenfield had written the Waverly Novels. General T. M. Forman's letter of inquiry in *AF*, July 22, 1826, with Tayloe's reply insisting on Diomed's sireship of Sir Archie in *ibid.*, July 20, 1826, are quoted in the present account. J. M. Selden's comprehensive account of his own researches and his conversation with Harrison was published in *ATR*, V, 601, in reply to the insinuations signed "Fair Play." Randolph's attempt to quiet the scandal, dated April 17, 1830, is in *ibid.*, I, 462.

Gabriel's respected career as racer and stallion is outlined in *ATR*, I, 173-74, in the same issue with memoirs of Sir Archie and Diomed. Gabriel's descent continued to run well on Western tracks for decades.

Files of the *National Intelligencer* carry announcements of the fall meetings of the Washington Jockey Club and the Maryland Association for 1827, and on September 11 of that year, the *Intelligencer* reprinted the protest in the Warrenton *Reporter* of September 6 with the disarming reply.

Notes

Comments of "A Bit of a Jockey" were reprinted in *AF*, December 2, 1825.

Announcement of entries in the 1830 National Colt Stake was first made in *ATR*, I, 362.

The story of Walk-in-the-Water's gallant old-age victory at Natchez is told by Balie Peyton in *Anderson*, pp. 355-57.

CHAPTER NINE

Sir Archie Fulfills His Destiny

CADWALLADER COLDEN thrillingly tells of the National Colt Stake, May, 1830, in *ATR*, III, 91-93.

Walk-in-the-Water's last race is mentioned by Balie Peyton in *Anderson*, pp. 354-55, and is fully described in *ATR*, III, 379.

The hot-blooded romance of young Junius Amis is related in *Blanchard*, IV, 227-29. In later years, Junius Amis served in the North Carolina Legislature and eventually followed his parents to the West. *Ibid.*, p. 217, tells of John Long and Mary Amis at the Virginia Hot Springs, crediting the story to their kinswoman, the widow of General Junius Daniel.

Davie's manifest dislike of the Amises, with its reflection in his attacks on the Amis method of horse breeding, is carefully considered in *ibid.*, pp. 50-59. See also *ATR*, IV, 517-18, and *ibid.*, VII, 9.

Mrs. Blanchard found and kept the hair from Sir Archie's tail as a family heirloom. Her efforts to trace the preserved hoof were unavailing.

CHAPTER TEN

Sir Archie Lives in His Descendants

THE riderless victory of Pelham and the impromptu race of three Sir Archies are described in *Blanchard*, IV, 204-5, quoting letters to *ATR*.

The rough-and-tumble adventures of young William Amis in Northampton County politics are vividly described in a typescript narrative

Notes

by the late Caldwell Hardy of Bertie County, *Northampton: An Historical Sketch of the County, Past and Present*, apparently meant for publication in a local paper. Amis, says Hardy, "was a Whig, and young, talented, brave and chivalrous."

The career of Trifle is well set forth in *Hervey*, II, 112-15. *Blanchard*, VI, 200-23, covers the career of Timoleon, and *ibid.*, VII, 103-99, that of Lexington. Among Mrs. Blanchard's notes is a diagrammed pedigree of Man O'War, tracing him back to Sir Archie through Lexington's daughter Aerolite. Man o'War, himself the most successful stallion of recent times, transmitted the Sir Archie blood to a host of later winners.

❦ BIBLIOGRAPHY ❦

Sources for the present work numbered hundreds of books, serial publications, and manuscripts. A few of the most important and most interesting are here listed.

Books and Pamphlets

Anderson, James Douglas. *Making the American Thoroughbred.* Norwood, Mass., 1916. Some good streamlined history of breeding and racing of horses in America, particularly the South, with republished reminiscences of Balie Peyton.

Bynum, Jesse A. *An Exposition of the Misrepresentation Contained in a Publication issued by Robert Potter....* Halifax, N.C., 1825. A pamphlet more restrained and therefore less fascinating than Potter's own publications of the political melodrama of the Bynum–Potter campaign for the legislature. Includes a fairly long and laudatory account of John D. Amis of Mowfield.

Cottom, Peter, (ed.). *The Gentleman's New Pocket Farrier, by Richard Mason, M.D....* Richmond, Va., 1830. This is the important little work known to collectors as Cottom. It includes a historical sketch called *Annals of the Turf*, the first published attempt at an

Bibliography

American stud book, and rules for training and racing as followed at the time.

Edgar, Patrick Nisbett. *The American Race-Turf Register, Sportsman's Record and General Stud Book....* New York, N.Y., 1833. Known as Edgar. Far more comprehensive than Cottom, but full of mistakes. Nevertheless invaluable.

Harrison, Fairfax. *Early American Turf Stock, 1720-1780,* Richmond, Va., 1934. Important for understanding the genesis of the American Thoroughbred.

────── *Equine F.F.V.'s.* Richmond, Va., 1928. Also important Thoroughbred history, with something about Diomed.

────── *The Roanoke Stud.* Richmond, Va., 1930. The turf career of John Randolph of Roanoke, discussing his part in the Sir Archie scandal.

Hervey, John Lewis. *Racing in America, 1665-1865.* 2 vols. New York, N.Y., 1944. Privately printed, this handsome and informative work is an absolute necessity for any student of American turf history. A large part of the work concerns Sir Archie and his descents.

Mackay-Smith, Alexander. *The Thoroughbred in the Lower Shenandoah Valley, 1785-1842.* Winchester, Va., 1948. This regional study provides some light on Sir Archie's early career, as well as information on early attempts at preparing a stud book.

Potter, Robert. *An Account of the Attempt Made by JESSE A. BYNUM, Attended by Several Armed Associates, to murder ROBERT POTTER....* Halifax, N.C., 1825. The Amis name gets into this diatribe, too.

────── *The Head of Medusa, a Mock-Heroic Poem....* Halifax, N.C., 1827. A veritable jewel of unrestrained invective in verse, with ill-tempered flavory preface and notes. Includes an assault on the character and appearance of John D. Amis that is fantastically insulting.

────── *A STATEMENT by ROB. POTTER of the circumstances connected with the affair between JESSE A. BYNUM and himself....* Halifax, N.C., 1824. The first publication in this grotesque

Bibliography

and delightful exchange. Between the angry lines shows a picture of the political times.

Scott, William Berryman. *Land Mammals of the Western Hemisphere.* New York, N.Y., 1937. Includes an authoritative essay on the descent of the horse.

Magazines and Publications

Most important by far are contemporary issues of the *American Farmer* and the *American Turf Register and Sporting Magazine*, both published in Baltimore and both full of news and information about Sir Archie. Of newspapers, chiefly informative were contemporary issues of the *Free Press*, Halifax, N.C.; the *Intelligencer*, Petersburg, Va.; the *National Intelligencer*, Washington, D.C.; and the *Reporter*, Warrenton, N.C.

Manuscripts

Mrs. Blanchard's papers include hundreds of photostats, photo-duplications, and typewritten copies of letters, notes, and family records. Among these are a number of items of Amis family correspondence, collected in many parts of the country. Her own writings of importance are seven bound volumes of typescript that include material for a biography of Sir Archie and a three-volume typewritten list of his sons and daughters, painstakingly annotated. All this material is now at the Louis Round Wilson Library of the University of North Carolina, Chapel Hill, N.C.

❧ INDEX ❧

(The Index has been divided into two parts: General Index and Horses)

General Index

Adams, Mrs. Howard, 196
Adams, Pres. John Quincy, 148
Alexander, Col. Mark, 58
Alexandria, Va. (racing at), 12
Allen, John, 96
Alsobrook, —, 117
Alston, William, 77
Alston, Willis, 51, 136
American Antiquarian Society, 196
American Farmer, 144, 148, 153, 156
American Notes, Charles Dickens, 140
American Stud Book, 167
American stud books, planned. *See* Stud books
American Turf Register, 167
American Turf Register and Sporting Magazine, 156
American Turf Register, Sportsman's Herald and General Stud Book, 177
Amis, Elizabeth, 179

Amis, John, 70
Amis, John Dillard, 66, 72, 73, 83, 85, 93, 107-21 *passim*, 131, 133, 134, 150, 160, 162, 166, 167, 170-72, 176, 178, 183
Amis, Junius, 109, 170-72, 174-75, 183
Amis, Mary (daughter of William Amis). *See* Mary Amis Long
Amis, Mary (daughter of John Dillard Amis), 108, 109, 111, 170, 175, 183; PORTRAIT OF, facing 162
Amis, Mary Dillard, 71
Amis, Susan, 107; PORTRAIT OF, facing 162
Amis, Thomas (of England), 70
Amis, Thomas (founder of family in America), 70
Amis, Thomas (of Virginia), 70
Amis, Thomas (son of John Amis), 71
Amis, Thomas (son of John Dillard Amis), 109, 170, 183

Index

Amis, William, 15, 39, 59, 68, 70-75, 107-9, 176
Amis, William (son of John Dillard Amis), 109, 111, 123-34 *passim*, 150, 170, 182; PORTRAIT OF, facing 162
Amis family, 70-74
Annals of the Turf, 149
Annapolis, Md. (racing at), 12
Annual Post Stakes, 42
Appomattox River, 14
Atherton, Col. Jephta, 13-14, 39
Atherton, Jesse, 39
Atherton, Wade, 39

Badger, Bela, 94
Baltimore, Md. (racing at), 12, 111, 154-56, 172, 181
Barnes, Lavinia, 122-23
Barnes family, 113
Barnum, Gen. —, 104
Barringer, Daniel L, 136
Barton Turf, England, 70
Belfield (racing at), 25, 46-47, 65, 83
Bell, John, 107, 109
Ben Lomond, 16, 17, 21
Benton, Sen. Thomas Hart, 149
Bey of Tunis, 7
Bioren, —, 83
"Bit of a Jockey, A" (pseud.), 147
Blair, the Rev. Dr. James, 10, 12
Bowling Green, the, 15
Boyd, R. J., 170
Bristol, Lord, 8
Broadnax, William Edward, 54, 56, 57, 59, 60, 67, 85
Broad Rock, Va. (racing at), 172, 181
Brown, Dr. Gustavus, 61, 82
Brown, Peter, 77, 80
Brunswick Co., Va., 54
Buckley, John, 98-99, 100, 101
Bullocke, James, 10
Bunbury, Sir Charles, 148
Burges, Thomas, 113-39 *passim*
Burnham, Michael, 91, 104
Burwell, Lucy, 21

Burwell, Col. Nathaniel, 21
Byerly, Captain —, 7
Bynum, Elizabeth, 73
Bynum, Jesse Atherton, 112-38, 150
Bynum, Wade, 66, 113-31 *passim*

"Cabin Point," 57
Carney, Gen. Stephen W., 13, 38, 46
Carter Hall, 21, 22
Caswell, Gov. Richard, 71
Central Course, Baltimore, 158
Charles I, 6
Charles II, 6
Charles (a slave), 144, 158
Charleston, S.C. (racing at), 77, 82-83, 93, 172
Cheney's *Racing Calendar*, 8
Chester, England (racing at), 6
Clairbourne, Phil, 64, 67, 81
Clanton, L., 127, 128
Clarke, Alexander, 11
Clay, Henry 149
Coates, Henry, 63
Colden, Cadwallader Rennselaer, 98, 100-2, 162-66
Coles, Gen. Nathaniel, 86
Colt Stake, 77
Colt Sweepstakes, 150
Columbia, S.C. (racing at), 172
Cottom, Peter, 166-67
Cox, Captain —, 96
Crafts, Billy, 97-99
Craig, John, 150, 172
Cromwell, Oliver, 6
Cutler, Dr. —, 59

"D" (pseud.), 177
Daniel, Judge J. J., 126, 128
Daniel, John, 117
Daniel, John Reeves Jones, 113-37 *passim*
Darley, —, 7
Davie, Allan Jones, 52-57, 60, 63-64, 67-68, 73, 176-77; PORTRAIT OF, facing 163
Davie, Sarah Jones, 51

Index

Davie, Gen. William R., 49-52, 67
Davis, Sarah, 183
Davis, Dr. Stephen, 183
Dawson, Jesse A., 119, 120
Dawson, John, 39
Dawson family, 113
Derby, first, 8
Dialectic Society, 55
Dickens, Charles, 140
Drew, John, 39
Drew, William, 128
Duke, –, 180
Duval, Dr. –, 155

Eaton, Benjamin C., 127, 128
Eaton, Maj. John R., 59
Edgar, Patrick Nisbett, 135, 177
Emmett, R., 104
Eohippus, 3, 185
Epsom, England (racing at), 8
Evans, Dr. George, 35
Evening Post (New York), 91

"F" (pseud.), 153
Fagen, Peter, 57
Fairfield Sweepstakes, 25, 29, 33
"Fair Play" (pseud.), 157
Fairview Course, 94
Faison, Herod, 182
Feild, Theophilus, 104, 121, 134-35, 145, 167
Fenner, Dixie C., 136
Fenner's Tavern, 113, 118, 122, 124, 130
Fisher, Alvan, 108, 110, 111
Forman, Gen. T. M., 146, 153
Forrest, Bedford, 20
Forrest, John, 60
Forrest, Jona, 62
Forrest, Jonathan, 58
Foxhall, Thomas, 168-69
Fulton, Robert, 91

Gazette (Virginia), 11
General Stud Book, of England, 11
General Stud Book, Weatherby, 83

Gentleman's New Pocket Farrier, 166
Gist, Samuel, 11
Godolphin, Lord, 7
Gogmagog Hall, 7
Goode, John, 81, 85
Goode, Thomas, 16, 25
Green, –, 77
Greenfield, William, 144, 149
Grove, the, 38, 115, 139
Gumberry District, Northampton Co., N.C., 71

Hagerstown, Md. (racing at), 82, 86
Halifax, N.C., 113; racing at, 83
Hall, Charles Henry, 108
Hamilton, John, 39
Hamlin, Col. W. J., 66
Hampton, Wade, I, 75
Hampton, Wade, III, 20
Handicap Purse, 84, 93
Hardy, Uncle (Sir Archie's groom), 108, 109, 110, 167, 198
Hare, Otway P., 92, 96, 102
Harrison, Archibald, 144, 145
Harrison, James, 76, 78, 88, 89
Harrison, James J., 58, 60, 62-63, 122, 135, 161, 166, 177
Harrison, Nathan, 58
Harrison, Nathaniel, 11
Harrison, Randolph, 21
Hascock, A., 104
Haskins, Thomas, 25
Hawkins, Celeste, 170-72
Hawkins, P., 59
Hawkins, Gov. William, 170
Haxall, William, 43
Head of Medusa, The, 137
Hempstead Plains, L.I. (racing at), 9, 87
Herbert, Henry William, 194
High Hills of Santee, the, 77
Highmettled Racer, The (song), 78
Holliday's Store, 125
Hoomes, Col. John, 15-16, 22, 25

Index

Hot Springs, Va., 145
Hyde Park, England (racing at), 6

Intelligencer (Petersburg, Va.), 52, 56, 149
Irby, Edmund, 64
Irby, Edmund, Jr., 148

Jackson, Andrew, 39
Jackson, Gen. Thomas J. ("Stonewall"), 12
Jamaica, N.Y. (racing at), 95
James I, 6
Jamestown, Va., 9
Jefferson, Pres. Thomas, 29
Jeffrey, George Washington, 122, 149, 167
Jockey Club Purse, 42, 172, 173, 181
Johnson, Marmaduke, 13, 32, 35-36, 38, 57-58, 63, 82, 92
Johnson, Mary, 35
Johnson, Robert, 83, 84, 92
Johnson, Samuel, 8
Johnson, William Ransom, 25, 32-33, 35, 39-40, 44-50, 54, 55, 59-64 *passim*, 76, 81-98 *passim*, 103-6, 112, 142, 161, 166, 172, 179, 183; PORTRAIT OF, facing 163
Jones, Col. Allan, 57
Jones, Allen, 13-14, 38
Jones, Harold, 54
Jones, Mary Montford, 115
Jones, Robert A., 116, 167, 172
Jones, Sarah, 51
Jones, Willie, 13, 38, 115, 117

Kendall's training track, 181
King George Court House (racing at), 62
King's Plates, 8

Lancaster, Pa. (racing at), 173
Lansford, S.C., 176
Lapham, J., 85
Larkin, Thomas, 17, 24, 26, 27, 29, 31, 40, 61, 158

Lee, Robert E., 20
Livingston, John, 91
Livingston, Robert, 91
Livingston, Walter, 161
Lockhart, Col. William B., 108, 182
Long, Benjamin S., 123
Long, James, 183, 184
Long, John, 175
Long, Lemuel, 73, 81, 92, 93, 109, 175
Long, Mary, 109
Long, Mary Amis, 72, 73, 112, 175
Long, Col. Nicholas, 73
Long Island, N.Y. *See* Union Course
Louis XV, 7
Lucy Walker (steamer), 183
Ludlow, —, 107

McClellan, George B., 20
MacKay-Smith, Alexander, 194
Macklin, Henry, 59
Macon, Nathaniel, 37-38, 142
McPherson, Gen. John, 77
Mansion House, 116
Markham, Gervase, 6
Marlborough, Md. (racing at), 85
Maryland Association, 154
Mason, Dick, 182
Mason, Dr. Richard, 167
Maughn, Peyton, 67
Moody, Banks, 42
Moore, Col. James, 54
Morton, Joseph, 11
Mosby, Wade, 25
Mount Airy, 15, 23; ILLUSTRATED, facing 146
Mount Gallant, 38-39
Mowfield Plantation, 66, 69-90, 107, 109, 110, 112, 188; ILLUSTRATED, facing 26
Mud Castle, 70

Nashville, Tenn. (racing at), 168-70
Nat (a slave), 17, 145, 158
Natchez, Miss. (racing at), 151-53
National Colt Stake. *See* Union Course

Index

National Intelligencer (Washington, D.C.), 155
New Hope Plantation, 50, 67, 73
New Market, England (racing at), 6
New Market, L.I. (racing at), 9
New Market, Va. (racing at), 14, 42-43, 60, 62-63, 65, 81-82, 86, 93, 111
New Orleans, La. (racing at), 184-85
Niblo, William, 91, 104
Nicolls, Gov. Richard, 9, 10
Norfleet, Thomas, 58
Nottaway, Va. (racing at), 93

Oakland, 35
Oaklands, 81
"Observator" (pseud.), 167-68

"Panton" (pseud.), 177
Parker, Edward, 155
Penn, William, 10
Perkins, Robert, 127
Petersburg, Va. (racing at), 14
Pettway, Sheriff —, 113, 117, 121, 125
Peyton, Balie, 169
"Philip" (pseud. of John Randolph of Roanoke), 157
"Pliny" (pseud.), 132
Plummer, Hannah, 37-38, 142
Plummer, Kemp, 35-36
Pocahontas, 21
"Political College," 136
Poseidon, 4
Potter, Robert, 114-40, 150, 153; PORTRAIT OF, facing 163
Price, Stephen, 91
Proprietor's Purse, 84
Purdy, Samuel, 97, 100-3

Quankey Place, 73
Quincy, Josiah, II, 96

Race Horse Region, The, 176
Race Week, Charleston, S.C., 75-77, 83-84
Racing Calendar of Cheney, 8

Randolph, Capt. Archie, 16, 21-22, 23, 59, 142-45, 149; PORTRAIT OF, facing 147
Randolph, John, of Roanoke, 12, 21, 29, 64, 92, 96, 101, 102, 106, 112, 135, 141-59, 167, 178; PORTRAIT OF, facing 163
Randolph, Nancy, 21
Randolph, Richard, 21
Ree, O., 79
Reporter (Warrenton, N.C.), 147, 154
Richard Coeur de Lion, 6
Richardson, Col. James B., 76-80, 93
Richmond, Va. (racing at), 14, 29
Ridgely, Gen. Charles, 96
Rienzi, 115
"Rienzi" (pseud.), 137
Roanoke Advocate, 171
Robinson, Abner, 60, 61-62
Rogers, Commodore —, 104
Rolfe, John, 21
Rosegill, 23

Salisbury, England (racing at), 6
Sandy (a jockey), 164-65
Sawyer, Lemuel, 136
Scotland Neck, N.C. (racing at), 47, 66, 83
Scott, Sir Walter, 144
Selden, James M., 17, 64, 144, 145, 158
Selden, Miles, 16, 25-30 *passim*, 42-49 *passim*, 54, 143, 144
"Senex" (pseud.), 168
Simmons, John W., 123
Shocco Springs, N.C., 171
Shrewsbury, Va. (racing at), 82
Silver Heels, 174, 183
Silver Plate Handicap, 80
Singleton, Col. Richard, 77, 79, 80, 81, 85, 121
Skinner, J. Stuart, 144, 149, 153, 156, 159, 178, 179
Smith, Harry Worcester, 196
South Carolina Jockey Club, 75, 77

Index

Southside, Va. (racing at), 14
Spann, Col. J. R., 92
Springfield, Ala. (racing at), 180-81
State Stakes, 184
Stevens, John C., 91
Stevens, John C., Jr., 90, 99, 104, 105-6, 161
Stevens, R. L., 161
Stockton, Commodore R. F., 155
Stuart, J. E. B., 20
Stud Book, General, of England, 11
Stud Book, General, Weatherby, 83
Stud books, Feild and Amis project, 112, 121-22, 134; Harrison project, 135; Randolph project, 135, 147-48
Stuyvesant, Peter, 9
Sully, Thomas, 108
Summeral, Hall, 167, 172, 178

Tarboro, N.C. (racing at), 65
Tayloe, Col. John, III, 15-16, 20, 23-24, 25, 61, 143, 147, 153-54, 178; PORTRAIT OF, facing 147
Taylor, Arthur, 40, 41, 48-49, 64, 93, 94, 96, 98, 102-3, 179
Taylor, Isabella, 139
Taylor, John, 77
Thoroughbred, definition, 8
Tree Hill, 16, 143, 144; racing at, 172, 181
Tucker's Paths (racing at), 13
Turner, Gov. James, 38

Union Course, Hempstead, L.I., 87-90, 95-104, 111, 150-51, 160-66, 173-74, 181
University of North Carolina, 50, 73, 136, 197

Van Mater, John, 161
Van Ness, Judge —, 104
Van Ranst, Cornelius, 87, 89-90, 97, 100

Virginia Herald (Fredericksburg, Va.), 26

Walden, John, 96-97, 98, 101, 102
War of 1812, 58
War of Independence, 12
Warren County, N.C., 34; racing at, 62, 65, 82
Warrenton, N.C., 32
Warrenton Academy, 35
Washington, George, 12, 29, 38
Washington, William, 75
Washington, D.C. (racing at), 64
Washington Course, 58, 75-77, 83-84
Washington Jockey Club, D.C., 154
Washington Sweepstakes, 27, 61
Watson, A. E. T., 5
Watson, Thomas, 77, 166
Waverly Novels, 144
Weatherby, James, 16
Weatherby's *General Stud Book*, 83
Weaver, Jared, 57, 58, 63, 66
White House (Amis residence), 73, 108
White's Hotel, Jackson, N.C., 182
Wickham, John, 64, 183
Wilburne, Susan, 71
Williams, Green Berry, 151-53, 168-69
Williams, William, 177
Williamsburg, Va. (racing at), 11-12, 14
Williamsburg Jockey Club, Va., 10
Wilson, Dr. —, 122
Wilson, Thomas Friend, 54
Wizer, —, 180
Wormeley, Ralph, IV, 23-27, 29, 31, 33, 178
Worsham, John, 62
Wyche, Dr. —, 104
Wynn, Gen. Williams, 59-66 *passim*, 76-84, 92, 93, 111

Index

Horses

Aerolite, 185
Alderman, 58
Alice Carneal, 184
Alice Gray, 181
Allan, 58, 59, 60
Allegranto, 38
Amanda, 25
American Eclipse. *See* Eclipse
Annoplede, 54
Arab, 151, 161
Archy Junior, 169

Babraham, 7
Bay Doe, 54
Beauty, 64
Bedford, 58, 59, 62, 77, 79, 160
Bellair, 73, 148
Bellona, 81
Bessy, 36
Bet Bounce, 57, 85
Betsey Abner, 176
Betsey Mitchel, 60, 62
Betsey Richards, 92-94, 105, 111
Black-Eyed Susan, 77-78, 79, 86
Black Maria, 61, 172, 173, 174, 181
Black Selima, 24
Blank, 7, 46-48, 49, 52, 63, 77, 79, 84
Blaze, 7
Blucher, 58, 59, 60, 111, 151-52
Bonnets of Blue, 161-66
Boston, 183-84; PORTRAIT OF, facing 106
Boxer, 81
Bright Phoebus, 29
Brown Bob, 58, 59
Bryan O'Lynn, 38
Bucephalus, 4
Bulle Rock, 10, 11
Butler, 20
Buzzard, 22, 58
Byerly Turk, 7, 8, 11

Calypso, 148
Camilla, 167, 172

Camsidel, 181
Carolinian, 64, 67, 85
Castel, 59, 60
Castianira, 16-17, 20, 21, 22, 24, 52, 135, 143-45, 146, 149, 150, 153, 157-58
Celer, Meade's, 35
Celerity, 16
Celeste, 161, 163
Centinel, 46
Chanticleer, 72-73
Childers, 89, 92-94, 106
Childers, Avery's, 61
Cicero, 172
Citizen, 38, 52, 59, 88
Cock of the Rock, 105
Columbia, 63, 64
Contention, 67, 85
Coquette, 63, 85, 150
Cormorant, 15
Corvisart, 93
Cripple, 7
Cypron, 8

Damsel, Miller's, 86
Dare Devil, 59, 64
Darley Arabian, 7, 8, 11, 59
Dimple, 7
Dinwiddie, 47
Diomed, 8, 15-16, 17, 20, 21, 24, 25, 30, 41, 47, 52, 54, 59, 64, 76, 86, 143-46, 153, 156, 157-58; PORTRAIT OF, facing 82
Diomeda, 16
Director, 56, 59, 60, 61, 62, 66, 76, 78, 107, 111
Dismal, 7
Doctor, 25
Dongolah, 57, 177
Dongolah saddle mare, J. Weaver's, 57, 63, 177
Dorimant, 156
Dormouse, 7
Druid, 59, 64, 81

Index

Duroc, 86, 106, 151, 161
Dutchess, 64

Eclipse, American, 85, 86, 87-88, 89, 90, 91, 94, 95, 97-106, 111, 146, 151, 161, 174
Eclipse, English, 8, 146
Eclipse, Richardson's, 77, 79

Fair Rosamond, 63
Fairy, 25
First Consul, 25, 85, 174
Flag of Truce, Schenck's, 87-88
Flirtilla, 111
Floretta, 25
Florizel, 8, 15
Florizel, Ball's, 24, 25, 27, 41, 60, 61, 64
Florizel, Worsham's, 83
Flying Childers, 7, 63, 173

Gabriel, 25, 143, 146-47, 149, 150, 153, 156, 157-58, 159
Gabriella, 148
Gallatin, 47, 151
Gamenut, 55
Gatiun, 52
General Jackson, 161, 163
Godolphin Arabian, 7, 8, 11, 145
Gohanna, 167
Grey Medley, 55

Harlequin, 147, 157
Harwood, 59, 60, 65, 82, 111
Heart of Oak, 87-88
Henry, 92-94, 96-106, 111, 146, 151, 172, 179
Hephestion, 22
Hermaphrodite, Price's, 161-66
Hermaphrodite (Swallow), 85-86
Highflyer, 8, 16
Hobgoblin, 7, 145, 146
Honeysuckle, 38

Industry, 181

Jane of the Green, 95, 106
Janus, 7, 35, 40, 85, 178
John Richards, 92-94, 151
Jonah, 25, 38

King Herod, 8
King Philip, 20
Kosciusko, 77, 180

Lady Bunbury, 64
Lady Burton, 63
Lady Jane, 77, 79
Lady Lightfoot, 60-61, 62, 64, 65, 66, 76, 77-78, 79, 80-81, 82, 85-86, 87-88, 172
Lady Rabbit, 59
Lady Relief, 173, 174
Lady Wilkinson, 173
Larry O'Gaff, 169
Lath, 7, 145
Lavinia, 16, 25
Lecomte, 184-85
Leonidas, 93
Lexington, 184-85; PORTRAIT OF, facing 182
Little Driver, 54
Little Johnny, 77, 80
Little Venus, 172
Little Witch, 78
Lottery, 59
Lycurgus, 77, 79

Madeira, 16
Magic, 38
Magnolio, 29
Magog, 54
Maid of the Oaks, 25
Man o' War, 185
Maria, 77-78, 80, 160
Maria, Haynie's, 25
Mark Anthony, 57
Markse, 8, 146
Marshall Ney, 169-70
Mary Dismal, 172
Mary Francis, 172
Mary Granville, 181

Index

Mary McHenry, 181
Matchem, 8
Matchless, 7
Medley, 36, 58, 63, 82
Meretrix, 54, 56, 59
Merino Ewe, 60-62, 76, 78, 80
Messenger, 29
Minerva, 44-46, 52
Miss Halifax, 64
Miss Monroe, 22, 54, 56
Miss Selden, 54
Moloch, 25, 30-31
Monkey, 11
Muckle John, 89
Mud Colt, 13
Mufti, 16

Northampton, 64

Optimus, 60, 61, 82
Orlando, Roe's, 78
Oscar, Ogle's, 25, 64, 143, 147, 156

Palafox, 25, 30-31, 52
Partner, 39
Peace Maker, 16, 25
Pegasus, 4
Pelham, 180-81
Phoenix, 38, 58, 64
Pilot (Wild-Bill-of-the-Woods), 160-66
Planter, 73
Playfair, 77, 79
Poll, 64, 81
Polly Pavell, 169
Postboy, 25, 143, 147, 156
Potomac, 25, 27, 44, 52, 60, 63, 77
Precipitate, 59
Princess, 93

Rainbow, 47
Rarity, 85
Ratler, Peeble's, 176
Rattray, 25, 44-45, 52
Reality, 63, 64, 65, 66, 81, 84, 85, 151, 161, 178

Reaphook, 63
Regulus, 7
Revenge, 61
Robert Burns, 20-21, 22, 23. *See also* Sir Archie
Robin Redbreast, 81, 85
Rockingham, 16
Roundhead, 7
Roxana, 7, 145
Rustic, 22

Saladin, 160
Sally Duffy, 59
Sally Waters, 184
Saltram, 62
Sambo, 63
Sarpedon, 184
Screamer, 172
Shakespeare, 146
Shark, 24, 41, 61
Sir Archie, breeding of, 17; birth of, 17; first named Robert Burns, 20; at Carter Hall, 22, at Mount Airy, 23; at Rosegill, 24; renamed, 24; sold, 24; described, 27; has distemper, 27-28; loses race, 29; sold to William Johnson, 33; at Warrenton, 33; wins at Richmond, 42; races Wrangler, 43; ends racing career, 49; sold to William R. Davie, 50; given to Allan J. Davie, 52; at stud, 52-53, 56-58; leased, 55, 56-58; leased to Edmund Irby, 64; sold to William Amis, 68; eight homes of, 69; at stud at Mowfield, 74-75; bequeathed to John D. Amis, 108; portrait painted, 108, 110; paternity debated, 143-59 *passim;* portrait published, 156; last foal of, 172; profits earned by, 176; death of, 178; sons and daughters of, 180; spelling of name, 187; ancestry, 189; birthplace and grave of, 191; racing record of sons and daughters, 194; location of MS records of sons and daughters, 197; PORTRAIT

231

Index

OF, frontispiece, facing 66, facing 67
Sir Charles, 67, 88-89, 111, 151, 161, 167, 178, 179, 181; PORTRAIT OF, facing 83
Sir Hal, 60, 62, 99, 111
Sir Harry, 58, 59
Sir Kirkland, 161, 163
Sir Peter, 25
Sir Sampson, 73
Sir William, 89, 93
Slim, 173
Slow and Easy, 106
Snip, 7
Spanking Roger, 7
Spiletta, 8
Spread-Eagle, 25
Spring Hill, 56, 59, 60, 181
Stockholder, 169
Stranger, 61, 64
St. Tammany, 25, 27
Stump-the-Dealer, 25
Swallow (Hermaphrodite), 85-86

Tabitha, 16
Tartar, 8
Tecumseh, 59, 60, 107, 111
Tickle Toby, 47
Timoleon, 62, 63, 65, 66, 76, 77, 79, 81-84, 87, 92, 107, 111, 167, 183; PORTRAIT OF, facing 82
Tom Tough, 44-46, 52
Top Gallant, 25
Transport, 77, 78, 80, 84; PORTRAIT OF, facing 83
Traveller, 11
Traveller, Lee's, 20

Trick'em, 14
Trifle, 172, 173, 174, 181; PORTRAIT OF, facing 44
True Blue, American, 25, 30-32, 41
True Blue, imported, 25, 38
Tuckahoe, 60, 64, 65, 82

Valentine, 6
Vanity, 63, 64-65, 66, 81, 82
Van Tromp, 89
Virginia, 20
Virginian, 60, 67, 169
Virginia Taylor, 150
Virginius, 25, 30-32, 76, 77, 78, 93

Walk-in-the-Water, 62
Walk-in-the-Water, Weaver's (Young Timoleon), 66, 107, 111, 151-53, 168, 169-70, 177
Washington, 92, 94, 107
Weaver's mare, 57
Whirlagig, 38
White Horse, 5
Wild-Bill-of-the-Woods (Pilot), 160-66
Wild Medley, 55
Woodpecker, 8
Wrangler, 25, 27, 30-32, 42-43, 44-46, 52

Yorick, 24
Young Florizel, 64
Young Lottery, 77-78, 79, 85
Young Selima, 24
Young Timoleon, Weaver's. *See* Walk-in-the-Water
Young Trumpator, 22

www.ingramcontent.com/pod-product-compliance
Lightning Source LLC
Chambersburg PA
CBHW021359290426
44108CB00010B/303